# Remember, Remember

LIFE-CHANGING TRUTHS FROM
THE BOOK OF MORMON

ALSO BY ROBERT L. MILLET

*Men of God*

*Becoming New*

*Whole in Christ*

*I Saw a Pillar of Light*

*The Holy Spirit*

*The Atoning One*

*Whatever Happened to Faith?*

*Precept upon Precept*

*Men of Covenant*

*Living in the Millennium*

*Living in the Eleventh Hour*

*Lehi's Dream*

*Coming to Know Christ*

*Making Sense of the Book of Revelation*

*Talking with God*

*Men of Influence*

*Holding Fast*

*Men of Valor*

*What Happened to the Cross?*

*Are We There Yet?*

*Getting at the Truth*

*Grace Works*

*When a Child Wanders*

# Remember, Remember

## LIFE-CHANGING TRUTHS FROM THE BOOK OF MORMON

ROBERT L. MILLET

SALT LAKE CITY, UTAH

Visit us at deseretbook.com

---

Library of Congress Cataloging-in-Publication Data

Names: Millet, Robert L., author.
Title: Remember, remember: lifechanging truths from the Book of Mormon / Robert L. Millet.
Description: Salt Lake City, Utah: Deseret Book, [2023] | Includes bibliographical references and index. | Summary: "Noted Latter-day Saint scholar Robert L. Millet summarizes fifty years of scholarship on the Book of Mormon"—Provided by publisher.
Identifiers: LCCN 2023022343 | ISBN 9781639932061 (hardback)
Subjects: LCSH: The Church of Jesus Christ of Latter-day Saints—Doctrines. | Book of Mormon—Criticism, interpretation, etc. | Mormon Church—Doctrines.
Classification: LCC BX8627. M553 2023 | DDC 289.3/22—dc23/eng/20230607
LC record available at https://lccn.loc.gov/2023022343

---

Printed in the United States of America
Publishers Printing, Salt Lake City, UT

10 9 8 7 6 5 4 3 2 1

# Contents

# Preface

There are many ways that a person may choose to study the Book of Mormon. President Russell M. Nelson observed: "I have read it many times. I have also read much that has been written about it. Some authors have focused upon its stories, its people, or its vignettes of history. Others have been intrigued by its language structure or its records of weapons, geography, animal life, techniques of building, or systems of weights and measures. Interesting as these things may be, study of the Book of Mormon is most rewarding when one focuses on its *primary* purpose—to testify of Jesus Christ. By comparison, all other issues are incidental. . . . When Mormon abridged these records, he noted that he could not write a 'hundredth part' of their proceedings. Thus *historical* aspects of the book assume *secondary* significance."[1]

Jacob, the son of Lehi, explained what his older brother Nephi instructed him to include in the sacred record: "And if there were *preaching which was sacred*, or *revelation which was great*, or *prophesying*, that I should engraven the heads [the most important parts] of them upon these plates, *and touch upon them as much as it were possible*, for Christ's sake, and for the sake of our people" (Jacob 1:4; emphasis added).

With the words of those two prophets ringing in my ears, I have chosen to focus in this book almost exclusively on the doctrine within the Book of Mormon. Elder Neal A. Maxwell taught that "doctrines believed and practiced do change and improve us, while ensuring our vital access to the Spirit. Both outcomes are crucial."[2]

Some members of the Church have proposed that the Book of Mormon basically reflects the teachings of the Bible and that there is very little within it that is doctrinally distinctive. My fifty-year experience with and study of the Book of Mormon, together with thirty years of working closely with marvelous men and women of other Christian denominations, leads me to disagree completely. To be sure, the teachings of the Book of Mormon are in harmony with the Bible; both books of scripture bear witness of God the Father; His Beloved Son, Jesus Christ; the Holy Ghost; and the message of the gospel—that salvation and redemption can come only in and through the Savior's atoning sacrifice and His Resurrection from the dead.

The Book of Mormon is not, however, simply a restatement or a reflection of the Holy Bible, for it teaches truths and propounds principles and precepts not found in the Bible. In the first appendix to this volume, I have provided a list of many of the important precepts found within the Book of Mormon and placed an asterisk (*) by those that, from my perspective, are distinctive to the Nephite-Jaredite record. As the reader will see, there are a surprising number of truths that are only to be found in the keystone of our religion. President Brigham Young once stated that "we, the Latter-day Saints, take the liberty of *believing more than our Christian brethren*: we not only believe . . . the Bible, but . . . the whole of the plan of salvation that Jesus has given to us. Do we differ from others who believe in the Lord Jesus Christ? No, *only in believing more*."[3]

One of the challenges I faced from the beginning of working on this project is the sheer volume of marvelous stories to be told, as well as precepts and doctrine to be discussed. My late friend and colleague Joseph Fielding McConkie and I coauthored a four-volume *Doctrinal Commentary on the Book of Mormon* from 1987 to 1992. Even in those volumes, because of limited space, we had to be selective with what we covered. It is inevitable, therefore, that in a one-volume work there will be a number of matters we will not have room to discuss. For that, I apologize. I sincerely hope, however, that readers will feel informed and inspired by what I *do* discuss in this short book.

I am indebted to far more people than I dare begin to mention. I have been blessed to sit at the feet of some of the most remarkable teachers in the Church, from general Church officers to Latter-day Saint professors of religion to trusted and valued colleagues in the Church Educational System. I only hope they know, somehow, how deeply grateful I am for the ways their counsel and teachings have shaped my life and impacted the way I study and teach the gospel of Jesus Christ. At this point in my life, it is extremely difficult to remember when I learned certain truths and from whom I learned them. Thus to one and all, I say, "Thank you, from the bottom of my heart."

Now, having given credit to those who taught me, I quickly add that this book is a private endeavor, expressing my own views, perspectives, and conclusions drawn from the evidence cited. While I have sought earnestly to be in harmony with both ancient and modern prophets and their teachings, this volume is not an official publication of The Church of Jesus Christ of Latter-day Saints.

# INTRODUCTION

# My Journey with the Book

I frequently hear people say that they have loved the Book of Mormon for as long as they can remember. I wish I could say that, but I can't. As a young missionary in the Eastern States Mission, our mission president was a great lover of the Doctrine and Covenants and had produced a very thorough study guide for that book of scripture. He made copies for all of the missionaries, and I enjoyed that study guide and spent a great deal of time with it. I too became a lover of the Doctrine and Covenants. For some reason, I found myself reading it again and again, memorizing favorite passages and keeping careful notes on which points of doctrine were found in which sections. A number of my companions and I quizzed one another on the Doctrine and Covenants as we walked along lonely roads or as we tracted from one door to another. I did read the Book of Mormon a couple of times while on my mission, but I did so more out of duty than enjoyment. I had a testimony that Joseph Smith was indeed a prophet of God and that the work he set in motion, including his translation of the Book of Mormon, was divine; but for reasons that I cannot now explain, I simply had not had a remarkable personal experience with the Book of Mormon.

When, after my mission, I transferred to Brigham Young University, I enrolled in a Pearl of Great Price class and was stirred and stretched intellectually and spiritually. I began to sense, more than I ever had before, the depth and breadth and reach of the restored gospel. Courses in the Doctrine and Covenants rekindled my excitement about the revelations given through the Prophet Joseph Smith. A semester before I was to graduate, I discovered that two courses on the Book of Mormon were required for graduation. I dutifully enrolled, though my heart wasn't in it. I somehow made it through the classes, received B grades in both, but was still unenthusiastic about the scripture known as the stick of Joseph.

After completing my master's degree at BYU, I began work with LDS Social Services as a counselor and later became employed by the Church Educational System (CES). After teaching full-time seminary in Salt Lake City for two years, I accepted a position as director of the institute of religion at Florida State University and as the local CES coordinator. In 1982, I read and relished the final volume of Elder Bruce R. McConkie's series on the Messiah. I noticed in *The Millennial Messiah* how often Elder McConkie turned to the Book of Mormon for doctrine, for interpretation, and for prophetic pronouncements. It was uncanny. He really used the Book of Mormon! This was especially the case when it came to discussing the destiny of the house of Israel. When I finished my second reading of *The Millennial Messiah*, I knew that I needed, eventually, to get serious about the Book of Mormon.

After living in Florida and Georgia for six years, I was invited to join the Religious Education faculty at BYU, which made me feel both thrilled and horrified. I found myself among many of the authors of Church books I had read over the last ten years or so. When the fall semester was about to begin, I learned that I had been scheduled to teach six classes of the first half of the Book of Mormon (1 Nephi through Alma 29). It was as if all things were in readiness for me.

The pages of the Book of Mormon exploded with feeling and meaning for me. I had known the Book of Mormon story for many years. When I was a young boy, my family had read and even listened to recordings of the Book of Mormon. But now it was different. Nephi came alive. Jacob seemed to be someone I had known but forgotten about. And Alma the Younger was larger than life. In short, I fell in love with the *story* of the Book of Mormon, the narrative and the characters. I felt the need to read it through, time after time, to get straight in my mind who was who and where they went and what they did. In the months and years that followed this experience, I became intimately acquainted with those voices from the dust, voices that now seemed not to be whispering but rather shouting to me that what they had to say was real and true. The witness came like fire into my heart that the Book of Mormon was a sacred record of a people who had once inhabited the Americas. I gained a witness of the truthfulness of the story.

My first phase of discovery soon merged into another phase. Over the years, I had heard more than one of the General Authorities remark that the Book of Mormon was the doctrinal standard for the Church, that in spite of the marvelous revealed truths contained in the Bible, the Doctrine and Covenants, and the Pearl of Great Price, it was to the Book of Mormon that we turn primarily to understand the *doctrine of Christ*. I had certainly heard them say that, but I wasn't sure. Now suddenly my eyes began to be opened to that reality.

It became clear that if we were to understand the Fall, the book of Genesis or even the book of Moses (which contain the accounts of *what* happened as part of the Fall) would be far less helpful than 2 Nephi 2 or Mosiah 16 or Alma 42. If we wanted to gain deeper insight into the Atonement of Jesus Christ, it was to 2 Nephi 9 and Mosiah 3 and Alma 34 that we should turn, to learn *why* those things had happened, rather than to the four Gospels or the epistles of Paul. It began to dawn on me that the teachings of Lehi, Nephi, Jacob, Mormon, and the risen Lord on the destiny of Israel far excelled in detail and spirit those wonderful teachings of Isaiah, Jeremiah, and Ezekiel. And so on and so on. As a teacher I found myself illustrating principles more and more often from the personalities and events (the story) of the Book of Mormon, but I also felt driven to teach and explain sacred matters (the doctrine) more frequently from the Nephite record.

Several years after I had come to recognize the infinite worth of the Book of Mormon as a doctrinal refuge and a source for theological understanding, I began to realize another phase of my own spiritual odyssey with this unusual scriptural record. That third phase might be called my *personal encounter*. I loved the story more than ever. I treasured the doctrine. But now I sensed that the prophet-writers were speaking directly to me—not only so that I might understand specific doctrinal details, but also that I might more fully conform my personal life with their teachings. For example, my study of the Fall now seemed to be an invitation from Lehi or Nephi or Benjamin or Abinadi to recognize my own fallen nature and seek to put off the natural man. My search of the scriptures pertaining to the Atonement of our Lord now became a pattern and an invitation to come unto Christ and for me to be changed, to become a new creature. In short, I now found myself driven beyond doctrinal understanding to personal engagement. The Book of Mormon became more than a book of religion; it *was* religion. The book was not simply something to be read and studied, though such activities are a necessary beginning; it was something to be *lived.* The Book of Mormon was not simply a collection of teachings about which we should speak (though we certainly needed to speak the word), but also something that we needed *to do* (see Doctrine and Covenants 84:57).

I have come to appreciate why the Book of Mormon has a spirit all its own. I love the Bible, both the Old and New Testaments. I cherish the Doctrine and Covenants and Pearl of Great Price and enjoy teaching from them more than I can say. These books of scripture—especially the books of modern scripture—are true and from God, and they convey a remarkable spirit. But the Book of Mormon is different. More than any other book, it is Christ-centered and gospel-centered. It leads men and women to the Lord and motivates them to become more like Him. There is a language, a logic, and a discernment that flow into the lives of those who drink deeply from the Book of Mormon. Within the reach of all those who become serious students of the book's pages and precepts is an interpretive key that opens hidden treasures of knowledge. God was and is its Author and its ultimate Editor. It was written and compiled by men who knew the Lord and had personally partaken of His goodness and grace, men who were seers who beheld our day and prepared the record with our obstacles, our challenges, and our personal difficulties in mind (see Mormon 8:35; 9:30). It is in this sense that the Book of Mormon is everlastingly relevant and perpetually pertinent. It speaks directly to us because it was written directly to us. President Ezra Taft Benson uttered this profound fact: "Not all truths are of equal value, nor are all scriptures of the same worth."[1]

I feel a tremendous love for the Book of Mormon. A spirit akin to coming home after a long vacation settles over me whenever I pick it up and begin reading. It speaks peace to my mind and heart. The Spirit of the Lord has borne witness to my soul that the Book of Mormon is not only true but faithful; its precepts are as current as they are consistent, as sanctifying as they are soothing. How deeply grateful I am that the "choice seer" (2 Nephi 3:6) named Joseph Smith translated and thereby made available an ancient record of a fallen people, "Another Testament of Jesus Christ," a divine message whose import can hardly be measured and whose total impact is yet to be seen and felt by the earth's inhabitants.

## CHAPTER 1

# "I Will Go and Do . . . , for I Know"

### 1 NEPHI 3

Chapter 3 of 1 Nephi begins with an announcement by Lehi that the Lord has commanded his sons to return to Jerusalem to obtain the plates of brass, a scriptural record of Genesis to Jeremiah (a contemporary of Lehi), much like our Old Testament. As seems to be their custom throughout 1 and 2 Nephi, Laman and Lemuel murmur against their father. Nephi had remarked earlier that "they did murmur because they knew not the dealings of that God who had created them" (1 Nephi 2:12). It is in the midst of this rebellion against Lehi and Jehovah, the God of the Old Testament, that Nephi utters one of the most well-known passages in all of scripture: "I, Nephi, . . . will go and do the things which the Lord hath commanded, for I know that the Lord giveth no commandments unto the children of men, save he shall prepare a way for them that they may accomplish the thing which he commandeth them" (1 Nephi 3:7).

Nephi's willingness to do whatever God calls upon him to do is a vivid demonstration of his faith. He believes in Jehovah, who will come to earth in six centuries as Jesus Christ. Further, he has a *total trust* in Him, *complete confidence* in Him, and a *ready reliance* upon Him. He will do what he is called upon to do because he has been visited by God and his heart has been softened (see 1 Nephi 2:16); he knows. When a woman of faith is called to serve as a Relief Society president, she sets aside her feelings of inadequacy, opens herself to being inconvenienced again and again, and moves forward because *she knows* she is called of God and therefore will be given the inspiration and the strength to magnify her calling. Because Nephi knew by the whisperings of the Holy Spirit that his father had been called by revelation, he could proceed toward Jerusalem and endure major opposition from Laman, Lemuel, and Laban, who possessed the brass plates. Nephi understood completely that since God had commanded him and his brothers to obtain the brass plates, the way would be opened to endure opposition and accomplish whatever was before them. Nephi *knew*, therefore he *did*. And as a result, his faith became even stronger.

We can also use verse 7 of chapter 3 to see faith from another angle. The Savior taught in the Old World: "My doctrine is not mine, but his that sent me. *If any man will do his will, he shall know of the doctrine*, whether it be of God, or whether I speak of myself" (John 7:16–17; emphasis added). Here the principle is this: do, then come to know. Members of the Lord's Church learn by experience that living the Word of Wisdom brings health of body and mind, as well as "great treasures of knowledge, even hidden treasures" (Doctrine and Covenants 89:18–19). A person gains a testimony of the value of paying a full tithe by paying a full tithe. That is, he or she does, then comes to know. As a person honestly and earnestly pays tithing, the promise of the Lord is affirmed: "Prove me now herewith . . . if I will not open you the windows of heaven, and pour you out a blessing, that there shall not be room enough to receive it" (Malachi 3:10).

In an address to new mission presidents, President Boyd K. Packer said: "It is not unusual to have a missionary say, 'How can I bear testimony until I get one? How can I testify that God lives, that Jesus is the Christ, and that the gospel is true? If I do not have such a testimony would that not be dishonest?'

"Oh, if I could teach you this one principle! A testimony is to be *found* in the *bearing* of it. . . . It is one thing to receive a witness from what you have read or what another has said; and that is a necessary beginning. It is quite another to have the Spirit confirm to you in your bosom that what *you* have testified is true. Can you not see that it will be supplied as you share it? As you give that which you have, there is a replacement, with increase!"[1]

Now let's get back to our original principle, that true faith is demonstrated when we act upon what we have come to know by revelation: we do, because we know. Over the last thirty years I have been involved in interfaith work and have had many, many opportunities to meet with large groups of people or classrooms of students not of our faith throughout the United States, as well as in Canada and Great Britain. I have usually been asked to speak about some of the beliefs and practices of The Church of Jesus Christ of Latter-day Saints and then respond to questions. On many, if not most, of those occasions, the audience has been respectful and the students' questions have been information-seeking. These gatherings have been absolutely delightful. Occasionally, however, I have encountered "gotcha" attempts to embarrass me or to malign the Church; these occasions have been much more difficult. In either case, while I certainly do not know the answers to all questions that might be raised, I have felt a confidence and a quiet assurance that things would turn out just fine.

In January of 2010, my dear Evangelical friend Richard J. Mouw and I were invited to speak to the students at Calvin College in Grand Rapids, Michigan. (If I may put it this way, Grand Rapids seems to me to be the Provo of Evangelical Christianity!) Richard spoke first for about twenty minutes, and then I spoke for the same amount of time. Then for about forty-five minutes the students were able to pose whatever questions they had. It was a large group of students, and the program was broadcast throughout different parts of the country. I and a Latter-day Saint couple who live in the area were the only members of our Church present, and as you might suppose, I was extremely nervous. During the time Rich was speaking, I prayed earnestly that I might represent the Church properly, that I could be cordial and nondefensive and provide answers to the audience members' queries that would be satisfying, even if they did not believe as I did.

As I began to speak, I suddenly felt a sweet peace that calmed my heart and settled my nerves. All fear left me, in spite of the fact that I was amid a group who could, if they chose to do so, put forward questions that could stump me or embarrass the Church. I knew with all of my heart that God lived and that Jesus was the Christ, the Only Begotten Son of God; that salvation comes in and through Christ and in no other way; that the boy Joseph Smith saw the Father and the Son in a grove of trees in upstate New York in the spring of 1820; that the Church to which I belonged was in fact the restoration of the first-century Christian Church; that, as Joseph Smith prophesied, no unhallowed hand could stop or stifle the work of the Restoration; and that it would spread to every nation and sound in every ear.[2] I knew these things by the power of the Holy Ghost, and no matter what happened, I would stand and defend the Restoration to the best of my ability. I knew, and therefore I proceeded without fear. Happily, the students were extremely cordial, and even their hard questions were asked in such a way that I did not in any way feel attacked. They were kind and respectful.

Now, to be sure, there are times when even though the Lord decrees that something shall be, those involved in bringing it to pass are blocked from accomplishing the will of God. This was the case with the prophesied temple that was to be erected in Jackson County, Missouri. In modern revelation we are told by the Savior that when "I give a commandment to any of the sons of men to do a work unto my name, and those sons of men go with all their might and with all they have to perform that work, and cease not their diligence, and their enemies come upon them and hinder them from performing that work, behold, it behooveth me to require that work no more at the hands of those sons of men, but to accept of their offerings" (Doctrine and Covenants 84:1–4; 124:49).

In the case of Nephi, son of Lehi, he went forward to retrieve the brass plates because he knew that the Lord would sustain and protect him and his brethren in accomplishing the difficult task. He went and did because he knew.

CHAPTER 2

# The Parable of the Paths

1 NEPHI 8, 11, 15

Early in this dispensation of the fullness of times, a revelation came to the Prophet Joseph Smith that we know as the Lord's preface to the Doctrine and Covenants. It provides a *description* of the state of the world in the early days of the restored Church. It also provides a *prescription* for how the God of Heaven had chosen to deal directly with a world gone astray. The voice of Jesus Christ declares: "And the anger of the Lord is kindled, and his sword is bathed in heaven, and it shall fall upon the inhabitants of the earth. And the arm of the Lord [His power] shall be revealed; and the day cometh that they who will not hear the voice of the Lord, neither the voice of his servants, neither give heed to the words of the prophets and apostles, shall be cut off from among the people."

Then follows the particulars of the apostasy: "For *they have strayed from mine ordinances, and have broken mine everlasting covenant*; they seek not the Lord to establish his righteousness, but *every man walketh in his own way*, and after the image of his own god, whose image is in the likeness of the world, and whose substance is that of an idol, which waxeth old and shall perish in Babylon, even Babylon the great, which shall fall" (Doctrine and Covenants 1:13–16; emphasis added).

The people of earth had not only broken the everlasting covenant—the fullness of gospel truths, covenants, and ordinances—but also had chosen to walk in their own way and after the image of their own God; in other words, they elected to "do their own thing" and fashion a god of their own choosing rather than attend to the soft but poignant voice of the Almighty, who beckons to each of us, "This is the way, walk ye in it" (Isaiah 30:21). God's loving invitation to each of us is to search diligently for the strait and narrow path, His covenant path, and to stay on it no matter what.

In many ways, Lehi's dream-vision in chapter 8 of 1 Nephi discloses the plight of the whole of humanity—all people choose to traverse the path that they assume will lead them to the greatest satisfaction and peace. Sadly, too often the outcome of their choice is deep disappointment, unhappiness, and existential despair. They continue, day in and day out, to lean their ladder against the wrong wall, to labor in secondary causes.

According to Nephi's account, his father beheld in vision four groups of people, each different from the other in important ways. *Group one* (see 1 Nephi 8:21–23) consists of "numberless concourses of people, many of whom were pressing forward, that they might obtain the path which led unto the tree by which I stood." These begin to make their way toward the tree of life—that is, they attempt to get onto the covenant path toward Christ the Savior and the salvation He offers—but they are soon encompassed in a mist of darkness, the temptations of the devil (1 Nephi 12:17). These did "lose their way, that they wandered off and were lost" (1 Nephi 8:23).

Many millions of people become aware of the restored gospel and feel some desire to investigate it and perhaps even accept it. Maybe they have heard good things about The Church of Jesus Christ of Latter-day Saints. Or perhaps the Light of Christ has prompted and led them toward a life of righteousness and devotion to God. Before they get serious about their spiritual quest, however, the father of lies and his minions find ways to distract many of them from the things of greatest worth and lure them onto paths that appear attractive but prove instead to be spiritually destructive. Unfortunately, they never make it to the tree of life, never perceive that all we do in this life is but a prelude to all that will come to pass in the life to come. Rather, as Lehi explained, they wander off and are lost.

Nephi recorded more about *group two* (see 1 Nephi 8:24–28) than any of the other three groups. These are folks who hear the message of the Restoration; are drawn to the principles, doctrine, and practices of the faith; and manage to get onto the covenant path. They take hold of the rod of iron (the word of God; see 1 Nephi 11:25; 15:24) and come to enjoy the sweet fruits of the Savior's atoning sacrifice and the supernal gifts and blessings that flow from membership in the Lord's Church and kingdom.

And yet sadly, tragically, they take their eyes away from the Lord and His gospel and begin to feel ashamed or embarrassed about the course they have taken. Nephi saw (as his father Lehi had) a great and spacious building on the other side of the river, which represents "the world and the wisdom thereof" as well as "vain imaginations" and "the pride of the world" (1 Nephi 11:35–36; 12:18). Those in the strange building—which is "high above the earth" (1 Nephi 8:26), meaning that it has no foundation or that the devil is the foundation—are jeering, mocking, and making fun of those who partook of the fruit of the tree. Perhaps these members of the Church cared too much about what others thought; perhaps they didn't want to appear "holier than thou"; or perhaps they had not undergone a deep conversion to Jesus Christ and His Church. They cared more about being approved and accepted by fickle mortals than they did about being worthy of the Lord's approbation, "Well done, thou good and faithful servant" (Matthew 25:21; see also Enos 1:27).

I want to turn our attention to *group four* before discussing group three. These people are absolutely unattracted to things of righteousness and totally uninclined toward the spiritual or religious life. They care precious little about the rod of iron, the tree of life, the fruit of the tree, or the Father's great plan of happiness. Instead, they choose to go, as a beloved teacher of mine once put it, "cross lots"—meaning by the most direct route—"to hell." These "feel their way" toward the great and spacious building. Why would they "feel" their way? Because they are blind to spiritual things, clueless about matters of greatest worth. As the Apostle Paul put it, "The natural man receiveth not the things of the Spirit of God: for they are foolishness unto him: neither can he know them, because they are spiritually discerned" (1 Corinthians 2:14). Or, as King Benjamin declared, "The natural [unredeemed] man is an enemy to God, and has been from the fall of Adam, and will be, forever and ever, unless he yields to the enticings of the Holy Spirit and putteth off the natural man" (Mosiah 3:19).

Very little is said in the scriptural text about *group three*. Nephi describes this group beautifully: his father "saw other multitudes pressing forward; and they came and caught hold of the end of the rod of iron; and they did press their way forward, continually holding fast to the rod of iron, until they came forth and fell down and partook of the fruit of the tree" (1 Nephi 8:30). Their love and unending gratitude, and their devotion to the Church and gospel of Jesus Christ, were such that they held to the rod and, in an act of reverential humility and overwhelming gratitude, they knelt, as it were, at the feet of the Savior and partook of His greatest of all gifts—salvation, or eternal life (see Doctrine and Covenants 6:13; 14:7). So what do we conclude about those in group three? That they took of the fruit, that they endured faithfully to the end, and that they were received into paradise when their mortal lives were over.

In a day when approximately eighty million Americans have cut all ties to any form of organized religion, who describe themselves as "spiritual but not religious," Lehi's vision is powerfully relevant. For one thing, too many of the members of the restored Church—who have in the past enjoyed the blessings and gifts of Christ's Atonement and participated in the highest ordinances of the temple—have chosen to leave the covenant path. They have shifted their allegiance and moral values from the word of God found in holy scripture and living prophets to the fleeting and ephemeral values of a secular society. They have trusted the shifting sands of a relativistic world that denies absolute truth and absolute values. For one thing, as the prophets have recently taught, we cannot simply keep the second great commandment (to love our neighbors as ourselves) while ignoring the first great commandment (to love God with all our hearts, souls, and minds and to keep His commandments).

Our only hope for spiritual safety is to hold tenaciously to the rod of iron, which is the word of God—holy scriptures, personal revelation, and the teachings of the prophets, seers, and revelators. In addition, we must never forget that Jesus Christ Himself is the Word of God (John 1:1; Revelation 19:13). We must, as Helaman counseled his two sons Nephi and Lehi, build our foundation of faith upon the rock of our Redeemer, who is Christ the Lord. Then, when the winds and waves of sin and persecution come, we can stand solid and firm on the only sure foundation "whereon if men build they cannot fall" (Helaman 5:12).

CHAPTER 3

# The Book of Mormon and the Bible

1 NEPHI 13–14

Early in the Restoration, the Saints were taught important truths about the Book of Mormon and the Bible. The Prophet Joseph Smith explained: "I believe the Bible as it read when it came from the pen of the original writers. Ignorant translators, careless transcribers, or designing or corrupt priests have committed many errors."[1] On a later occasion, he stated that "from Sundry revelations which had been received, it was apparent that many important points touching the salvation of man had been taken from the Bible, or lost before it was compiled."[2] Nephi saw in vision that many plain and precious truths and many covenants of the Lord would be taken away or kept back from the Bible before it was compiled. This was done intentionally by persons with wicked motives—to distort the truth and confuse people. "And all this have they done that they might pervert the right ways of the Lord, that they might blind the eyes and harden the hearts of the children of men" (1 Nephi 13:24–28). This would become a great "stumbling block" to the Gentiles in the centuries ahead (see 1 Nephi 13:29; 14:1).

I would suggest that some of the following points of doctrine were among what was excised: the nature of God and His relationship to Christ and to all of the Father's children; the importance of the Fall of Adam and Eve in the plan of salvation; that there is no original sin that has tainted all who were born into this life; the necessity of certain ordinances; the Aaronic and Melchizedek Priesthoods; covenants and ordinances such as eternal marriage and the sealing of families for time and eternity; our premortal existence as spirits; the postmortal spirit world and the work that goes on there; the precious knowledge that every child of God will have a valid opportunity to hear and accept the gospel of Jesus Christ, either in this life or the next; the three degrees of glory hereafter; and so on. It's possible that what was taken away from the Bible has been made known through what is restored.

The vision of Nephi was thus not a dismal picture, for he learned that many of the lost plain and precious truths would be restored through the teachings within the Book of Mormon and latter-day scripture. In referring specifically to the Book of Mormon, Nephi wrote the words of the Savior regarding His future appearance to the Nephites: "I [Christ] will manifest myself unto thy seed, that *they shall write many things which I should minister unto them, which shall be plain and precious*; and after thy seed shall be destroyed, . . . these things shall be hid up, to come forth unto the Gentiles, by the gift and power of the Lamb. And *in them shall be written my gospel*, saith the Lamb, and my rock and my salvation" (1 Nephi 13:35–36; emphasis added).

As a young missionary, my leaders often stressed the need to get copies of the Book of Mormon into the hands of people everywhere, because it was a "second witness of Christ" or, as Church leaders taught many years later, "Another Testament of Jesus Christ." When the restored Church was organized in 1830, an important revelation was received and recorded. In speaking of young Joseph Smith, the revelation stated: "After it was truly manifested unto this first elder that he had received a remission of sins"—which is mentioned specifically in the 1832 and 1835 accounts of the First Vision—"he was entangled again in the vanities of the world; but after repenting, and humbling himself sincerely, through faith, God ministered unto him by an holy angel [Moroni], whose countenance was as lightning, and whose garments were pure and white above all other whiteness; . . . and gave unto him commandments which inspired him."

The revelation continues by mentioning how the Book of Mormon was translated by the gift and power of God. Then, the revelation asserts that the Nephite record "*[proves] to the world that the holy scriptures are true*, and that God does inspire men and call them to his holy work in this age and generation, as well as in generations of old" (Doctrine and Covenants 20:5–7, 11; emphasis added). Stated simply, one of the major purposes and functions of the Book of Mormon is *to establish the essential truthfulness of the Bible*. That is, the Book of Mormon attests that the Bible is a true account of God's dealings with ancient prophets, a faithful record of the coming of the Only Begotten Son of God into mortality to accomplish the work of salvation, and a confirming witness of what is taught within the Acts of the Apostles and the New Testament epistles.

In the very last chapter of Nephi's second book, as a crucial part of his concluding testimony, he records: "And now, my beloved brethren, and also Jew, and all ye ends of the earth, hearken unto these words and believe in Christ; and if ye believe not in these words [the messages of the Book of Mormon] believe in Christ. And *if ye shall believe in Christ ye will believe in these words*, for they are the words of Christ" (2 Nephi 33:10; emphasis added). What a powerful statement! We are being taught that anyone who truly believes in the Lord Jesus Christ—anyone who accepts His divine Sonship and His atoning work, who has received the spiritual witness that He is the Son of God and God the Son, and who is a genuine seeker after truth—will recognize through the Holy Spirit the words of Christ as they are found throughout the entire Book of Mormon. On the other hand, a person who believes in the Bible but refuses to read, study, or pray earnestly about the truthfulness of the Book of Mormon will never recognize that same sweet, certifying Holy Spirit that someone feels when they read and ponder the Book of Mormon.

Toward the end of the Nephite record, Mormon, the chief compiler and editor of the gold plates, bears a similar testimony: "Therefore repent, and be baptized in the name of Jesus, and lay hold upon the gospel of Christ, which shall be set before you, not only in this record [the Book of Mormon], but also in the record which shall come unto the Gentiles from the Jews, which record [the Bible] shall come from the Gentiles unto you." Now, ponder on these words: "For behold, *this [the Book of Mormon] is written for the intent that ye may believe that [the Bible];* and if ye believe that ye will believe this also; and if ye believe this ye will know concerning your fathers, and also the marvelous works which were wrought by the power of God among them" (Mormon 7:8–9; emphasis added).

In speaking at a symposium on the value and blessing of the Joseph Smith Translation of the Bible, President Dallin H. Oaks referred to what he called "the royal family of scripture"[3]—the Bible, Book of Mormon, Doctrine and Covenants, and Pearl of Great Price. Now in my own family, the Millet family, we have six children—two girls and four boys. Though I may not relate to each of my children the same way, or have as many things in common with one than another, I love them all. They are a part of our family, and I do not love one member more than another. So it should be with holy scripture: though we might relate to one scriptural record more than another, we should love the Bible just as we do the other three books within the standard works, our royal family of scripture.

President M. Russell Ballard explained that "it is a miracle that the Bible literally contains within its pages the converting, healing Spirit of Christ, which has turned men's hearts for centuries, leading them to pray, to choose right paths, and to search to find their Savior. . . . Members of The Church of Jesus Christ of Latter-day Saints believe that 'all scripture is given by inspiration of God, and is profitable' (2 Timothy 3:16). . . . [The Bible] is one of the pillars of our faith. . . . The more we read and study the Bible and its teachings, the more clearly we see the doctrinal underpinnings of the restored gospel of Jesus Christ. *We tend to love the scriptures that we spend time with. We may need to balance our study in order to love and understand all scripture.*" President Ballard continued, "*Those who join this Church do not give up their faith in the Bible—they strengthen it. The Book of Mormon does not dilute nor diminish nor de-emphasize the Bible. On the contrary, it expands, extends, and exalts it. The Book of Mormon testifies of the Bible, and both testify of Christ.*"[4]

Oh, how I look forward to the grand day when the Bible and the Book of Mormon "grow together, unto the confounding of false doctrines and laying down of contentions, and establishing peace," in bringing honest truth seekers and people of goodwill "to the knowledge of their fathers in the latter days, and also to the knowledge [of the Lord's] covenants" (2 Nephi 3:12).

# CHAPTER 4

## "There Are Save Two Churches Only"

2 NEPHI 10

Some time ago I was speaking to a combined group of Evangelical Christians and Latter-day Saints in Southern California. The meeting was held in a Latter-day Saint chapel. After an Evangelical associate and I had spoken about the great value of developing friendships with persons of other faiths, we allowed the audience to ask any questions they might have. Among the very first questions raised was one from a full-time missionary who was sitting with his companion on the front row. He said: "My question is for Brother Millet." He then proceeded to ask the following: "If I remember right, the Book of Mormon states that there are really only two churches—the Church of the Lamb of God and the church of the devil. So I suppose that means we as Latter-day Saints are the Church of the Lamb of God and all others are the church of the devil. Is that correct?"

I paused momentarily and thought about how unwise it was for the missionary to make such a comment, especially when about 40 percent of those in attendance were not members of our Church. Not exactly a way to endear an audience to you, especially the men and women not of our faith. I replied: "No, that is not true." I then attempted to explain how to understand 1 Nephi 14:10, which says that "there are save two churches only." Jesus Himself taught in the Old World that "*he that is not with me is against me*; and he that gathereth not with me scattereth abroad" (Matthew 12:30; emphasis added). A similar episode is found in the Gospel of Mark. We read that "John answered him, saying, Master, we saw one casting out devils in thy name, and he followeth not us. . . . But Jesus said, Forbid him not: for there is no man which shall do a miracle in my name that can lightly speak evil of me. For *he that is not against us is on our part* [side]" (Mark 9:38–40; emphasis added).

In a modern revelation given to Joseph Smith, Oliver Cowdery, and David Whitmer, Jesus Christ spoke directly: "Contend against no church, save it be the church of the devil" (Doctrine and Covenants 18:20). In offering commentary on this verse, Elder B. H. Roberts taught: "I understand the injunction to Oliver Cowdery to 'contend against no church, save it be the church of the devil' to mean that he shall *contend against evil, against untruth, against all combinations of wicked men. They constitute the church of the devil, the kingdom of evil, a federation of unrighteousness*. . . . But, let it be understood, we are not brought necessarily into antagonism with the various sects of Christianity as such. So far as they have retained fragments of Christian truth—and each of them has some measure of truth—that far they are acceptable unto the Lord. . . . Wherever we find truth, whether it exists in complete form or only in fragments, we recognize that truth as part of that sacred whole of which the Church of Jesus Christ is the custodian."

Elder Roberts emphasized that "our relationship to the religious world is not one that calls for the denunciation of sectarian churches as composing the church of the devil. *All that makes for truth, for righteousness, is of God*; it constitutes the kingdom of righteousness—the empire of Jehovah; and, in a certain sense at least, constitutes the Church of Christ. *All that makes for untruth, for unrighteousness constitutes the kingdom of evil—the church of the devil.* With the kingdom of righteousness we have no warfare."[1]

Decades ago I was teaching a class at BYU in which we studied the second half of the New Testament, Acts through Revelation. Something was said by one of the students about how those who are not members of our Church cannot really accomplish much without the fullness of the gospel and the gift of the Holy Ghost. I had recently finished reading the autobiography of Billy Graham, believed by many to be the greatest evangelist of the twentieth century. I replied to the young man that I had been deeply moved by what I had read and sensed that this simple preacher from North Carolina had been raised up by God for a special purpose—to help lead many souls to Christ. The young man then responded: "Well, if he was such a good man, why didn't he accept the restored gospel and join the true Church?"

I then paraphrased a statement made by Elder Orson F. Whitney of the Quorum of the Twelve Apostles. His exact words are, "Perhaps the Lord needs such men [noble men and women] on the outside of His Church to help it along. They are among its auxiliaries, and *can do more good for the cause where the Lord has placed them, than anywhere else.* . . . Hence, some are drawn into the fold and receive a testimony of the truth; while others remain unconverted . . . *the beauties and glories of the gospel being veiled temporarily from their view, for a wise purpose. The Lord will open their eyes in His own due time.*" Now note this particularly poignant message: "*God is using more than one people for the accomplishment of His great and marvelous work. The Latter-day Saints cannot do it all.* It is too vast, too arduous for any one people." Elder Whitney then stated that we have no quarrel with those of other faiths who love the Lord. "They are our partners in a certain sense."[2]

In 2001, I was invited by the Latter-day Saint students at Harvard and MIT to address a group consisting of members of our Church, faculty members, and interested students from other faith traditions. I delivered a fifty-minute presentation on "The Christ of the Latter-day Saints." Questions and answers followed. One faculty member made a comment early in the Q&A session: "I do have questions for you, but frankly I have great difficulty taking seriously any religious group that dismisses out of hand two thousand years of Christian history." His question sobered me at the time, and it still haunts me. It has elicited in my mind a host of issues: Do we as members of The Church of Jesus Christ of Latter-day Saints in fact dismiss the whole of Christian history as "apostate"? Is such a position necessary in light of a belief in a restoration of the gospel? Is it really the case that "the lights went out" in AD 100 and did not come on again until 1820? Was this period of time actually the "Dark Ages" in the sense that no spiritual light, no sacred truth, and no divine manifestations were had or enjoyed by men and women for some seventeen centuries?

Having discussed the passing of the primitive Church and the flickering and dimming (not dousing) of the flame of Christian faith, President Boyd K. Packer stated: "But always, as it had from the beginning, the Spirit of God inspired worthy souls. We owe an immense debt to the protesters and the reformers who preserved the scriptures and translated them. They knew something had been lost. They kept the flame alive as best they could."[3]

And so in the broadest sense, yes, there are only two churches—those who choose to follow God and strive to keep His commandments and those described by Nephi: "Wherefore, he that fighteth against Zion, both Jew and Gentile, both bond and free, both male and female, shall perish; . . . for they who are not for me are against me" (2 Nephi 10:16). Each of us are essentially on trial, to determine which side to be on, to be a friend of Jesus or an enemy. From a Book of Mormon perspective, there are no other possibilities.

CHAPTER 5

# The Scattering and Gathering of Israel

1 NEPHI 15; 2 NEPHI 6, 10

In a very significant message to the youth of the Church in June of 2018, entitled "Hope of Israel," President Russell M. Nelson extended an invitation and a charge: "Now, we would like to talk with you about *the greatest* challenge, *the greatest* cause, and *the greatest* work on earth. And we want to invite *you* to be part of it! . . . My dear young brothers and sisters, these surely *are* the latter days, and the Lord is hastening His work to gather Israel. That *gathering is the most important thing taking place on earth today. Nothing else compares in magnitude, nothing else compares in importance, nothing else compares in majesty.* And if you choose to, if you want to, you can be a big part of it. . . . When we speak of the *gathering*, we are simply saying this fundamental truth: every one of our Heavenly Father's children, on both sides of the veil, deserves to hear the message of the restored gospel of Jesus Christ. They decide for themselves if they want to know more.

"Those whose lineage is from the various tribes of Israel are those whose hearts will most likely be turned to the Lord. He said, 'My sheep hear my voice, and I know them, and they follow me' (John 10:27). *Those who are of the house of Israel will most easily recognize the Lord Jesus Christ as their Savior and will desire to be gathered into His fold.* They will want to become members of His Church, make covenants with Him and Heavenly Father, and receive their essential ordinances."

President Nelson went on to teach a simple truth that has enormous implications: "*Anytime* you do *anything* that helps *anyone*—on either side of the veil—take a step toward making covenants with God and receiving their essential baptismal and temple ordinances, you are helping to gather Israel. It is as simple as that."[1]

Looking back to the beginning of this earth's history, we learn that our first parents were given a very significant commandment: "*Thou shalt do all that thou doest in the name of the Son*, and thou shalt repent and call upon God in the name of the Son forevermore" (Moses 5:8; emphasis added). We can grasp the purpose and thrust of the gathering of Israel only when we understand that people are gathered, not just to lands and locations, not just to *a place*, but to *a Person*, namely, to the Lord Jesus Christ—to Him, to His doctrine, and to His Church and kingdom.

Because Lehi was of the tribe of Manasseh (Alma 10:3), the son of Joseph, the promises that God had made to Father Abraham continued through Lehi's descendants. Nephi reminds his wayward brothers that their father, Lehi, declared that in the latter days the gospel of Jesus Christ would come to his descendants through the Gentiles. "Wherefore, our Father hath not spoken of our seed alone, but also of all the house of Israel, *pointing to the covenant which should be fulfilled in the latter days; which covenant the Lord made to our father Abraham, saying: In thy seed shall all the kindreds of the earth be blessed*" (1 Nephi 15:17–18; emphasis added).

Because of their wandering ways, ancient Israel became scattered—alienated from Jehovah, from the people of the covenant, and from the ways of righteousness and displaced from their identity as covenant representatives and from the lands set aside for their inheritance. Israel was scattered because of apostasy, because they strayed from the ordinances and broke the everlasting covenant (compare Doctrine and Covenants 1:15).

Although Israel is almost always scattered because of apostasy, there are times when the Lord scatters or leads away certain branches of His chosen people to various parts of the earth in order to accomplish His purposes—to spread the blood and influence of Abraham throughout the globe. This was certainly the case with the Lehite colony, a branch of Joseph that was led away from their Palestinian homeland to another hemisphere because of wickedness in Jerusalem.

Nephi taught that God raises up a righteous nation "and destroyeth the nations of the wicked. And *he leadeth away the righteous into precious lands*, and the wicked he destroyeth, and curseth the land unto them for their sakes" (1 Nephi 17:37–38; emphasis added). Even more plainly, Jacob explained that "*the Lord God has led away [groups of people] from time to time from the house of Israel, according to his will and pleasure*. And now behold, the Lord remembereth all them who have been broken off, wherefore he remembereth us also" (2 Nephi 10:22; compare 1:5).

Now, just as Israel is *scattered* through transgression, Israel is *gathered* through turning to the Lord and repenting of sin. Individuals were gathered in ancient days when they aligned themselves with the people of God, with those who practiced the religion of Jehovah and received the ordinances of salvation. They were gathered when they gained a sense of tribal identity, when they came to know who and whose they were. They were gathered when they congregated in those places set apart as sacred sites for the people of promise.

Nephi wrote that "after the house of Israel should be scattered they should be gathered together again; or, in fine, after the Gentiles had *received the fulness of the Gospel* the natural branches of the olive-tree, or the remnants of the house of Israel, should be grafted in, or *come to the knowledge of the true Messiah*" (1 Nephi 10:14; emphasis added; see also 1 Nephi 15:13–14; 2 Nephi 10:6–7; 30:5).

As Nephi, the son of Lehi, was about to close his first book, he wrote of the great millennial day and the gathering that would take place during those one thousand years of peace: "And the time cometh speedily that the righteous must be led up as calves of the stall, and the Holy One of Israel must reign in dominion, and might, and power, and great glory. And *he gathereth his children from the four quarters of the earth*; and he numbereth his sheep, and they know him; and *there shall be one fold and one shepherd*; and he shall feed his sheep, and in him they shall find pasture. And *because of the righteousness of his people, Satan has no power*; wherefore, he cannot be loosed for the space of many years" (1 Nephi 22:24–26; emphasis added).

Coming unto Christ, accepting His gospel, joining His Church, and associating with the Saints are not the final steps toward exaltation. "While salvation is an individual matter," President Russell M. Nelson explained, "exaltation is a family matter. Only those who are married in the temple and whose marriage is sealed by the Holy Spirit of Promise will continue as spouses after death and receive the highest degree of celestial glory, or exaltation. . . . To be exalted—or to gain exaltation—refers to the highest state of happiness and glory in the celestial realm. These blessings can come to us after we leave this frail and mortal existence. The time to prepare for our eventual salvation and exaltation is now."[2]

The Prophet Joseph Smith delivered a most significant message on June 11, 1843: "What was the object of gathering the Jews, or the people of God, in any age of the world? . . . The main object was *to build unto the Lord a house whereby He could reveal unto His people the ordinances of His house and the glories of His kingdom, and teach the people the way of salvation.*"[3] Thus the final phase of the gathering of the members of the house of Israel is the gathering to holy temples or, as Isaiah expressed it, to "the mountain of the Lord's house" (Isaiah 2:2; 2 Nephi 12:2).

In April 1995, President Nelson delivered a message in general conference entitled "Children of the Covenant." He taught: "*We are . . . children of the covenant.* We have received, as did they of old, the holy priesthood and the everlasting gospel. *Abraham, Isaac, and Jacob are our ancestors. We are of Israel.* We have the right to receive the gospel, blessings of the priesthood, and eternal life. *Nations of the earth will be blessed by our efforts and by the labors of our posterity.*"[4]

On another occasion, President Nelson declared: "This is the

Church of Jesus Christ, restored in these latter days so that the families of scattered Israel can be gathered into the fold of the Lord. They don't have to be gathered physically into any one place. The gathering place for the people of India is *India*. The gathering place for the people of Sri Lanka is *Sri Lanka*. The gathering place for the people of Nepal is *Nepal*. The gathering place for the people of China is *China*. Our job is to be gathered into the fold of Christ—wherever that is—and to live by His precepts from now on."[5]

The Book of Mormon bears a powerful testimony of the supernal gift of God's never-ending love for and infinite patience with the house of Israel. Jacob, the son of Lehi, quotes from the complex but profound allegory of Zenos. He then rejoices in the mercy of God, "for he remembereth the house of Israel, both roots [ancestry] and branches [posterity]; and he stretches forth his hands unto them all the day long." Jacob then pleads with his people, and with all people for that matter, to repent "and come with full purpose of heart, and cleave unto God as he cleaveth unto you" (Jacob 6:4–5).

We speak often of those who are descendants of Abraham, Isaac, and Jacob as the "chosen people." We must never forget, however, that true chosenness is based, not just on one's lineage, but especially upon one's choices. "God does not have a list of favorites to which we hope our names will some day be added," Elder David A. Bednar clarified. "He does not limit the 'chosen' to a restricted few. Instead, *our* hearts, *our* desires, *our* honoring of sacred gospel covenants and ordinances, *our* obedience to the commandments, and, most importantly, the Savior's redeeming grace and mercy determine whether we are counted as one of God's chosen."[6]

The allegory of Zenos says it all—God simply will not let Israel go! To be involved in the gathering of Israel in these latter days is a sacred and sobering responsibility, but it is also a supernal and soul-satisfying opportunity and privilege. As we do our part in this, the greatest work in all the world, we are being loyal to the royal within us and thereby helping to fulfill God's promises to Father Abraham.

CHAPTER 6

# The Merits, Mercy, and Grace of Christ

2 NEPHI 2

During the last forty years, I have noticed a much stronger emphasis in The Church of Jesus Christ of Latter-day Saints on the saving mission of Jesus Christ and the grace or divine assistance He offers us. Don't misunderstand me. When I was a boy living in the 1950s our leaders spoke with deep reverence for the Savior and encouraged the Saints to study His life and repent of our sins by means of His Atonement. We as a people have always believed that; these central teachings have been in our standard works since the Church was organized in April of 1830.

Yet since the mid-1980s, it's as though we have discovered a treasure trove of truth, encouragement, and comfort that can be ours through relying upon the Lord's merits, mercy, and grace. I sense that a significant reason for that discovery is the repeated emphasis that President Ezra Taft Benson and his prophetic successors have placed upon the importance of reading, searching, and applying the soul-satisfying and sanctifying messages of the Book of Mormon.

Whether a person is a Latter-day Saint, a Roman Catholic, a follower of Eastern Orthodoxy, a Protestant, or a member of a non-Christian faith, one doesn't travel very far in reading and studying the Book of Mormon before becoming aware that the book is drenched in what I call *redemptive theology*—the importance of the Fall and its very real consequences; the need to exercise faith in the Lord Jesus Christ; the crucial need to take full advantage of the Lord's infinite and eternal Atonement; the necessity of repentance—of turning away from sin and turning toward God, acquiring a new mind, a new heart, and new eyes; the repeated invitation and charge to be born again and become a new creature; and, finally, the peace and comfort that can flow into our souls as we reach out to receive the grace of Jesus Christ.

References to the merits of men and women in the Book of Mormon are few and far between. Instead, we find verses like this: "Aaron [the son of King Mosiah] did expound unto him [the father of King Lamoni] the scriptures from the creation of Adam, laying the fall of man before him, and their carnal state and also the plan of redemption, which was prepared from the foundation of the world, through Christ, for all whosoever would believe on his name." Now notice what follows: "And *since man had fallen he could not merit anything of himself*, but the sufferings and death of Christ atone for their sins, through faith and repentance, and so forth" (Alma 22:13–14; emphasis added).

In the same spirit, look carefully at the following passages:

> "Wherefore, how great the importance to make these things known unto the inhabitants of the earth, that they may know that there is no flesh that can dwell in the presence of God, *save it be through the merits and mercy and grace of the Holy Messiah*, who layeth down his life according to the flesh, and taketh it again by the power of the Spirit." (2 Nephi 2:8; emphasis added)
>
> "After ye have gotten into this strait and narrow path, I would ask if all is done? Behold, I say unto you, Nay; for ye have not come thus far save it were by the word of Christ with unshaken faith in him, *relying wholly upon the merits of him who is mighty to save*." (2 Nephi 31:19; emphasis added)
>
> "I [Anti-Nephi-Lehi] also thank my God, yea, my great God, that he hath granted unto us that we might repent of

> these things, and also that he hath forgiven us of those our many sins and murders which we have committed, and taken away the guilt from our hearts, *through the merits of his Son.*" (Alma 24:10; emphasis added)
>
> "If ye believe on his name [the name of Christ] ye will repent of all your sins, that thereby ye may have a remission of them *through his merits.*" (Helaman 14:13; emphasis added)
>
> "And after they had been received unto baptism, and were wrought upon and cleansed by the power of the Holy Ghost, that they were numbered among the people of the church of Christ; and their names were taken, that they might be remembered and nourished by the good word of God, to keep them in the right way, to keep them continually watchful unto prayer, *relying alone upon the merits of Christ, who was the author and the finisher of their faith.*" (Moroni 6:4; emphasis added)

Now, while I don't want to weary the reader with a multitude of passages from the Book, I do want to make it clear that the writers and preachers within the Book of Mormon taught that men and women simply cannot save themselves—cannot do enough good deeds or serve long and hard enough to merit the celestial kingdom. This truth should not discourage us or make us want to throw in the towel and admit that we are just not celestial-kingdom types. On the contrary, I have taken the time to list these significant passages from the Book of Mormon to help us recognize and always remember that we cannot do this on our own, and, thankfully, we need not even try to do it on our own. The Son of God stands ready and willing to forgive our sins, to change our hearts, and to empower and strengthen us to do what we could never, ever do by ourselves. In short, this is a team effort, a team made up of the Savior and us. We are working together with Him to save our souls. This is what the Apostle Paul taught so profoundly in his letter to the Philippian Saints—we work out our salvation by working with

God and allowing Him, through the power of the Holy Spirit, to do a marvelous work and a wonder within our hearts (Philippians 2:12–13).

President Dallin H. Oaks taught: "Men and women unquestionably have impressive powers and can bring to pass great things. But after all our obedience and good works, we cannot be saved from death or the effects of our individual sins without the grace extended by the atonement of Jesus Christ. . . . In other words, salvation does not come simply by keeping the commandments. . . . Man cannot earn his own salvation."[1]

Now of course you and I need to be about the business of doing good works—attending Church meetings and being an active part of the body of Christ; serving our brothers and sisters, seeking to lighten their burdens; being involved regularly in temple worship; and helping to gather Israel on both sides of the veil. But if salvation comes to us through the goodness and grace of the Almighty, then why should we be involved in good works? Because in serving and doing and striving to the best of our ability to obey Him, we are expressing both our love ("If ye love me, keep my commandments" [John 14:15]) and our gratitude ("Thou shalt thank the Lord thy God in all things" [Doctrine and Covenants 59:7]) for all that the Father, Son, and Holy Ghost have done and will continue to do for us and with us.

President Dieter F. Uchtdorf put it this way: "Salvation cannot be bought with the currency of obedience; it is purchased by the blood of the Son of God. Thinking that we can trade our good works for salvation is like buying a plane ticket and then supposing we own the airline. Or thinking that after paying rent for our home, we now hold title to the entire planet earth.

"If grace is a gift of God, why then is obedience to God's commandments so important? Why bother with God's commandments—or repentance, for that matter? Why not just admit we're sinful and let God save us? . . . Brothers and sisters, we obey the commandments of God—out of love for Him! . . .

"Therefore, our obedience to God's commandments comes as a

natural outgrowth of our endless love and gratitude for the goodness of God. This form of genuine love and gratitude will miraculously merge our works with God's grace. . . . Grace is a gift of God, and our desire to be obedient to each of God's commandments is the reaching out of our mortal hand to receive this sacred gift from our Heavenly Father."[2]

I once heard someone define mercy as "not getting what you deserve" and grace as "getting what you don't deserve." Both sides of that equation manifest the tender regard and infinite love our Heavenly Father has for each one of us. Rather than getting discouraged because the journey is so long and we seem to have made little progress in our difficult climb up the mountain of spirituality, let's do our best and then trust the Lord more. "We can contemplate how far we have already come in the climb on the pathway to perfection," Elder Neal A. Maxwell wrote. "It is usually much further than we acknowledge, and such reflections restore resolve. . . . We can know that when we have *truly* given what we have, it is like paying a full tithe; it is, in that respect, *all* that was asked. . . . Finally, we can accept this stunning, irrevocable truth: Our Lord can lift us from deep despair and cradle us midst any care. . . . This is a gospel of grand expectations, but God's grace is sufficient for each of us if we remember that there are no *instant* Christians."[3]

"My fellow disciples of Jesus Christ," Sister Michelle D. Craig of the General Young Women Presidency declared, "with all my heart, I choose to stand with the Lord. I choose to stand with His chosen servants . . . for they speak for Him and are the stewards of the ordinances and covenants that tie me to the Savior.

"When I stumble, I will keep getting up, relying on the grace and enabling power of Jesus Christ. I will stay in my covenant with Him and work through my questions by study of God's word, by faith, and with the help of the Holy Ghost, whose guidance I trust. I will seek His Spirit every day by doing the small and simple things. This is my path of discipleship."[4]

I have been a serious student of the Apostle Paul for almost fifty years, and I am very grateful for the understanding of the goodness and grace of God he provided in his life and in his epistles. My journey through Paul's teachings and writings have assisted me greatly in perceiving the majesty of our Lord's atoning sacrifice and the grace that He proffers me. It has been my love affair with the Book of Mormon, however, that has sharpened my views, shaped my comprehension, and provided a doctrinal understanding of the balance of and vital relationship between people's good works and their total reliance upon the Lord. The Book of Mormon shines a bright light on what it means for us to be saved by "the merits and mercy and grace of the Holy Messiah" (2 Nephi 2:8). The Book of Mormon is a priceless possession, one we must continue to offer to the world, a testament that will tighten men's and women's focus on Jesus Christ and make known how they may inherit the precious gift of eternal life that He freely offers.

CHAPTER 7

# Life in Eden before the Fall

2 NEPHI 2

When I transferred from Louisiana State University to Brigham Young University after returning from my mission, I was still uncertain about what I wanted to do with my life and thus what I should major in. For a time I thought I might major in English, then later decided that I would like to be a mathematician, then even later a historian. I took an introduction to psychology class and was absolutely fascinated with what I read and learned. So I became a psychology major. A few semesters later, in a class on motivation, we were required to read and report on a book about either the life or life's work of a well-known behavioral scientist. I happened upon a book in the university bookstore entitled *Ye Shall Be as Gods*, written by Eric Fromm.

To my surprise, very early in the book, Dr. Fromm described Adam and Eve's partaking of the forbidden fruit as an obvious case of rebellion against Deity, the grossest illustration of pride and unbridled ambition. He even accused them of blasphemy, supposing that they could, in some evil way, "become like God." Needless to say, my eyes were opened! This was a view of the Fall that I not only had never heard but also could never have conceived.

After receiving my master's degree, I chose to leave the study of psychology and pursue a PhD in religious studies, and my understanding of "orthodox" or Nicene Christianity expanded even more. I remember being bowled over as I read St. Augustine's *Confessions*, Martin Luther's *The Bondage of the Will*, and excerpts from John Calvin's *Institutes of the Christian Religion*. I discovered why so many Roman Catholics and Protestants today believe that men and women are depraved by nature; that little children are born corrupt, inheriting the "original sin" of Adam and Eve; that the hearts of all human beings are twisted, even warped by the Fall; and that mortals are actually incapable of choosing good until God transforms and empowers them to do so.

I am reminded of a conversation I had once with a Protestant minister who was basically taking shots at the "strange" view of the Fall held by the Latter-day Saints. I remember very well him saying something like, "The difference between you folks and 'real Christians' is that if and when you are ever allowed to meet Adam or Eve in the next life, you want to rush up to them and give them a high five. You want to embrace Eve and thank her for partaking of the forbidden fruit and congratulate Adam for following her lead. If I ever have the opportunity to see them, I'll scream at them, condemn them, maybe even take a swing at them. It's because of them that our world is as corrupt and wicked as it is today." As you can see, there's quite a difference between what most of our Christian friends think and what we as Latter-day Saints think about Adam and Eve and the Fall.

Let's spend a minute more on contrasting a Restoration perspective of the Fall and thus the nature of humankind with what many in our world believe. John Calvin, the leader of the Protestant Reformation in Switzerland, taught, "After the heavenly image was effaced [through the Fall], he not only was himself punished by a withdrawal of the ornaments in which he had been arrayed, i.e., wisdom, virtue, justice, truth, and holiness, and by the substitution in their place of those dire pests, blindness, impotence, vanity, impurity, and unrighteousness, but he involved his posterity also, and plunged them in the same wretchedness. This is the hereditary corruption to which early Christian writers gave the name original sin, meaning by the term the depravation of a nature formally good and pure. . . . Augustine labored to show that we are not corrupted by acquired wickedness, but bring an innate corruption from the very womb. . . . All of us, therefore descending from an impure seed, come into the world tainted with the contagion of sin. . . . We thus see that the impurity of parents is transmitted to their children, so that all, without exception, are originally depraved."[1]

This is why Emile Brunner, a prominent twentieth-century Christian theologian, explained: "There is no greater sense of distance than that which lies in the words Creator-Creation. Now this is the first and fundamental thing which can be said about man: He is a creature, and as such he is separated by an abyss from the Divine manner of being. The greatest dissimilarity between two things which we can express at all—more dissimilar than light and darkness, death and life, good and evil—is that between the Creator and that which is created."[2]

As to the guilt or innocence of children, the prophet Enoch spoke of Adam conversing with the Lord: "And our father Adam spake unto the Lord, and said: Why is it that man must repent and be baptized in water? And the Lord said unto Adam: Behold *I have forgiven thee thy transgression in the Garden of Eden.* Hence came the saying abroad among the people, that the Son of God hath atoned for original guilt, wherein the sins of the parents cannot be answered upon the heads of the children, for *they [children] are whole from the foundation of the world*" (Moses 6:53–54; see also Moroni 8:11–12, 19, 22; Doctrine and Covenants 29:46–48; 74:7). One wonders just how different the Christian religious life would be if that salient truth were understood by followers of Jesus Christ all over the world!

In speaking to his son Jacob, Lehi said: "If Adam had not transgressed he would not have fallen, but he would have remained in the Garden of Eden. And all things which were created must have remained in the same state they were after they were created; and they must have remained forever, and had no end" (2 Nephi 2:22). Before the Fall, all life within the Garden of Eden existed in what we would call a paradisiacal condition—that is, a terrestrial state. In a future day, when the Son of God returns to earth and the great Millennium begins, the earth will return to that paradisiacal condition (see Articles of Faith 1:10). President Joseph Fielding Smith taught that although Adam and Eve possessed a physical body, they were spiritual in nature; they were not subject to death. He describes them as physical-spiritual. They had tangible, physical bodies, but within their veins flowed spirit, not blood.[3] We often say that they were immortal, but, strictly speaking, since immortality only comes to us through death and the resurrection, we might instead consider them as being in an *amortal* (nonmortal) condition.

Lehi is explaining that if our first parents had not chosen to partake of the fruit of the tree of knowledge of good and evil and thereby initiate the Fall, they would have remained in their amortal condition; they would still be there, some 6,000+ years later. Notice Lehi's words: "And they would have had no children; wherefore they would have remained in a state of innocence, having no joy, for they knew no misery; doing no good, for they knew no sin" (2 Nephi 2:23). In their physical-spiritual condition, they could not produce mortal children, and thus all of the Father's spirit children would have remained in their premortal first estate, and the Father's plan of salvation would have been foiled. As found in the book of Moses (Joseph Smith's inspired translation of the early chapters of Genesis), we read: "And in that day [following the Fall] Adam blessed God and was filled, and began to prophesy concerning all the families of the earth, saying: Blessed be the name of God, for *because of my transgression my eyes are opened, and in this life I shall have joy*, and again in the flesh I shall see God. And Eve, his wife, heard all these things and was glad, saying: *Were it not for our transgression we never should have had seed, and never should have known good and evil, and the joy of our redemption*, and the eternal life which God giveth unto all the obedient" (Moses 5:10–11; emphasis added).

The scriptures of the Restoration are consistent in describing what our first parents did in Eden as a *transgression*, not a sin. The Prophet Joseph is reported to have stated that "Adam did not commit sin in eating the [forbidden] fruits, for God had decreed that he should eat and fall. . . . Therefore the Lord appointed us [the human family] to fall and also redeemed us."[4] While most within the Christian world condemn Mother Eve in particular, Latter-day Saints understand the vital role she played within the Father's plan.

President Dallin H. Oaks offered inspired prophetic commentary on the scriptural account of the Fall: "When Adam and Eve received the first commandment, they were in a transitional state, no longer in the spirit world but with physical bodies not yet subject to death and not yet capable of procreation. They could not fulfill the Father's first commandment without transgressing the barrier between the bliss of the Garden of Eden and the terrible trials and wonderful opportunities of mortal life. . . .

"It was Eve who first transgressed the limits of Eden in order to initiate the conditions of mortality. Her act, whatever its nature, was formally a transgression but eternally a glorious necessity to open the doorway toward eternal life. Adam showed his wisdom by doing the same. And thus Eve and 'Adam fell that men might be' (2 Nephi 2:25).

"Some Christians condemn Eve for her act, concluding that she and her daughters are somehow flawed by it. Not the Latter-day Saints! *Informed by revelation, we celebrate Eve's act and honor her wisdom and courage in the great episode called the Fall.*"[5] Contrary to the feelings of my pastor friend, if I live worthy enough to be introduced to Adam and Eve in the world to come, I will express my undying gratitude and deepest appreciation for their Fall, for if there had been no Fall of Adam and Eve, there would have been no Atonement of Christ. All would have been lost, and no amount of human goodness and faithfulness could make up for the loss.

## CHAPTER 8

# The Choice Seer

### 2 NEPHI 3

Chapter 3 of 2 Nephi is an excerpt from a larger prophecy by Joseph who was sold into Egypt. We can read that prophecy in its entirety in chapter 50 of Joseph Smith's Translation of the Bible. Lehi seems to be drawing upon this prophecy when he delivers his final words of blessing to his youngest son, Joseph.

In verse 4, Lehi states that "great were the covenants of the Lord which he made unto Joseph." We know, of course, of the covenant that God made with Abraham and his posterity, that if they chose to follow Jehovah, observe His laws and statutes, and keep themselves from the beliefs and practices of the nations surrounding them, they would (1) have the blessings of the priesthood; (2) have the gospel in their lives; (3) receive exaltation, or the continuation of the family unit into eternity; and (4) be given a land inheritance (Abraham 2:8–11, 19).

Lehi explains that out of the lineage of Joseph who was sold into slavery, "a seer shall the Lord my God raise up, who shall be a choice seer unto the fruit of my loins [descendants of Joseph]." The Lord spoke to Joseph of old: "A choice seer will I raise up out of the fruit of thy loins; and he shall be esteemed highly among the fruit of thy loins. And unto him will I give commandment that he shall do a work for the fruit of thy loins, his brethren, which shall be a great worth unto them, even to the bringing of them to the knowledge of the covenants which

I have made with thy fathers" (2 Nephi 3:6–7). This language reminds us of what we discussed in chapter 3, that the Lord would, in the last days, restore not only precious truths that had been lost from the Bible but also many covenants of the Lord that had been lost through the centuries.

What Joseph of old saw was the call and prophetic ministry of Joseph Smith Jr., and he prophesied that this choice seer "shall do none other work, save the work which I shall command him" (verse 8). In a revelation given to the Prophet in July 1830, Jesus Christ instructed Joseph Smith: "Thou shalt devote all thy service in Zion; and in this thou shalt have strength. . . . And in temporal labors thou shalt not have strength, for this is not thy calling. Attend to thy calling and thou shalt have wherewith to magnify thine office, and to expound all scriptures, and continue in the laying on of the hands and confirming the churches" (Doctrine and Covenants 24:7–9).

Lehi goes on to declare more of the words of the Savior about this choice seer: (1) he will bring forth the word of the Lord, which will convince people of the truthfulness of the Bible (verse 11); (2) he will be involved in restoring or gathering the house of Israel (verses 7, 13); (3) those who seek to destroy him will be confounded (verse 14); (4) his name, as well as his father's, will be the same as Joseph of old (verse 15); and (5) he will be an instrument in the hands of the Lord to do mighty wonders, including bringing about "much restoration unto the house of Israel" (verse 24). Verses 18 and 19 deserve a bit more discussion. Joseph, son of Lehi, learns that as it was with Moses, so it will be with the choice seer: he will not be mighty in speaking at first but will be given spokesmen, called by God to declare the words of the seers. With Moses, this was his older brother, Aaron (Exodus 4:10–16; see also JST, Genesis 50:35).

In 2 Nephi 3:18–19, we read more of the prophecy of Joseph of old: "And the Lord said unto me also: I will raise up [a man] unto the fruit of thy loins; and I will make for him a spokesman. And I, behold, I will give unto him that he shall write the writing of the fruit of thy loins, unto the fruit of thy loins; and the spokesman of thy loins shall declare it. And the words which he shall write shall be the words which are expedient in my wisdom should go forth unto the fruit of thy loins. And it shall be as if the fruit of thy loins had cried unto them from the dust; for I know their faith."

Over the years, many Latter-day Saints have concluded that Oliver Cowdery was the prophesied spokesman for Joseph; the Lord indicated as much at the time the restored Church was organized. Oliver was called as "the first preacher of this church" (Doctrine and Covenants 21:12). In section 28, Oliver is instructed by Christ: "And thou shalt be obedient unto the things which I shall give unto him [Joseph], even as Aaron, to declare faithfully the commandments and the revelations, with power and authority unto the Church" (verse 3). Later, in October of 1833, Sidney Rigdon was also called to be a spokesman for the Prophet (Doctrine and Covenants 100:9).

In his last book, published just after his death in 1985, Elder Bruce R. McConkie suggested an alternative interpretation of the prophecy of Joseph of old about the choice seer. In what follows, the bracketed information is from Elder McConkie, not me. "Mormon wrote the Book of Mormon, quoting, condensing, and summarizing from many ancient records as the Spirit directed. And Joseph Smith translated the ancient word by the gift and power of God and proclaimed it to all men, and to the seed of Joseph in particular, as the mind and will and voice of Him by whom salvation comes."

"With this in mind," Elder McConkie continued, "note these words of the Lord: 'And I, behold, I will give unto him [Mormon] that he shall write the writing of the fruit of thy loins [the Nephites], unto the fruit of thy loins [the Lamanites]; and the spokesman of thy loins [Joseph Smith] shall declare it.'"[1] My impression is that these two explanations are not necessarily mutually exclusive; perhaps they are both correct.

I have saved for last a brief consideration of 2 Nephi 3:12. In the words of our Redeemer, "Wherefore, the fruit of thy loins [descendants of the ancient Joseph] shall write [the Book of Mormon]; and the fruit of the loins of Judah shall write; and that which shall be written by thy loins, and also that which shall be written by the fruit of the loins of Judah *shall grow together, unto the confounding of false doctrines and laying down of contentions, and establishing peace among the fruit of thy loins,* and bringing them to the knowledge of their fathers in the latter days, and also to the knowledge of my covenants, saith the Lord" (emphasis added).

Let me share a personal experience here. Some years ago, while I was a member of the BYU Religious Education faculty, I taught a semester-long course on the four Gospels—Matthew, Mark, Luke, and John. The first day of class we were to discuss John 1, concerning Jesus being the Word who was made flesh and came and dwelt among His people. Our class went well; we had a mentally and spiritually invigorating discussion about several verses of scripture. It was one of those moments when the Spirit of the Lord was felt in an unusually powerful way, an occasion when you feel deeply grateful to be able to study and teach the gospel of Jesus Christ.

As I was walking from the building where I taught back to my office in the Joseph Smith Building, I reflected on what my students and I had just experienced. We had discussed the King James Version of John 1:1–18, as well as the Joseph Smith Translation of those verses. We read from section 93 of the Doctrine and Covenants, which proved to be an enlightening commentary on John's writings. I quoted from Elders Orson Pratt, John Taylor, and Bruce R. McConkie on their belief that in John 1, John the Beloved Apostle was drawing upon the writings of John the Baptist.[2] It occurred to me that we had just experienced an approximation of what took place when the risen Lord taught the Nephites—He "expounded all the scriptures in one" (3 Nephi 23:6, 14). That is, by our broadened study, we had expounded all the scriptures in one. We had demonstrated to ourselves how each of our books within the standard works, coupled with the teachings of modern apostles and prophets, bears a distinctive but united testimony of the Lord Jesus Christ and His eternal gospel.

To some extent, through our use of the Latter-day Saint edition of the King James Bible and triple combination, which contains thousands of cross-references to all the books within our standard works, we can, when properly inspired, expound all the scriptures in one. What a grand and joyous day it will be when we can meet cordially with our friends from other faiths and discover that when brought together, these sacred volumes will, more than ever before, unite to confound false doctrines and contention, all to the edification and blessing of God's children.

Some thirty years after the death of the Joseph Smith Jr., President Brigham Young remarked about the choice seer: "When I first heard him preach, he brought heaven and earth together; and all the priests of the day could not tell me anything correct about heaven, hell, God, angels or devils. . . . When I saw Joseph, he took heaven, figuratively speaking, and brought it down to earth; and he took the earth, brought it up, and opened up, in plainness and simplicity, the things of God; and that is the beauty of his mission."[3]

CHAPTER 9

# Resurrection and Judgment

2 NEPHI 9; ALMA 11; HELAMAN 14

As we search the pages of the Book of Mormon, we detect very early on that the doctrine of the Fall and the doctrine of the Savior's Atonement are companions; in almost every case in which the prophets or teachers speak of the Lord's Atonement, the concept of the Fall of humankind is either taught directly or implied. So it is with the doctrine of the Resurrection and the doctrine of eternal judgment. They are companions and, in most cases, are taught together.

Lehi's declaration that Christ will be the "firstfruits" of the resurrection (2 Nephi 2:9) is akin to what the Apostle Paul wrote to his beloved Corinthian Saints: "If in this life only we have hope in Christ, we are of all men most miserable. But now is Christ risen from the dead, and become the firstfruits of them that slept" (1 Corinthians 15:19–20). Now hear Lehi's words that link the two companions: "And because of the intercession for all, *all men come unto God; wherefore, they stand in the presence of him, to be judged of him* according to the truth and holiness which is in him" (2 Nephi 2:10; emphasis added).

Jacob learned well from his father, for in 2 Nephi 9:15, we read: "And it shall come to pass that *when all men have passed from this first death unto life*, insomuch as they have become immortal, *they must appear before the judgment seat of the Holy One of Israel*; and then cometh the judgment, and then must they be judged according to the holy judgment of God" (emphasis added). Only six verses later Jacob repeats himself: "And he [Jesus Christ] cometh into the world that he may save all men if they will hearken unto his voice; for behold, he suffereth the pains of all men, yea, the pains of every living creature, both men, women, and children, who belong to the family of Adam. And he suffereth this that the resurrection might pass upon all men, *that all might stand before him at the great and judgment day*" (2 Nephi 9:21–22; emphasis added).

As Alma will later teach, the Savior suffered all of the stresses and strains and challenges of life in this second estate (pains, afflictions, temptations, sicknesses, and infirmities—see Alma 7:11–12). He also suffered what myriads of people through the millennia have considered to be the greatest pain of all—physical death. Just as He suffered spiritual death—alienation from the Father's sustaining Spirit[1]—so He needed to face and experience what every other mortal will face when their life on earth comes to an end.

While we could go on and on in listing the powerful teachings of the Book of Mormon prophets regarding resurrection and judgment, I will refer to just one more, one I consider to be the most informative. Near the end of the Nephite nation, Moroni bears witness that the God of Abraham, Isaac, and Jacob is a God of miracles. He then instructs us: "Behold he [God] created Adam, and by Adam came the fall of man. And because of the fall of man came Jesus Christ, even the Father and the Son; and *because of Jesus Christ came the redemption of man. And because of the redemption of man, which came by Jesus Christ, they are brought back into the presence of the Lord; yea, this is wherein all men are redeemed,* because the death of Christ bringeth to pass the resurrection, which bringeth to pass a redemption from an endless sleep, from which sleep all men shall be awakened by the power of God when the trump shall sound; and they shall come forth, both small and great, and *all shall stand before his bar [of judgment], being redeemed and loosed from this eternal band of death,* which death is a temporal death. And then cometh the judgment of the Holy One upon them" (Mormon 9:11–14; emphasis added).

Now, let us reason together. Those who respond positively to the message of salvation in Christ, repent of their sins, are baptized by water, receive the gift of the Holy Ghost, and remain faithful to their covenants until death will enter paradise (the abode of righteous spirits). There they will rest from their earthly labors and pressures, be taught and undergo further refinement, and, when Christ returns to the earth in glory, come to earth with Him as celestial, resurrected beings. Their judgment will be a sweet experience.

Those who reject the message of salvation when they had valid opportunities to receive it, who spurned and made light of righteousness and goodness, who violated God's commandments regularly, and who pursued an evil course until the time of their death will leave this life and be admitted into what is variously called spirit prison, hell, or outer darkness (see 1 Peter 3:18–19; 2 Nephi 9:10–12; Alma 40:13). In the October 2019 general conference, President Dallin H. Oaks said: "The scriptures . . . teach that this spirit world is divided between those who have been 'righteous' or 'just' during life and those who have been wicked. They also describe how some faithful spirits teach the gospel to those who have been wicked or rebellious (see 1 Peter 3:19; Doctrine and Covenants 138:19–20, 29, 32, 37). Most important, modern revelation reveals that the work of salvation goes forward in the spirit world (see Doctrine and Covenants 138:30–34, 58), and although we are urged not to procrastinate our repentance during mortality (see Alma 13:27), *we are taught that some repentance is possible there* (see Doctrine and Covenants 138:58)."[2]

Here is the principle we need to understand: those who reject the gospel, both in this life and the next, suffer a spiritual death and are cast out of the presence of God and cut off as to things pertaining to righteousness (see Alma 12:16, 32; Helaman 14:16, 18). And yet the infinite love of the Father and the Son is manifest in the fact that even these, the wicked, will for a short time, be allowed to stand in the presence of God once more, this time to be judged.

The Book of Mormon teaches the same doctrine as the Bible

concerning the fact that the Father commits all judgment unto the Son (see John 5:22; Acts 17:31; 2 Nephi 9:41; Mosiah 3:10). And yet there are scriptural passages that speak of judgment by the Twelve Apostles in the Old World (see Matthew 19:28) and the Twelve Apostles in the New World (see 3 Nephi 27:27). In a revelation given to the Church in September of 1830, the Lord stated: "And again, verily, verily, I say unto you, and it hath gone forth in a firm decree, by the will of the Father, that *mine apostles, the twelve which were with me in my ministry at Jerusalem*, shall stand at my right hand at the day of my coming in a pillar of fire, being clothed with robes of righteousness, with crowns upon their heads, in glory even as I am, *to judge the whole house of Israel, even as many as have loved me and kept my commandments*" (Doctrine and Covenants 29:12; emphasis added).

The Nephite prophets give us singular insights into the nature of the resurrected body. Amulek, Alma's missionary companion, taught the wicked people of Ammonihah that the Savior will "come into the world to redeem his people; and he shall take upon him the transgressions of those who believe on his name; and these are they that shall have eternal life, and salvation cometh to none else. Therefore the wicked remain as though there had been no redemption made, except it be the loosing of the bands of death; for behold, the day cometh that *all shall rise from the dead and stand before God, and be judged according to their works. . . . The spirit and the body shall be reunited again in its perfect form*; both limb and joint shall be restored to its proper frame, even as we now are at this time; and we shall be brought to stand before God" (Alma 11:40–41, 43; emphasis added).

Later, Alma taught his errant son, Corianton, that "the soul [spirit] shall be restored to the body, and the body to the soul; yea, and every limb and joint shall be restored to its body; yea, even a hair of the head shall not be lost; but all things shall be restored to their proper and perfect frame" (Alma 40:23). These teachings are consistent with revelation we have received in this final dispensation (see Doctrine and Covenants 88:14–16; 138:16–17).

Finally, I'd like to return to Jacob's teachings on the Resurrection, to a passage that is rather difficult to understand. Very often the Book of Mormon prophets, in order to highlight and dramatize the plight of humankind if Christ had not redeemed us, essentially ask readers, "What if there had been no Atonement of Christ?" In 2 Nephi 9, Jacob rejoices in the wisdom, mercy, and grace of God. He testifies that "if the flesh should rise no more [if there were no resurrection of the dead] our spirits must become subject to that angel who fell from before the presence of the eternal God, and became the devil, to rise no more. And our spirits must have become like unto him, and we become devils, angels to a devil, to be shut out from the presence of our God, and to remain with the father of lies, in misery, like unto himself" (2 Nephi 9:8–9). But *why* would we become devils, angels to a devil, if there had been no resurrection of Jesus Christ?

My late friend and colleague Robert J. Matthews shared a personal experience with me many years ago. He explained that when he was a teenager, he and his friends sat in their Sunday School class listening to their teacher speak about the Lord's atoning work, including the Resurrection. One of the members of the class asked the teacher: "What would happen if we all died and Jesus had never risen from the dead? What would be our situation?" The instructor hemmed and hawed a bit, quietly pondered, and then responded: "I suppose that, when we died, we would go into the spirit world and that, at the right time, our spirits would be assigned to one of the three kingdoms of glory." Bob looked around the room and saw his fellow classmates nodding their head in agreement. He said to me: "It sounded like a pretty good answer to a good question." But a few years later, when he stumbled across 2 Nephi 9:8–9 he realized that the teacher had not really given a good (or correct) answer to what had been a pretty good question.

Well then, what is the answer? If Jesus Christ had not risen from the tomb, why would we all be in Satan's power? The following answer illustrates how, when we acquaint ourselves with all of the books within our standard works, we discover that the greatest commentary on scripture is scripture. Matters that are difficult to understand in one scriptural text are often cleared up in another book of scripture. Regarding the Resurrection, consider the challenge that the Apostle Paul faced in preaching Christ. Many people living in Corinth, including some of the Saints, were influenced by Greek philosophy, which had a dualistic perception of the world—the physical, the tangible, the flesh, was something that was to be discarded, despised, and transcended, while spiritual things led one to understand sacred, saving knowledge that the bulk of humanity would never know. Thus there were times when the Resurrection of Jesus of Nazareth sounded foolish, illogical, or strange to some listeners. If the flesh is evil, something that must be put away or transcended, why in the world would anyone want a resurrection in which they would get their carnal and spiritually worthless physical bodies back? This idea of a resurrection, of receiving our bodies once again, was simply not reasonable.

In 1 Corinthians 15, Paul attempts to help the Saints see the oddity and tragedy of believing that Jesus Christ is the Savior and Redeemer and yet rejecting the idea that we can one day have our spirits and our bodies reunite. Notice his reasoning: "Now if Christ be preached that he rose from the dead, how say some among you that there is no resurrection of the dead? But if there be no resurrection of the dead, then is Christ not risen: and if Christ be not risen, then is our preaching vain, and your faith is also vain. Yea, and we are found false witnesses of God. . . . And if Christ be not raised, your faith is vain: *ye are yet in your sins*" (verses 12–17; emphasis added). Being forever sinful, we could never enter into the presence of the Lord; we would be subject to Satan.

To put this another way, if Jesus did not have the power to rise from the tomb into immortality, as He said He did, why should we suppose that He has the power to forgive our sins? The Resurrection is the capstone of the Atonement of the Redeemer, and thus it is closely linked with other facets of His Atonement, including faith in Christ, repentance, and forgiveness. In other words, if no Resurrection, then no Atonement.

CHAPTER 10

# Beware the "Precepts of Men": Evil Attitudes

2 NEPHI 28–29

President Ezra Taft Benson declared that "the Book of Mormon brings men to Christ through two basic means. First, it tells in a plain manner of Christ and His gospel. It testifies of His divinity and the necessity for a Redeemer and the need of our putting trust in Him. . . . Second, the Book of Mormon exposes the enemies of Christ. It confounds false doctrines and lays down contention (see 2 Nephi 3:12). It fortifies the humble followers of Christ against the evil designs, strategies, and doctrines of the devil in our day. The type of apostates in the Book of Mormon is similar to the type we have today. God, with His infinite foreknowledge, so molded the Book of Mormon that we might see the error and know how to combat false educational, political, religious, and philosophical concepts of our time."[1]

In this chapter and the next we will study some of the evil attitudes and perspectives which have been spawned by Satan and which are ever before us in our modern world. In 2 Nephi 28 and 29, we encounter some of those mental and spiritual traps about which the prophets still warn us, almost three millennia after the time of Nephi.

Nephi wrote of a day and time when churches "shall contend one with another; and their priests shall contend one with another" (2 Nephi 28:4). It is not difficult today to hear the squabbles and witness the contention between Christian denominations about how the gospel should be preached in church or what kind of music is best for worship services. The more important questions, however, deal with what doctrine should be taught and emphasized. How and how often should sin and repentance be taught? Do we believe in freedom of the will or predestination? What role, if any, do good works play in one's salvation? Is a person literally consuming the body and blood of Christ or remembering Him during the communion or eucharist (sacrament)? Should the congregation adhere to and regularly repeat creeds and theological formulations? What about the nature of authority—does one's authority come through succession from the time of the Apostle Peter, or do we subscribe to the Protestant concept of a priesthood of all believers?

Disagreements on content or procedure or policy are one thing, but large disagreements on the nature of God and the Godhead are very serious. Should a church hold tenaciously to traditional moral values on gender, marriage, and family or rather yield to the values of society? This is a crucial decision. Should Christians accept and participate in spiritual gifts or conclude that such matters ceased with the first-century Apostles? This is a crucial decision. Are men and women depraved creatures, absolutely incapable of recognizing truth and receiving divine guidance, or are they the sons and daughters of God, created in His image and likeness, open to divine guidance and answers to prayer? This is a crucial decision. And on and on. Nephi saw that in the last days priests, ministers, or religious leaders would "teach with their learning, and deny the Holy Ghost, which giveth utterance" (2 Nephi 28:4). When there is no central or priestly hierarchy in a church to which members may look for answers and clarity, chaos and great confusion are the result.

In what might well be called the "law of the teacher," the Lord in February 1831 counseled the Latter-day Saints that "the elders, priests and teachers of this church shall teach the principles of my gospel, which are in the Bible and the Book of Mormon, in the which is the fullness of the gospel. And they shall observe the covenants and church articles [the revelations and particularly what is taught in Doctrine and Covenants 20] to do them, and these shall be their teachings, as they shall be directed by the Spirit. And the Spirit shall be given unto you by the prayer of faith; and *if ye receive not the Spirit ye shall not teach*" (Doctrine and Covenants 42:12–14; emphasis added). This last phrase could mean a number of things. The Lord could be saying, in essence, "If you do not have the Spirit accompanying you when you speak or teach, your presentation will not be effective, will not accomplish what you hope to accomplish." It could mean that the message will not be well received, that the person will not really be teaching, or that true learning will not take place. In this sense, verse 14 of section 42 seems to be a *prophecy* of what will or will not take place if the speaker does not have the Spirit with her.

Now let's look at verse 14 from a different angle. Perhaps the Lord is saying, "If the Holy Spirit does not attend you in your presentation, *you should not teach*; you really ought not plan to speak if the Spirit is not with you." Or, "Don't try to press your message upon listeners if you are not spiritually prepared." From this perspective, verse 14 would be a *command*, a divine injunction.

Lessons, sermons, articles, or books on sacred matters that are essentially exercises in intellectual showboating never touch or warm the heart or inspire the listener to do good or serve God and fellowman. What is taught may be interesting, but it does not inspire. It may cause a listener to reconsider certain things in life, but it does not fan the flame of faith or bring conviction. In a modern revelation, the Lord Jesus Christ asks members of His Church this question: "Unto what were ye ordained [or called or set apart]?" He then provides the answer: "To preach my gospel by the Spirit, even the Comforter which was sent forth to teach the truth. . . . Verily I say unto you, he [or she] that is ordained of me and sent forth to teach the word of truth by the Comforter, in the Spirit of truth, doth he [or she] preach it by the Spirit of Truth or some other way? And if it be by *some other way* it is not of God" (Doctrine and Covenants 50:13–14, 17–18; emphasis added). What is "some other way"? It is to teach by the power of the intellect alone.

The prophecy in verses 7 and 8 of 2 Nephi 28 can regularly be seen in people all about us who suggest strongly that we shouldn't be too religious, too spiritual, or too intense; that we shouldn't take life so seriously; that we should take it easy and enjoy the pleasures of the world. "Yea, and there shall be many," Nephi recorded, "which shall say: *Eat, drink, and be merry, for tomorrow we die*; and it shall be well with us. And there shall also be many which shall say: Eat, drink, and be merry; nevertheless, fear God—*he will justify in committing a little sin*; yea, lie a little; take the advantage of one because of his words, dig a pit for thy neighbor; there is no harm in this; and *do all these things, for tomorrow we die*; and if it so be that we are guilty, God will beat us with a few stripes, and at last we shall be saved in the kingdom of God" (emphasis added).

"Eat, drink, and be merry, for tomorrow we die." Some years ago there was a beer commercial in which handsome and well-built men and beautiful women were sitting around a table, consuming their alcohol, seemingly enjoying themselves. One man spoke up and said: "We need to grab for all the gusto that we can!" This attitude would certainly fit persons who were agnostics or atheists, who may not believe in life after death, who definitely have rejected the idea of absolute truths and absolute values. These have no worry about what the consequences of their current lifestyle will be after they pass through the veil of death and are confronted with what they have done, which was basically waste their lives. It will surely be a rude awakening. As Amulek beckoned to the Zoramites, "I beseech of you that ye do not procrastinate the day of your repentance until the end; for after this day of life, which is given us to prepare for eternity, behold, if we do not improve [make wise use of] our time while in this life, then cometh the night of darkness wherein there can be no labor performed" (Alma 34:33).

Let's attend to one more of the devilish precepts about which we are warned in the Book of Mormon. Nephi continues: "Because of pride, and because of false teachers, and false doctrine, their churches have become corrupted, and their churches are lifted up; because of pride they are puffed up. . . . They wear stiff necks and high heads; yea, and because of pride, and wickedness, and abominations, and whoredoms, they have all gone astray save it be *a few, who are the humble followers of Christ: nevertheless, they are led, that in many instances they do err because they are taught by the precepts of men*" (2 Nephi 28:12, 14; emphasis added). I suppose these last words of warning could pertain to noble men and women of various churches who truly love the Lord and do a great deal of good in the world. But I find myself reading and rereading and reflecting on these painful words—that there are humble followers of Christ who are led astray because they absorb and inculcate the precepts of men. I honestly believe these words pertain to Latter-day Saints just as well (compare Doctrine and Covenants 45:26–29).

We live in a strange day, unlike any time I can recall. So many words have been redefined in our culture. For example, the word *tolerance* has always been used this way: "I don't agree with your perspective on this matter, but I respect your right to express your views." But today, in many different communities, the word *tolerance* is used as follows: "If you disagree with me, you are intolerant." Too many otherwise faithful members of The Church of Jesus Christ of Latter-day Saints have been snared in what might be called the "tolerance trap." In the name of tolerance, many of our own people have stated publicly their disagreements with the Church's leaders and teachings; they have adopted the moral values of a culture that is gradually sinking toward Sodom.

President Boyd K. Packer, in addressing the J. Reuben Clark Law Society at Brigham Young University, told the assembled group: "I charge each of you . . . and put you on alert: These are days of great spiritual danger for this people. The world is spiraling downward at an ever-quickening pace. I am sorry to tell you that it will not get better. I know of nothing in the history of the Church or in the history of the world to compare with our present circumstances. *Nothing happened in*

*Sodom and Gomorrah which exceeds the wickedness and depravity which surrounds us now.*"[2]

President Gordon B. Hinckley likewise stated: "No one need tell you that we are living in a very difficult season in the history of the world. Standards are dropping everywhere. Nothing seems to be sacred any more. . . . The traditional family is under heavy attack. *I do not know that things were worse in the times of Sodom and Gomorrah.* At that season, Abraham bargained with the Lord to save these cities for the sake of the righteous. Notwithstanding his pleas, things were so bad that Jehovah decreed their destruction. They and their wicked inhabitants were annihilated. We see similar conditions today. They prevail all across the world. I think our Father must weep as He looks down upon His wayward sons and daughters. In the Church we are working very hard to stem the tide of this evil. But it is an uphill battle."[3]

Now, before we kick the dog, throw in the towel, and thrust up our hands in complete frustration, let me refer to a powerful message from a great man to his righteous son. Mormon, writing at a time somewhat similar to our own, pleaded with his son Moroni: "And now, my beloved son, notwithstanding [the people's] hardness, *let us labor diligently*; for if we should cease to labor, we should be brought under condemnation; for *we have a labor to perform* whilst in this tabernacle of clay, *that we may conquer the enemy of all righteousness, and rest our souls in the kingdom of God*" (Moroni 9:6; emphasis added).

CHAPTER 11

# Beware the "Precepts of Men": Treasuring Every Word of God

2 NEPHI 28–29

As we continue our search in the Book of Mormon for evil attitudes of the last days or for the inclination of some to give heed to the precepts of men, we come to a series of verses that are stunningly accurate. "For behold, at that day"—the last days, the final dispensation—"shall he [Satan] rage in the hearts of the children of men, and stir them [the people] up to anger against that which is good" (2 Nephi 28:20). This passage also describes the actions of some men and women in our day who have chosen to reject the restored gospel and leave the restored Church. Elder Neal A. Maxwell said: "Church members will live in this wheat-and-tares situation until the Millennium. Some real tares even masquerade as wheat, including the few eager individuals who lecture the rest of us about Church doctrines in which they no longer believe. They criticize the use of Church resources to which they no longer contribute. They condescendingly seek to counsel the Brethren whom they no longer sustain. Confrontive, except of themselves, of course, they leave the Church, but they cannot leave the Church alone."[1]

But Lucifer is versatile and often takes a different approach, as Nephi illustrates: "And others will he pacify, and lull them away into carnal security, that they will say: All is well in Zion; yea, Zion prospereth, all is well" (2 Nephi 28:21). This evil attitude—this enemy of Christ—seems to largely apply to the Latter-day Saints, although the mindset could certainly be a trap into which persons of many faiths might fall. To be led into "carnal security" is to become complacent, smug, satisfied with the present way of life, and uninterested and unwilling to leave the spiritual plateau on which a person has been pausing for a long, long time. While the Savior has counseled us not to be unduly weighed down with worry concerning the future, He also desires that we seek first to build up the kingdom of God and to establish His righteousness (see JST, Matthew 6:35–39). We cannot afford to pause on spiritual plateaus for very long. Nephi's counsel is direct and pertinent here: "Therefore, I would that ye should be steadfast and immovable, always abounding in good works, that Christ, the Lord Omnipotent, may seal you his, that you may be brought to heaven, that you may have everlasting salvation and eternal life" (Mosiah 5:15). In that sense, we must never be "at ease" in Zion (2 Nephi 28:24); we need to continually progress toward the abundant life (see John 10:10).

Finally, it seems as though Nephi chose to leave the worst and most evil attitude and precept of humankind for the very last. It is this: "Yea, woe be unto him that saith: We have received, and we need no more! . . . Woe be unto him that shall say: We have received the word of God, and we need no more of the word of God, for we have enough!" (2 Nephi 28:27, 29). Jesus countered the satanic temptation to turn stone into bread with this reply: "Man shall not live by bread alone, but by *every word that proceedeth out of the mouth of God*" (Matthew 4:4; emphasis added; see also Doctrine and Covenants 84:44). Not every other word, not every tenth word, but *every word.* This is a message for those outside the restored Church as well as those within.

Most of Christianity believes that the Bible is the word of God, the *essential* word of God, the *sufficient* word of God, the *final* word of God. Others would contend that the Holy Bible is the *inerrant* and *infallible* word of God. They are perfectly happy with what they have and feel no desire for further institutional revelation (or holy scripture) beyond the Bible. The Lord Himself has responded to this perspective of biblical sufficiency. In 2 Nephi 28:30, we read: "I will give unto the children of men line upon line, precept upon precept, here a little and there a little; and blessed are those who hearken unto my precepts, and lend an ear unto my counsel, for they shall learn wisdom; for unto him that receiveth I will give more; and from them that shall say, We have enough, from them shall be taken away even that which they have."

What we have in 2 Nephi 29 is the Lord's own and very direct feelings toward those who refuse revelation, meaning holy scripture beyond the Bible. When confronted with the teachings of the Restoration and thus the additional scripture possessed by the Latter-day Saints, many people of the nineteenth century said essentially, "A Bible! A Bible! We have got a Bible, and there cannot be any more Bible." It is just so today. Modern revelation is often rejected because people already possess ancient revelation. The question is whether the people of the world are open to the word of God in modern times, and Jesus Christ reasons with those who are skeptical: "*Know ye not that there are more nations than one?* Know ye not that I, the Lord your God, have created all men, and that *I remember those who are upon the isles of the sea;* . . . and *I bring forth my word unto the children of men, yea, even upon all the nations of the earth?* . . . And because that I have spoken one word ye need not suppose that I cannot speak another; for *my work is not yet finished; neither shall it be until the end of man,* neither from that time henceforth and forever" (2 Nephi 29:3, 6–10; emphasis added).

And then, to illustrate the principles He has been teaching, He adds this powerful remark: "For behold, I shall speak unto the Jews and they shall write it; and I shall also speak unto the Nephites and they shall write it; and I shall also speak unto the other tribes of the house of Israel which I have led away, and they shall write it; and I shall also speak unto all nations of the earth and they shall write it [these records are unknown by us].

"And it shall come to pass that the Jews shall have the words of the Nephites, and the Nephites shall have the words of the Jews; and the Nephites and the Jews shall have the words of the lost tribes of Israel;

and the lost tribes of Israel shall have the words of the Nephites and the Jews" (2 Nephi 29:12–13).

In an address delivered in 1995 at a symposium on Joseph Smith's Translation of the Bible, President Dallin H. Oaks made these significant remarks: "*Those who understand that the importance of the scriptures is what the Lord would have us understand today are anxious for revelatory insight into the current significance of scriptural texts and concepts.* They understand that some things we have already received are hard to understand without the Lord's help (see 1 Nephi 15:1, 3, 8, 11), and that *we can never receive enough of the word of God. Persons with this attitude are anxious to have every source of revelation to help us know what the Lord would have us understand from the scriptures today.* Such persons will welcome the revelatory insights—even additions—by the prophets of this dispensation."[2] Such words regarding an expanding canon of scripture are thrilling.

We might ask ourselves: Just how grateful am I that God has chosen to speak in the last days through living prophets? How do I show my gratitude for the scriptures of the Restoration? How do I demonstrate my appreciation for apostles and prophets today, for "watchmen on the tower," revelators who can see "things . . . not visible to the natural eye" (Moses 6:36)? What are some ways that I can lovingly share my gratitude for modern and continuing revelation with friends and family who have not yet accepted the restored gospel? Pondering such questions may lead us to rejoice over what God has given us and thereby motivate us to share our pearls of great price with a world that desperately needs additional light and truth.

## CHAPTER 12

# Confronting the Anti-Christs: Sherem and Nehor

JACOB 7; ALMA 1

The Book of Mormon not only reveals the person and redeeming power of Jesus Christ but also provides vital insight into the persons and perspectives of the enemies of Christ. We need to know what it takes to draw closer to the Redeemer and Savior, but we also need to know how to avoid, recognize, and confront those whose purpose is to thwart the progress of the Lord's Church and kingdom. In this chapter and the next we will look carefully at three major anti-Christs—Sherem, Nehor, and Korihor—what they taught, what they did, and how the servants of God and God Himself dealt with them.

Jacob, son of Lehi, does not tell us what year Sherem the anti-Christ entered the Nephite community. The last verse of Jacob 6 reads simply: "I bid you farewell, until I shall meet you before the pleasing bar of God, which bar striketh the wicked with awful dread and fear. Amen." Clearly Jacob had planned to end his book, but after "some years had passed away" (Jacob 7:1), something took place that he felt needed to be recorded on the gold plates. That something was, of course, his confrontation with Sherem.

We are told that Sherem "began to preach among the people, and to declare unto them that there should be no Christ" (Jacob 7:2). Early in the small plates, Nephi taught that in six hundred years from the time his father, Lehi, left Jerusalem, "a prophet would the Lord God raise up among the Jews—even a Messiah, or, in other words, a Savior of the world" (1 Nephi 10:4). We do not refer to Jesus Christ very often as a prophet, but that is surely what he is—a spokesman for His Heavenly Father. "He was the Word, even the messenger of salvation—the light and the Redeemer of the world" (Doctrine and Covenants 93:8–9). He is the Messiah, the Anointed One, the Redeemer who was sent into the world to save the world from sin and death. He was and is the Prophet to all prophets.

Sherem "preached many things which were flattering unto the people" (Jacob 7:2). To *flatter* is to soothe or satisfy, to make people feel comfortable, or to raise false hopes.[1] It is to whisper in the people's ears that all is well. And we are told that Sherem flattered the people in order to "overthrow the doctrine of Christ" (Jacob 7:2). That is, he sought to dissuade the people from receiving and applying the gospel of Jesus Christ. Obviously the first and perhaps the most obvious characterization of an anti-Christ is that he or she denies the reality or necessity for Jesus Christ. Prior to the meridian of time, the anti-Christ contended that there would be no Christ and that no man had the ability to speak authoritatively concerning future things.

Sherem accused Jacob of perverting the gospel and of uttering false prophecies concerning the coming of Christ. Surely some Nephites who were in tune with the Spirit must have discerned in Sherem the spirit of one who was an "accuser of [the] brethren" (Revelation 12:10), who was guilty of evil speaking of the Lord's anointed. When persons refuse to exercise faith—to have hope in that which is unseen but true (Alma 32:21)—they thereby deny themselves access to the spiritual world, another realm of reality. Their vision of things is at best deficient and at worst perverse; they cannot see things "as they really are" (Jacob 4:13; Doctrine and Covenants 93:24). They are seekers of truth with insufficient data; their methodology is limited by their approach, and their conclusions must surely be suspect.

Sherem's naturalistic view of reality prevented him from comprehending the unseen and discovering the unknown. Those who rely exclusively upon human sensory experience and human reason to determine truth do not find a place in their tightly enclosed epistemological system for such matters as spirit and revelation and prophecy. Further, when people's faith centers on that which can be seen and heard and felt through natural means only, they tend to generalize beyond their own experience; what they have not experienced they assume no one else has either. Because they do not know, surely no one does. Often those who dare not believe dare not allow others to believe.

Sherem professed to know and believe in the scriptures (Jacob 7:10–11), but lacking that elevated perspective that comes only by study and faith, he was unable to understand the true meaning and messages of the scriptures. He seemed to have been afflicted with a means-to-an-end sickness. He was obsessed with the here and now and refused to look beyond the present to greater and grander ends. Like the priests of King Noah (see Mosiah 12:31–32), Sherem believed that the law of Moses was sufficient and that salvation would come through observing the law without any reference whatsoever to Christ the Lawgiver. It is ironic that Sherem argued for the sufficiency of the law of Moses when in fact the law was given to point people to the coming of Jesus Christ.

Like most (but not all) anti-Christs, Sherem insisted that Jacob prove his point by demonstrable and measurable means—he demanded a sign (Jacob 7:13). We are taught in modern revelation that "faith cometh not by signs, but signs follow those that believe" (Doctrine and Covenants 63:9). You may remember that Jesus taught that it is a wicked and adulterous generation that seeks after signs (Matthew 12:39). Why is this the case? Simply stated, those who have given in to their lusts, who desire that which will satiate the flesh, and who have exhausted their passions in searching for the sensual also seek for physical manifestations of spiritual sensations. They demand proof! Unable to recognize and acknowledge eternal certainties, they insist that spiritual truths, with which they are unfamiliar, be manifest and translated into that realm they have come to know more surely than any other—the fanciful and the physical.

Sign seekers do have one thing going for them when it comes to convincing an audience: the servants of the Lord will generally not stoop to cheap theatrics to win the hearts of observers. Why? Because signs and miracles fan the flame of faith *already burning* in the hearts of believers. Signs and wonders and miracles do not create faith; they come as a result of or as a byproduct of faith that already exists. Seldom will God perform a notable miracle through his true servants to titillate sign seekers. And sign seekers know enough about the Lord and the prophetic past to know this. Unfortunately for Sherem, once in a great while the Lord *does* choose to bare His mighty arm in response to the taunting imps of uncleanness. In such cases, however, it is in wrath and the sign condemns the thrill seekers (see Doctrine and covenants 63:11). In Sherem's case, "the power of the Lord came upon [Sherem], insomuch that he fell to the earth" (Jacob 7:15). Sherem was struck down dramatically, even as Korihor was (who is discussed in the next chapter).

Presumably unable to care for himself, Sherem was "nourished for the space of many days" (Jacob 7:15)—perhaps meaning that he was fed and clothed and sheltered, and hopefully even educated and instructed in the true way of salvation. This kind act alone demonstrates Christianity and discipleship in their highest and deepest forms: a group of Saints who had been the object of a very unchristian intellectual attack provided succor for the man who had formerly wielded the sword of Satan. When Sherem recovered, he asked that the believers gather together, for he had a message to deliver. Sherem "spake plainly unto them, that he had been deceived by the power of the devil" (compare Alma 30:53). He spoke of hell, eternity, and eternal punishment (Jacob 7:18). Such doctrine would normally be scoffed at by the learned and ignored by the sophisticated. Sherem now spoke of these things because they weighed upon his mind: hell and eternal punishment were to him no longer religious rhetoric, but reality. After he had spoken the words he wanted to deliver, "he gave up the ghost" (Jacob 7:20).

In Nehor, we find a very different kind of anti-Christ. He is described as being "large and was noted for his much strength." He went about teaching what he declared to be the word of God, "bearing down against the church; declaring unto the people that every priest and teacher ought to become popular; and they ought not to labor with their hands, but that they ought to be supported by the people" (Alma 1:3). Nephi, son of Lehi, had defined priestcraft many years before: "Priestcrafts are that men preach and set themselves up for a light unto the world, that they may get gain and praise of the world; but they seek not the welfare of Zion" (2 Nephi 26:29). In other words, one is guilty of priestcraft when his or her deepest motives and desires in teaching the gospel are popularity, prominence, and financial gain.

Interestingly, with Nehor we find one who is teaching doctrine—that "all mankind [will] be saved at the last day" and that the people should "lift up their heads and rejoice; for the Lord had created all men, and had also redeemed all men; and in the end, all men [will] have eternal life." We are also told, however, that Nehor "began to be lifted up in the pride of his heart, and to wear very costly apparel, yea, and even began to establish a church after the manner of his preaching" (Alma 1:2–6).

Let's look more carefully at what he is teaching. While seemingly good, his invitation for the people to lift up their heads and rejoice was another way of saying, "Don't get caught up with feelings of guilt, for such is completely unnecessary. Lift up your heads, for the Lord has forgiven everyone, and thus all persons will receive eternal life" (see Alma 1:4). This is of course what is known as *universalism*, the belief that because God possesses all divine attributes, including an infinite patience, He will wait as long as He needs to for individuals to come around. In other words, "Everyone will eventually receive eternal life, so don't sweat it!" One can understand why Nehor's doctrine was so popular and so well received. We learn later in the Nephite record that the people of the wicked city of Ammonihah "remained a hard-hearted and a stiffnecked people; and they repented not of their sins, ascribing all the power of Alma and Amulek to the devil; for *they were of the profession of Nehor, and did not believe in the repentance of their sins*" (Alma 15:15; emphasis added).

That Nehor's "attractive" teachings began to spread is clear from later accounts. When Aaron, the son of King Mosiah, came to the city of Jerusalem, he "first began to preach to the Amalekites. And he began to preach to them in their synagogues, for *they had built synagogues after the order of the Nehors; for many of the Amalekites and Amulonites were after the order of the Nehors.*" Aaron entered into their synagogues and began to call the people to repentance. Their response? "How knowest thou that we are not a righteous people? Behold, we have built sanctuaries, and we do assemble ourselves together to worship God. *We do believe that God will save all men*" (Alma 21:4, 6; emphasis added).

We soon learn that Nehor's pride proved to be his undoing. When Gideon, who had been responsible for helping to save many people, confronted Nehor and "withstood him with the words of God," Nehor drew his sword and slew Gideon. The anti-Christ was then brought before Alma the Younger, who was then serving as the governor, or chief judge. Alma explained to Nehor that this was the first time that priestcraft had made its way into the Nephite culture. He then added that "thou art not only guilty of priestcraft, but hast endeavored to enforce it by the sword. . . . Therefore thou art condemned to die, according to the law which has been given us by Mosiah." Nehor was led to the top of the hill Manti and he there "suffered an ignominious death" (Alma 1:9–15), meaning a death that is humiliating, contemptible, or shameful.

Tragically, the teachings of Nehor the anti-Christ did not die with him. Indeed, as we read the remainder of the Book of Mormon, we see that the worldview and doctrine and practices of Nehor continued to be felt throughout much of Nephite history (see Alma 14:16; 24:28). Sherem and Nehor were not, however, the only anti-Christs in the Book of Mormon. We turn our attention in the next chapter to the anti-Christ whose teachings and methods are spelled out in more detail than those of his predecessors—namely, Korihor.

## CHAPTER 13

# Confronting the Anti-Christs: Korihor

### ALMA 30

In the latter part of the seventeenth year of the reign of the judges in the Nephite society, "there came a man into the land of Zarahemla, and he was Anti-Christ, for he began to preach unto the people against the prophecies which had been spoken by the prophets, concerning the coming of Christ" (Alma 30:6). Mormon is careful to instruct readers that no one in Nephite society was forced to believe a certain way; he writes, "There was no law against a man's belief" (Alma 30:7; see also verse 11).

In verse 12 of chapter 30 we begin to learn of Korihor and his beliefs (or nonbeliefs). First, of course, is that "there should be no Christ." In the next chapter, we learn of the Zoramites, who did not believe that God would come to earth and take a body; that is, they did not believe in the Incarnation of God (the condescension of Christ). They prayed atop the Rameumptom: "Holy, holy God; we believe that thou art God, and we believe that thou art holy, and that *thou wast a spirit, and that thou art a spirit, and that thou wilt be a spirit forever*" (Alma 31:15; emphasis added). But for now let's look carefully at what Korihor teaches, as detailed in chapter 30.

*First,* there should be no Christ (verse 6).

*Second,* the Nephites are "yoked" and "bound down under a foolish and a vain hope." The Nephite prophets' prophecies "are foolish traditions of your fathers" (verses 13–14). This is to say, Korihor contends that the predictions of a coming Savior and Redeemer are simply silly and foolish (meaning only a fool would believe such things). Because the anti-Christ cannot conceive of himself knowing, by the power of God's Spirit, things which will come to pass in the future, he thinks surely no one else can either.

*Third*, there is no way the Nephites can know of the truthfulness of the prophecies, since one *cannot know* such things (verse 13; see also verses 15, 24). Sadly, this is something I hear bantered about even among some members of The Church of Jesus Christ of Latter-day Saints. We can in fact come to *know* spiritual things. And what does it mean to *know* something in the spiritual realm? The scriptures and the prophets proclaim that it is by means of the Holy Spirit that we come to know spiritual truths:

> "*The things of God knoweth no man, except he has the Spirit of God.* Now, we have received, not the spirit of the world, but the Spirit which is of God; *that we might know* the things that are freely given to us of God. . . . For who hath known the mind of the Lord, that he may instruct him? But *we have the mind of Christ.*" (JST, 1 Corinthians 2:11–12, 16; emphasis added)
>
> "By the Spirit are *all things made known.*" (1 Nephi 22:2; emphasis added)
>
> "He that believeth these things which I have spoken, him will I visit with the manifestations of my Spirit, and *he shall know and bear record.* For *because of my Spirit he shall know* that these things are true; for it persuadeth men to do good." (Ether 4:11; emphasis added)
>
> "And by the power of the Holy Ghost *ye may know* the truth of all things." (Moroni 10:5; emphasis added)
>
> "Verily, verily, I say unto you, *I will impart unto you of my Spirit*, which shall enlighten your mind, which shall fill your

> soul with joy; and *then shall ye know, or by this shall you know,* all things whatsoever ye desire of me, which are pertaining unto things of righteousness, in faith believing in me that ye shall receive." (Doctrine and Covenants 11:13–14; emphasis added)
>
> "To some it is given by the Holy Ghost *to know that Jesus Christ is the Son of God* and that he was crucified for the sins of the world." (Doctrine and Covenants 46:13; emphasis added)
>
> "Be still and *know that I am God.*" (Doctrine and Covenants 101:16; emphasis added)

What if I were to stand and bear witness that Jesus Christ lives, that He is our Lord and Savior, that He has the power to forgive our sins, purify our hearts, and equip us to live comfortably and everlastingly in a celestial realm hereafter? How could I know these things? I could know, first of all, because both ancient and modern prophets have attested these truths; their conviction is shared regularly, consistently, and powerfully. I could also know that Jesus has power to forgive sins by personal experience—I know what it feels like to be in sin, and I know, conversely, what it feels like to have my sins remitted by the Savior through the gracious process of repentance. I know that Jesus Christ lives and that He is the Redeemer because He has redeemed me. I can know that the restored gospel is true because of the happiness, peace, light, and truth that come into my mind and heart as I do my best to live the gospel. I can know that the Holy Priesthood is the power and authority of God because I have witnessed and been the recipient of healing miracles.

*Fourth*, believing that one can receive a remission of sins "is the effect of a frenzied mind" or a "derangement of your minds" (verse 16). Here Korihor resorts to psychologizing, throwing out impressive-sounding words to explain what he is not capable of comprehending. To be frenzied is to be "wildly excited" or subject to "violent mental agitation."[1] If people cannot fathom spiritual experiences or supernatural phenomena, they might attempt to explain them away as being bizarre, abnormal, or even dangerous.

*Fifth*, there is no need for an atonement, since "every man fared in this life according to the management of the creature; therefore every man prospered according to his genius, and that every man conquered according to his strength" (verse 17). This is a classic example of *humanism*, the philosophical view that if people succeed in life or accomplish great things, they do so by themselves, without being enabled by some supposed divine power. Humanism declares that man is the measure—that if people improve, make progress, or even overcome tremendous odds, it is because they pulled themselves up by their own bootstraps. Humanism denies divine intervention, including the grace of a supreme being. At its worst, humanism is a hollow perspective on life that can lead a person to become absolutely ego driven.

*Sixth*, whatever a person does is no crime (verse 17). This is no more nor less than *moral* or *ethical relativism*, the belief that there is no one divine standard, no one right and wrong; everything is relative. It is a denial of absolute truth, absolute values, and thus, very often, individual responsibility. We often hear someone chant that "there are no absolutes." Now that's a pretty absolute statement, don't you think? For such a person, there are no rights and wrongs except when someone does damage or harm to them; then relativism flees.

In speaking to CES religious educators about Doctrine and Covenants 93:30 ("All truth is independent in that sphere in which God has placed it"), Elder D. Todd Christofferson said: "I take this to mean that all truth, including the truth that governs our present sphere, exists independent and apart. It is unaffected by my preference or your opinion. It stands independent of any effort to control or change it. It cannot be lobbied or influenced in any way. It is a fixed reality. . . .

"In much of the world, relativist thinking has become a dominant philosophy. By relativism I mean the view that ethical or moral truths are relative, that they depend on the attitudes and feelings of those who hold them, and that no one can judge the validity of someone else's 'truth.' You hear a lot of talk these days about 'my truth' and 'his truth' or 'her truth.' . . .

"Moral relativism just doesn't work if there is to be order and justice in society. Can murder be wrong for most but right for some? Is a thief entitled to keep what he steals and continue stealing because he believes robbery is right for him, especially since he grew up in an underprivileged circumstance? . . .

"Our calling, and it is ever more urgent in this environment, is to teach the truth of moral concepts: what they are and how far they extend. . . . Eternal truth, especially as it bears on the meaning and the purpose and the conduct of life, we must obtain from God. Moral relativists generally see no role or relevance for God in this discussion and typically doubt that He even exists. It would be most inconvenient for them if He does exist, and even more so if He speaks to man. One can only think about truth as relative as long as God is not around."[2]

President Russell M. Nelson explained that the leaders of the Church "are commanded to teach truth! . . . That commission does *not* give us the authority to modify divine law. . . . Ask your Heavenly Father if we truly are the Lord's apostles and prophets. Ask if we have received revelation on this and other matters."[3] President Nelson also said: "There really *is* such a thing as right and wrong. There really *is* absolute truth—eternal truth. One of the plagues of our day is that too few people know where to turn for truth."[4]

One year later in general conference, President Nelson stated that "some would have us believe that truth is relative—that each person should determine for himself or herself what is true. Such a belief is but wishful thinking for those who mistakenly think they will not also be accountable to God.

"Dear brothers and sisters, God is the source of all truth. The Church of Jesus Christ of Latter-day Saints embraces *all* truth that God conveys to His children, whether learned in a scientific laboratory or received by direct revelation from Him."[5]

*Seventh*, when a person is dead, that is the end of existence (verse 18).

This is sometimes called *nihilism*—namely, that all things are moving toward dissolution. There is no life to come, no hereafter, no heaven or hell; there are no consequences for one's actions. And thus one can sin and break the laws of society without concern for consequences hereafter.

In the land of Gideon, Korihor voiced a couple of other arguments against religion and spiritual things. "Ye say that this people is a free people. Behold, I say they are in bondage" (verse 24). How often do we hear that religion or religious values rob people of their agency? This is pure foolishness. People who pray, attend church, minister to others, study the scriptures, fast, attend the temple, and in general abide by the commandments of God, *choose* to do so. It is their choice to be religious, their preference to attend to spiritual things. The irony of this whole matter is that when people reach the point where they have chosen to turn their lives over to God, yield their hearts to Him, have an eye single to His glory, and trust in His mercy and grace—such people are becoming truly free.

It is in verse 25 that we read of Korihor's effort to twist or distort doctrine and thereby confuse the Saints. "Ye say that this people is a guilty and a fallen people because of the transgression of a parent. Behold, I say that a child is not guilty because of its parents." This is a fascinating move on the part of the anti-Christ. Clearly the Nephites were taught by their prophets about the Fall of Adam and Eve and of the consequences, both physical and spiritual, that came upon humankind because of that Fall—namely, physical and spiritual death. But to say that each of us is *affected* by the Fall is not to say that we are *guilty of* or *accountable* or *responsible for* what happened in Eden. Adam was instructed by God: "Behold, I have forgiven thee thy transgression in the Garden of Eden. Hence came the saying abroad among the people, that the Son of God hath atoned for original guilt, wherein *the sins of the parents cannot be answered upon the heads of the children*, for they [the children] are whole from the foundation of the world" (Moses 6:53–54; emphasis added; see also Moroni 8).

Alma's response to Korihor is powerful. He asks Korihor whether he believes there is a God, and the anti-Christ responds negatively. Alma then bears testimony that there is a God and that Jesus Christ would indeed come to earth. "And now what evidence have ye that there is no God, or that Christ cometh not? I say unto you that ye have none, save it be your word only. But, behold, I have all things as a testimony that these things are true; and ye also have all things as a testimony unto you that they are true." Alma then states that he knows that Korihor does in fact believe but that he is "possessed of a lying spirit" and has "put off the Spirit of God that it may have no place in [him]; but the devil has power over [him]" (verses 37–42).

At this point Korihor demands a sign. Alma replies that "thou hast had signs enough." He has had access to the scriptures and the words of holy prophets, as well as evidence that there is a God found in the order within the cosmos. Alma affirms that "all the planets which move in their regular form do witness that there is a supreme Creator" (verses 43–44). This is what for centuries has been known as "cosmological proof" for the existence of God.

Korihor is struck dumb, and it's possible his hearing was taken away also since people wrote to him in order to communicate (verse 51; compare Luke 1:20, 62). Korihor pleads with Alma to have the curse removed, but Alma discerns that if the curse were to be lifted, Korihor would return to his path of perverse teaching. Korihor admits that he always knew there was a God but that the devil had appeared to him in the form of an angel and instructed him on what he should teach the people. The angel bore witness that there was no God. Thus Korihor taught things that were pleasing to the carnal mind, insomuch that he began to believe what he was teaching (verses 50–53). The account comes to an end in a rather gruesome way: Korihor goes about begging food from the people until he is "run upon and trodden down, even until he was dead" (verses 58–59). The group responsible for his death was the Zoramites, whom Alma and his missionary associates will meet and teach in chapter 31.

The prophet-editor Mormon, the major purveyor of the "and thus we see" messages throughout the Book of Mormon, brings this sobering story to an end with the following: "And thus we see the end of him who perverteth the ways of the Lord; and thus we see that the devil will not support his children at the last day, but doth speedily drag them down to hell" (verse 60).

## CHAPTER 14

# The Sufferings and Death of Christ

MOSIAH 3, 14; ALMA 7, 34

It was understood long before the earth was created and inhabited that the Son of God would be sent to earth to suffer and die. Why did He need to suffer? Why did He need to die? The prophet Abinadi either quoted or read from what we know as Isaiah 53 to the wicked King Noah and his priests about the Suffering Servant. Note how He would suffer:

"He is despised and rejected of men; a man of sorrows, and acquainted with grief" (Mosiah 14:3). To be despised and rejected by people all about you brings a kind of suffering that is closely linked to loneliness. Surely few things are more painful than to have a profound message to deliver and a power to extend that would transform people and bring them great joy and happiness, only to have your message spurned and your offer of deliverance rejected. Jesus of Nazareth knew, more than any other mortal woman or man, what it felt like for people to despise Him and then to reject Him. Truly, throughout His mortal ministry in the Old World, He became well acquainted with grief.

"Surely he has borne our griefs, and carried our sorrows" (Mosiah 14:4). As a fellow mortal, Jesus went about His mission of mercy and encountered all types of people and every imaginable reaction to His precious offering of salvation or eternal life. Like every one of us, Jesus came face to face with grief and sorrow—grief and sorrow of His own, as well as those who came unto Him and received Him and His gospel. Possessed of perfect love, He also experienced perfect empathy for His suffering and troubled fellow mortals.

"But he was wounded for our transgressions, he was bruised for our iniquities" (Mosiah 14:5). These words refer specifically to the Savior's atoning suffering, the suffering that was heaped upon his shoulders in both Gethsemane and on Golgotha, as though He had been the one who committed the sins in the first place. He was our substitute, our stand-in, our personal representative. As the Apostle Paul put it, God the Father made one who knew no sin to be sinful for us, as though He had committed the sins Himself (2 Corinthians 5:21). This is what theologians and Christian church leaders have through the centuries called "the great reversal" or "the great exchange." Christ essentially says to each of us: "If you will but come unto me, repent of your sins, and enter into my gospel covenant, I will take the sins you have committed upon myself and give to you my righteousness." We are redeemed because of the righteousness of Jesus Christ (see 2 Nephi 2:3).

"The chastisement of our peace was upon him; and with his stripes we are healed" (Mosiah 14:5). Another way of saying this is that "the punishment that brought us peace was on him" (Isaiah 53:5, New International Version). "With his stripes we are healed" means that with or through His welts, wounds, and scars of His suffering in Gethsemane, followed by His scourging and Crucifixion, we are healed of sin and purged of guilt.

"Yet it pleased the Lord to bruise him; he hath put him to grief; when thou shalt make his soul an offering for sin he shall see his seed" (Mosiah 14:10). Surely our Father in Heaven was not "pleased" to witness the torture and awful agony of His Only Begotten Son, but the Father received and accepted the Son's offering because it made it possible for men and women, both noble people and horribly wicked souls, to be cleansed and renewed. The Father saw the travail of His Beloved Son and accepted Christ's atoning offering.

When Christ's soul was made an offering for sin—once He had

suffered and agonized in Gethsemane and on Golgotha and His atoning suffering was "finished"—He died and entered instantly into the post-mortal spirit world. There He saw His "seed"—the faithful prophets and those persons through the centuries who had given heed to the words of the prophets (see Mosiah 15:11–17). There he beheld, in the words of President Joseph F. Smith, "an innumerable company of the spirits of the just" (Doctrine and Covenants 138:12). He taught these spirits and organized and prepared for the glorious Resurrection. By means of this precious and singular redeeming act, billions of our Father's spirit children are justified—cleansed, renewed, pardoned, exonerated, and made free from sin.

An angel explained to King Benjamin that the Savior would "suffer temptations, and pain of body, hunger, thirst, and fatigue, even more than man can suffer; except it be unto death; for behold, blood cometh from every pore, so great shall be his anguish for the wickedness and the abominations of his people" (Mosiah 3:7; compare Luke 22:39–44; Doctrine and Covenants 19:15–19). Jesus had to suffer so that He could know and understand perfectly the painful suffering of the children of God, what they encounter in coming into this second estate. As Alma taught in later years, Jesus suffered pains, afflictions, temptations, sicknesses, and infirmities—all of the kinds of things His mortal brothers and sisters face—"that he may know according to the flesh how to succor his people according to their infirmities" (Alma 7:11–12).

What was the "bitter cup" spoken of in scripture that Jesus was required to imbibe? It is not uncommon to hear ministers, priests, or scholars remark that Jesus's anguish in Gethsemane was caused by His dread or fearful anticipation of the cross. To be sure, crucifixion was a brutal form of torture. It included, in many cases, the grossly painful process of having nails driven into the hands and feet, hanging on the cross for what could stretch into days, and then eventually dying from asphyxiation. It also entailed the ignominy and the scandal of being stripped of clothing, insulted and harangued, and ridiculed as a common criminal.

Jesus needed to suffer physical death (1) so that He could

experience what every other son or daughter of God must face as mortal life comes to an end and (2) so that He could, some three days after His death, rise from the tomb of Joseph of Arimathea as a glorified, immortal being. And, as a result of the Savior's rise from the dead, every other son or daughter of God might one day do the same. "For since by man [Adam] came death, by man [Jesus Christ] came also the resurrection of the dead. For as in Adam all die, even so in Christ shall all be made alive" (1 Corinthians 15:21–22).

We frequently hear that our Master suffered so that we might not suffer. So does that mean if we sin and then repent, we need not suffer for sin? No, not at all, for some degree of suffering is naturally a part of the repentance process. The promise here is that if we sin and then repent, we will not be required to suffer the way the Savior suffered. President Dallin H. Oaks explained: "Sinners who are repenting will experience some suffering, but, because of their repentance and because of the Atonement, they will not experience the full 'exquisite' extent of eternal torment the Savior suffered for that sin."[1]

The immediate consequence of sin is withdrawal of the Spirit (see Mosiah 2:36; Alma 34:35). It may be that this withdrawal is what causes an individual to feel guilt, pain, emptiness, and alienation. Jesus Christ, in taking upon Himself the effects of the sins of all humankind, was thus exposed to the awful (and, to Jesus, unusual) withdrawal of the Spirit, which had been His constant companion from the beginning. In speaking of the events of the Atonement, President Brigham Young explained: "The Father withdrew His Spirit from His Son, at the time he was to be crucified. Jesus had been with his Father, talked with Him, dwelt in His bosom. . . . The light, knowledge, power, and glory with which he was clothed were far above, or exceeded that of all others who had been upon the earth after the fall, consequently at the very moment, *at the hour when the crisis came for him to offer up his life, the Father withdrew Himself, withdrew His Spirit. . . . That is what made him sweat blood.* If he had had the power of God upon him, he would not have sweat blood."[2] Christ descended below all things (see

Ephesians 4:8–10; Doctrine and Covenants 88:6). The Redeemer has thus "trodden the wine-press alone, even the wine-press of the fierceness of the wrath of Almighty God" (Doctrine and Covenants 76:107; see also Isaiah 63:3; Doctrine and Covenants 88:106; 133:50).

So did the Father really leave His Only Begotten Son during the hours of agony? Elder Jeffrey R. Holland spoke tenderly of those stirring moments in the Master's final hours:

"With all the conviction of my soul I testify that He *did* please His Father perfectly and that a perfect Father did *not* forsake His Son in that hour. Indeed, it is my personal belief that *in all of Christ's mortal ministry the Father may never have been closer to His Son than in these agonizing final moments of suffering.* Nevertheless, that the supreme sacrifice of His Son might be as complete as it was voluntary and solitary, the Father briefly withdrew from Jesus the comfort of His Spirit, the support of His personal presence. . . . For His Atonement to be infinite and eternal, He had to feel what it was like to die not only physically but spiritually, to sense what it was like to have the divine Spirit withdraw, leaving one feeling totally, abjectly, hopelessly alone."[3]

In the *Lectures on Faith*, we read that the Savior "descended in suffering below that which man can suffer; or, in other words, suffered greater sufferings, and was exposed to more powerful contradictions than any man can be. But, notwithstanding all this, he kept the law of God, and remained without sin."[4] Aaron, the son of King Mosiah, "began to open the scriptures unto them [the father of Lamoni and his household] concerning the coming of Christ, and also concerning the resurrection of the dead, and that *there could be no redemption for mankind save it were through the death and sufferings of Christ, and the atonement of his blood*" (Alma 21:9; emphasis added).

"'Infinite and eternal' [Alma 34:10], 'stronger than the cords of death' (Doctrine and Covenants 121:44)," Elder Gerrit W. Gong taught, "Jesus Christ's Atonement can help us bring *peace to our past and hope to our future.*"[5] We will surely spend eternity singing praise to our Lord and Redeemer and expressing undying gratitude for His sufferings and death. He did for us what we could never, ever do for ourselves.

CHAPTER 15

# Obtaining and Retaining a Remission of Sins

MOSIAH 4

We learn from the various accounts of Joseph Smith's First Vision that one important reason that young Joseph entered the Sacred Grove (in addition to wanting to know which church he should join) was to find out how to have his sins removed, how to become clean before God. In the earliest (1832) account of the vision we read: "While in the attitude of calling upon the Lord, in the sixteenth year of my age, a pillar of light above the brightness of the sun at noonday came down from above and rested upon me. I was filled with the Spirit of God, and the Lord opened the heavens upon me, and I saw the Lord. And he spake unto me, saying, 'Joseph, my son, thy sins are forgiven thee.'"[1]

In the 1835 account we find the following: "A pillar of fire appeared above my head. It presently rested down upon me and filled me with joy unspeakable. A personage appeared in the midst of this pillar of flame, which was spread all around, and yet nothing consumed. Another personage soon appeared like unto the first. He said unto me, 'Thy sins are forgiven thee.'" Orson Pratt's account (1840) contains this same insight.[2]

In the atrium of the Joseph Smith Building on the Brigham Young University campus, there is a beautiful statue of young Joseph Smith kneeling in the grove. I recall clearly that, during the time I was serving as dean of Religious Education, the grounds crew at BYU made an extensive effort to plant trees and shrubs in such a way that each time students or visitors passed that quiet and beautiful spot, they would be prompted to reflect on the theophany in Palmyra. I was asked to conduct the brief dedication ceremony of the area and make a few comments. Before offering a dedicatory prayer, President Henry B. Eyring, then the commissioner of Church Education and a member of the Quorum of the Twelve Apostles, spoke to those gathered. "From studying the various accounts of the First Vision," he said, "we learn that young Joseph went into the grove not only to learn which church he should join but also to obtain forgiveness for his sins, *something he seems not to have understood how to do*. And in more than one account the Lord addressed the young truth seeker and said, 'Joseph, my son, thy sins are forgiven thee.'

"I hope that as young people through the generations see this statue," Elder Eyring continued, "they will realize . . . [that] this piece of art represents *that moment when Joseph Smith learned there was a way for the power of the Atonement of Jesus Christ to be unlocked fully*. Because of what Joseph saw and what began at this moment, the Savior was able, through this great and valiant servant and through others He sent, to restore power and privilege. That power and privilege allow us, and all who will live, to have the benefit of Jesus Christ's Atonement work in our lives."[3]

As discussed earlier in this work, the Book of Mormon is drenched in redemptive theology—the plight of fallen humanity, the need for redemption, the Atonement of Jesus Christ, repentance and forgiveness, spiritual rebirth, and salvation by the grace of God. There are a number of instances in the Book of Mormon where people seek for and obtain a remission of their sins. For example, King Benjamin delivered his final major address as he came to the close of his life. He preached on our divine indebtedness to God, the need to look to and acknowledge the goodness of God and our own nothingness without Him, the coming of the Savior to the earth and how He would minister among the people, and the need to put off the natural man and put on Christ.

Chapter 4 of the book of Mosiah contains the response of the people to Benjamin's message. Mormon describes in important detail that the people fell to the earth, "for the fear of the Lord had come upon them. And they had viewed themselves in their own carnal state, even less than the dust of the earth" (Mosiah 4:1–2). That is, their hearts had been pricked, and they sensed the need to repent and bring their lives into conformity with the gospel of Jesus Christ. They cried out: "O have mercy, and apply the atoning blood of Christ that we may receive forgiveness of our sins, and our hearts may be purified; for we believe in Jesus Christ, the Son of God" (Mosiah 4:2). Look carefully at what the people most desired: (1) forgiveness of their sins and (2) the purification of their hearts. In other words, they wanted to have their sins remitted (to be justified) and they wanted their hearts to be purified (to be sanctified).

Verse 3 of chapter 4 contains precious insights into how we may know when our sins have been forgiven: "And it came to pass that after [the people] had spoken these words the Spirit of the Lord came upon them, and they were filled with joy, having received a remission of their sins, and having peace of conscience, because of the exceeding faith which they had in Jesus Christ who should come." Notice that, first, the Spirit of the Lord came upon them. One of the immediate consequences of sin is the removal of the Holy Spirit from a person (see Mosiah 2:36; Alma 34:35; Helaman 13:8). Thus when individuals genuinely and honestly repent and are forgiven, they begin to notice the Holy Ghost working within them again. Second, the people were filled with joy. The burden that had weighed upon their souls as a result of their sinful practices had been lifted. Instead of guilt, they felt a joy that signaled the Lord's acceptance. In speaking of joy in a modern revelation, the Lord asked the question: "What greater witness can you have than from God?" (Doctrine and Covenants 6:23). Third, the people had peace of conscience. The feelings of guilt, disappointment with themselves, and discomfort in the presence of righteous and God-fearing persons were swept away.

*Obtaining* a remission of sins is a precious gift. It feels good to be clean. It feels comforting to be right with God. It is so nice to have a clear conscience. The problem, of course, is, how do we stay that way? How do we remain clean and free from sin? We may be tempted to lock all the doors, turn off the phones, and block out any and all spiritual distractions and every temptation to violate the laws of God. But of course we can't do that; we must re-enter society each day and strive with all our hearts to remain free from transgression.

In chapter 4 of Mosiah, Benjamin continues his sermon. It is in this chapter that we learn how to *retain* (that is, keep or maintain) a remission of sins. First, Benjamin says: "As ye have come to the knowledge of the glory of God, or if ye have known of his goodness and have tasted of his love, and have received a remission of your sins, which causeth such exceedingly great joy in your souls, even so I would that *ye should remember, and always retain in remembrance, the greatness of God, and your own nothingness, and his goodness and long-suffering towards you, unworthy creatures*, and humble yourselves even in the depths of humility, calling on the name of the Lord daily, and standing steadfastly in the faith of that which is to come, which was spoken of by the mouth of the angel. And behold, I say unto you that *if ye do this ye shall always rejoice, and be filled with the love of God, and always retain a remission of your sins*" (verses 11–12; emphasis added). To distill this significant teaching, we might say that once we have obtained a remission of our sins, we should, in the words that Alma spoke a half century later, remain humble and "acknowledge [our] unworthiness before God at all times" (Alma 38:14); we should continually acknowledge and confess God's goodness and greatness and, in summary, live in a state of gratitude all our days.

Benjamin mentioned another way to retain a remission of sins—by looking to the needs of those who are less fortunate. He stated: "And now, for the sake of these things which I have spoken unto you—that is, for the sake of retaining a remission of your sins from day to day, that ye may walk guiltless before God—*I would that ye should impart of your substance to the poor*, every man according to that which he hath, such as *feeding the hungry, clothing the naked, visiting the sick and administering to their relief*, both spiritually and temporally, according to their wants" (Mosiah 4:26, emphasis added; compare Alma 4:11–14).

Members of The Church of Jesus Christ of Latter-day Saints have yet another way to retain a remission of their sins—through partaking of the sacrament of the Lord's Supper each week in our main worship service. Elder David A. Bednar explained that "as members of the Lord's restored Church, we are blessed both by our *initial cleansing from sin* associated with baptism and by the potential for an *ongoing cleansing from sin* made possible through the companionship and power of the Holy Ghost—even the third member of the Godhead. . . .

"That we might more fully keep ourselves unspotted from the world, we are commanded to go to the house of prayer and offer up our sacraments upon the Lord's holy day (Doctrine and Covenants 59:9–12). Please consider that the emblems of the Lord's body and blood, the bread and the water, are both blessed and sanctified. . . . To sanctify is to make pure and holy. The sacramental emblems are sanctified in remembrance of Christ's purity, of our total dependence upon His Atonement, and of our responsibility to so honor our ordinances and covenants that we can 'stand spotless before [Him] at the last day' [3 Nephi 27:20].

"The ordinance of the sacrament is a holy and repeated invitation to repent sincerely and to be renewed spiritually. The act of partaking of the sacrament, in and of itself, does not remit sins. But as we prepare conscientiously and participate in this holy ordinance with a broken heart and a contrite spirit, then the promise is that we may *always* have the Spirit of the Lord to be with us. And by the sanctifying power of the Holy Ghost as our constant companion, we can *always* retain a remission of our sins."[4]

While it is not possible for us to live completely flawless lives in mortality, we can live in such a way as to be worthy and acceptable before God, sufficiently clean before Him, and to enjoy the gift of the Holy Ghost, to attend the temple, and to participate fully in all of the programs of the Church. Through obtaining and retaining a remission of sins from day to day, we maintain our place on the strait and narrow path, the gospel path, the covenant path, and continue our course toward the tree of life.

CHAPTER 16

# The Mighty Change of Heart

MOSIAH 5; ALMA 5

Alma posed the following questions to the members of the Church at Zarahemla in ancient America: "Have ye spiritually been born of God? Have ye received his image in your countenances? Have ye received this mighty change in your hearts?" (Alma 5:14). These questions, though posed in 83 BC, are everlastingly relevant to men and women of all ages and in all places. Religion deals with things of eternal import, with things of the heart, with the change each of us must undergo to become more Christlike and thus more serviceable in the Lord's kingdom.

Because Jesus Christ is a living God, He is forevermore involved in this business of change. In the beginning He spoke, chaotic matter responded, and the heavens and the earth were formed. The placement of Adam and Eve and all forms of life on earth thereby changed the nature of existence on this planet. Because of the Fall of our first parents and because men and women are often enticed to wander from the covenant path, the Father sent His Only Begotten Son into the world to change things, both cosmically and individually. As a sacred volume of scripture filled with redemptive theology, the Book of Mormon addresses spiritual change again and again, throughout the history of the Jaredites and the Nephites.

This change is much more than personal improvement or development (though these are significant matters) and much more than a cosmetic alteration. John Stott, a beloved Christian theologian, explained: "We may be quite sure that Christ-centeredness and Christlikeness will never be attained by our own unaided efforts. How can self drive out self? As well expect Satan to drive out Satan! For *we are not interested in skin-deep holiness, in a merely external resemblance to Jesus Christ.* We are not satisfiewd by a superficial modification of behavior patterns in conformity to some Christian sub-culture which expects this, commands that, and prohibits the other. No, what we long for is *a deep inward change of character, resulting from a change of nature and leading to a radical change of conduct.* In a word we want to be like Christ, and that thoroughly, profoundly, entirely. Nothing less than this will do."[1]

Very early in our story of the Nephites, we witness the kind of change to which Stott referred. Nephi, "being exceedingly young, nevertheless being large in stature, and also having great desires to know of the mysteries of God, . . . did cry unto the Lord." "And behold," said Nephi, "*he did visit me, and did soften my heart that I did believe all the words which had been spoken by my father*; wherefore, I did not rebel against him like unto my brothers." Nephi then communicated to his older brother Sam "the things which the Lord had manifested unto [Nephi] by his Holy Spirit. And it came to pass that [Sam] believed in [his] words" (1 Nephi 2:16–17; emphasis added). We cannot tell from the text if by "he did visit me," Nephi referred to a personal appearance of the Savior or rather a great outpouring of the Spirit that transformed him into a man with a believing heart. Either way, Nephi was changed, as was Sam.

Nephi's younger brother Jacob underwent a slightly different kind of spiritual change. Jacob was a believer from the beginning and one who faced many afflictions—most of which were caused by the rebellion of Laman and Lemuel. In spite of opposition, Jacob came to know the greatness of God, and his afflictions were consecrated for his good (see 2 Nephi 2:2). As a much older man, Jacob contended with Sherem, the anti-Christ, and through that encounter we learn something about the kind of spiritual growth that Jacob had undergone over the years. Sherem approached Jacob in hopes of shaking his faith and thereby leading many of the Nephites astray. Notice these words from Jacob: "And he had hope to shake me from the faith, *notwithstanding the many revelations and the many things which I had seen* concerning these things; for *I truly had seen angels, and they had ministered unto me*. And also, I *had heard the voice of the Lord speaking unto me in very word*, from time to time; wherefore, I could not be shaken" (Jacob 7:5; emphasis added). There's a significant lesson to be learned through this experience: the way you and I can remain secure in the faith and have an unshakable testimony and conversion is through regular, ongoing, spiritual experiences—encounters with the Holy Spirit of God—and remembering them always.

After Benjamin had finished his powerful address to his people, he sent some of his servants to see if the people believed his words. "And they all cried with one voice, saying: Yea, we believe all the words which thou hast spoken unto us; and also, we know of their surety and truth, because of *the Spirit of the Lord Omnipotent*, which *has wrought a mighty change in us, or in our hearts, that we have no more disposition to do evil, but to do good continually*" (Mosiah 5:1–2; emphasis added). This is a powerful statement about the change that takes place in human hearts when honest truth seekers, faithful disciples, seek for, gain, and bear witness of this mighty change.

Benjamin had taught that the natural man or woman—the unredeemed person, the selfish and self-centered person, the unclean and impure person, the person driven by carnal instincts, the person who takes cues from a fallen world—is an enemy to God and would remain an enemy until they recognized their spiritual plight, called upon God for deliverance, and sought for and received the cleansing power of Jesus Christ (Mosiah 3:19). *The natural man* wants to sin, is easily drawn into sin, and has little interest in changing. On the other hand, *the spiritual man or woman*, the one who has truly been born again; who has exercised faith in Christ; who has sincerely repented, sought for, and obtained forgiveness; and who now enjoys the lifting and liberating power of the Holy Spirit—this person is no longer enticed by evil but wants to do good. As time passes, sin and the sinful life become less and less attractive, even repulsive (see 2 Nephi 4:31; Alma 13:12; 19:33).

Do we suppose, then, that the converted people of Benjamin never sinned again? No, of course not, for only Jesus was able to remain free from sin (see 1 Peter 2:22; Hebrews 4:15; 1 John 3:5). These good people did make mistakes, and they did sin in the future, but they didn't want to, and they repented quickly (see Doctrine and Covenants 109:21). They sinned, but as the Apostle John taught us, those who are born again *do not continue in sin* (JST, 1 John 3:9).

Among the most powerful sections of the Book of Mormon are the missionary efforts of Alma and the sons of Mosiah following their own conversion. In chapters 17–20 of the book of Alma, Ammon, one of the sons of Mosiah, is led to the land of Ishmael, where he meets King Lamoni. Ammon teaches Lamoni about God, heaven, the Creation, the Fall, and the Atonement of Christ (Alma 18:24–40). Lamoni prayed: "O Lord, have mercy; according to thy abundant mercy which thou hast had upon the people of Nephi, have upon me, and my people. And now, when he had said this, he fell unto the earth, as if he were dead. And it came to pass that his servants took and carried him in unto his wife, and laid him upon a bed; and he lay as if he were dead for the space of two days and two nights" (Alma 18:41–43).

While we as modern Saints are not very familiar with the kind of spiritual trance that King Lamoni experienced (see also Alma 22, which deals with the missionary efforts of Ammon's brother Aaron), it is clear that during that space of time, a meaningful change happens within the person's soul. Mormon explained: "King Lamoni was under the power of God; he knew that *the dark veil of unbelief was being cast away from his mind*, and the light which did light up his mind, which was the light of the glory of God, which was a marvelous light of his [God's] goodness—yea, this light had infused such joy into his [Lamoni's] soul, *the cloud of darkness having been dispelled*, and that *the light of everlasting light was lit up in his soul*, yea, he knew that this had overcome his natural frame, and he was carried away in God" (Alma 19:6; emphasis added).

We could add example after example of people in the Book of Mormon who were changed by Christ—changed, in fact, quite dramatically and rather quickly. President Ezra Taft Benson taught: "The scriptures record remarkable accounts of men whose lives changed dramatically, in an instant, as it were: Alma the Younger, Paul on the road to Damascus, Enos praying far into the night, King Lamoni. Such astonishing examples of the power to change even those steeped in sin give confidence that the Atonement can reach even those deepest in despair.

"But we must be cautious as we discuss these remarkable examples. *Though they are real and powerful, they are the exception more than the rule.* For every Paul, for every Enos, and for every King Lamoni, there are hundreds and thousands of people who find the process of repentance much more subtle, much more imperceptible. Day by day they move closer to the Lord, little realizing they are building a godlike life. They live quiet lives of goodness, service, and commitment."[2]

Sister Kristen M. Yee of the General Relief Society Presidency spoke tenderly of the power of Jesus Christ to heal hearts that have been broken by those close to us. "As my love for the Savior has grown, so has my desire to replace hurt and anger with His healing balm. It has been a process of many years, requiring courage, vulnerability, perseverance, and learning to trust in the Savior's divine power to save and heal. I still have work to do, but my heart is no longer on a warpath. I have been given 'a new heart' [Ezekiel 36:26]—one that has felt the deep and abiding love of a personal Savior, who stayed beside me, who gently and patiently led me to a better place, who wept with me, who knew my sorrow."[3]

How comforting it is to know that no matter how far we have strayed, no matter how distant we seem to be from God, no matter how guilty we may feel for all that we have done or not done, there is a way back. No matter what we have done, we are never beyond the reach of the Good Shepherd who knows and loves His sheep, even those who have wandered. In short, we can change. The gospel of Jesus Christ is all about change. Joseph Smith, the Prophet of the Restoration, taught this simple yet profound truth: "There is never a time when the spirit is too old to approach God. All are within the reach of pardoning mercy, who have not committed the unpardonable sin."[4]

CHAPTER 17

# No Salvation by the Law Alone

MOSIAH 13

From the days of Adam until the time of Moses—some 2,600 years—the only priesthood that existed on earth was the Melchizedek, or Higher, Priesthood, which administers *the everlasting gospel* of Jesus Christ. The Prophet Joseph Smith taught that all the ancient prophets held the Melchizedek Priesthood.[1] In the days of Moses, however, the children of Israel failed to live up to their spiritual privileges and fulfill their covenantal obligations. They chose not to enjoy the power of godliness in their midst (see Doctrine and Covenants 84:19–21) and refused to prepare themselves to come into the divine presence and thereby see the face of God (see Exodus 20:19).

Therefore, Jehovah "took Moses out of their midst, and the Holy Priesthood also; and the lesser [or Aaronic] priesthood continued, which priesthood holdeth the key of the ministering of angels and *the preparatory gospel*; which gospel is the gospel of repentance and of baptism, and the remission of sins, and the law of carnal commandments, which the Lord in his wrath caused to continue with the house of Aaron among the children of Israel until John [the Baptist]" and the coming of the Savior to the earth (Doctrine and Covenants 84:25–27; emphasis added).

"When the Lord took Moses out of Israel," President Joseph Fielding Smith explained, "he took the higher priesthood also and left

Israel with the lesser priesthood which holds the keys to the temporal salvation of mankind—the temporal gospel—that which deals with repentance and baptism particularly, but does not have to do with the higher ordinances which have been revealed in the dispensation in which we live.

"Therefore, in Israel, the common people, the people generally, did not exercise the functions of priesthood in its fulness, but were confined in their labors and ministrations very largely to the Aaronic Priesthood. The withdrawal of the higher priesthood was from the people as a body, but the Lord still left among them men holding the Melchizedek Priesthood, with power to officiate in all its ordinances, so far as he determined that these ordinances should be granted unto the people."[2]

The law of Moses consisted of strict dietary laws, health laws, and laws of reparation, equity, and justice. Abinadi taught the wicked priests of King Noah that "it was expedient that there should be a law given to the children of Israel, yea, a very strict law; for they were a stiffnecked people, quick to do iniquity, and slow to remember the Lord their God.

"Therefore there was a law given them, yea, a law of performances and of ordinances, a law which they were to observe strictly from day to day, to keep them in remembrance of God and their duty towards him" (Mosiah 13:29–30; emphasis added; compare 2 Nephi 25:30).

Professor Andrew C. Skinner has written that the law of Moses "was a comprehensive religious and legal system revealed to the prophet-lawgiver-deliverer on Mount Sinai. It replaced, for a time, the higher law and fulness of the gospel that had operated from Adam to Moses and that the Lord had intended to reconfirm to Israel after their Egyptian sojourn had ended. But because Israel kept rebelling against sacred things, including the requirements of the higher law, the law of Moses, or lesser law, was 'added because of transgressions,' as Paul taught (Galatians 3:19). . . . Besides prescribing moral, ethical, and physical behavior, the law of Moses contained an elaborate system of sacrifices that included animals, grains, and other commodities (Leviticus 1–7). These were to remind the Israelites of their duties to God and to point them to the great and last sacrifice of Jesus Christ, which ended sacrifice by the shedding of blood."[3]

It is important to understand that the law of Moses "was a higher and more perfect order of worship than any system of worship other than the fulness of the everlasting gospel. . . . *Those who lived the law of Moses had revelation, were led by prophets, held the priesthood, and did the things that started them in the direction of the celestial kingdom. . . .* Theologically speaking, *those who received and lived the law of Moses might be said to have been walking in a celestial course, to have been taking some of the initial steps leading to eternal life*, to have been preparing themselves for that eternal fulness out of which eternal life comes."[4]

To what degree did the Nephites observe and keep the law of Moses? Did the Nephites officiate in what we would call the Levitical rituals? For one thing, we need to keep in mind that there were no Levites among them.[5] Were the Nephites under a religious obligation to perform the intricate system of sacrifices that had been given ancient Israel, and did they perform daily sacrifices? Consistent with what Joseph Smith taught, all the prophets—which would certainly include Lehi and Nephi—held the Melchizedek Priesthood. My study of the Book of Mormon for the last fifty years leads me to believe that the Nephites lived the law in the sense that they followed the laws and ordinances of the everlasting gospel, participated in simple animal sacrifice (as was carried out from the days of Adam and Eve to the time of Moses [see Moses 5:1–8]), kept the Ten Commandments, and were obedient to principles and standards of justice, equity, and reparation. There is no indication, however, in the text of the Book of Mormon that the Nephites were required to observe dietary laws, laws of purification, or the elaborate system of sacrificial offerings.[6]

The prophet Abinadi challenges the insistence of King Noah and his wicked priests to live the law of Moses. Abinadi asserts: "If ye teach the law of Moses why do ye not keep it?" Now notice what Abinadi mentions specifically: "Why do ye set your hearts upon riches? Why do ye commit whoredoms and spend your strength with harlots, yea, and cause this people to commit sin, that the Lord has cause to send me to prophesy against this people, yea even a great evil against this people?" (Mosiah 12:28–29.) Abinadi next asks why they do not "keep the commandments which the Lord delivered unto Moses in the mount of Sinai." Abinadi then reads the Ten Commandments to Noah and his priests (Mosiah 12:33–36; 13:11–24).

Abinadi does not mention dietary or health laws or laws of justice and reparation. To put this simply, Abinadi denounces them because they are not keeping the Ten Commandments. Abinadi testifies that "it is expedient that ye should keep the law of Moses as yet; but I say unto you, that the time shall come when it shall no more be expedient to keep the law of Moses. And moreover, I say unto you, that *salvation doth not come by the law alone; and were it not for the atonement, which God himself shall make for the sins and iniquities of his people, that they must unavoidably perish, notwithstanding the law of Moses*" (Mosiah 13:27–28; emphasis added).

In one of his last addresses to Brigham Young University students, Elder Bruce R. McConkie offered a modern application of Abinadi's words: "Suppose we have the scriptures, the gospel, the priesthood, the Church, the ordinances, the organization, even the keys of the kingdom—everything that now is down to the last jot and tittle—and yet there is no atonement of Christ? What then? Can we be saved? Will all our good works save us? Will we be rewarded for all our righteousness?

"Most assuredly we will not. We are not saved by works alone, no matter how good; we are saved because God sent his Son to shed his blood in Gethsemane and on Calvary that all through him might ransomed be. We are saved by the blood of Christ.

"To paraphrase Abinadi: '*Salvation doth not come by the Church alone*: and were it not for the atonement, given by the grace of God as a free gift, all men must unavoidably perish, and this notwithstanding the Church and all that appertains to it.'"[7]

This principle—expounded by Abinadi and a modern Apostle—is not just about the law of Moses. It is about law in general—the laws and commandments of God set forth in the fullness of the gospel of Jesus Christ. Of course we are expected to obey God and to keep His commandments, but let us never be so naïve as to suppose that our own goodness and obedience and faithfulness are sufficient to save us. They are not. As Lehi explained to Jacob, salvation is free (2 Nephi 2:4; see also 26:27), and as the Savior declared through the Prophet Joseph Smith, salvation, or eternal life, is the greatest of all the gifts of God (Doctrine and Covenants 6:13; 14:7). We keep the commandments to express and demonstrate our love and gratitude to a gracious Savior and a beloved Heavenly Father (see John 14:15, 21). As we are counseled in a modern revelation, "Thou shalt love the Lord thy God with all thy heart, with all thy might, mind, and strength; and in the name of Jesus Christ thou shalt serve him. . . . Thou shalt thank the Lord thy God in all things" (Doctrine and Covenants 59:5, 7). That is our duty and our privilege.

## CHAPTER 18

# Jesus Christ: the Father and the Son

MOSIAH 14–15

Isaiah 53 is, without question, the most detailed Messianic prophecy in the Old Testament. It is a beautiful description of the coming Redeemer's mission and ministry. The *mission* of Christ was His alone in the sense that what He needed to accomplish in our behalf was something that could only be carried out by one who was more than man, who was God. His mission comprised His sufferings in the Garden of Gethsemane and on the cross of Calvary. It was climaxed by His glorious rise from the tomb of Joseph of Arimathea. His mission was the redemption of the whole human family—deliverance from both spiritual and physical death.

The *ministry* of Christ included how He served His brothers and sisters on earth—how He taught His gospel with power and persuasion; reached out to others and lifted and strengthened those who were weak and helpless; and ministered to those who were lonely, shunned, or otherwise on the outskirts of society. In general, the ministry of the Master entailed His comforting, lifting, and liberating all who came unto Him by faith. Each of us, as His followers, are called upon to do these very things—to participate in the ministry of Jesus and to devote ourselves untiringly to the imitation and emulation of Jesus Christ the Savior.

One matter with which both Jewish and Christian people have

wrestled for centuries was how Jehovah, or Jesus of Nazareth, could be both a Suffering Servant and a Conquering King. In other words, some struggle to comprehend how He could be both man and God, both flesh and spirit, both Father and Son. Isaiah addressed this issue in what we have as the 53rd chapter of his book of scripture. When the prophet Abinadi addressed the wicked priests of King Noah, a significant portion of his sermon was a doctrinal commentary on Isaiah 53, which is the answer to the seeming contradiction of the Messiah being both man and God. Mosiah 15 is essentially an extended commentary on Isaiah 53. It is deep and powerful doctrine that was not understood at all by Noah's priests some 150 years before the coming of the Messiah and often not grasped by many persons living in the twenty-first century either. When one ponders and prays over the twelve verses of Isaiah 53 and looks to Abinadi for his helpful and heart-warming commentary and explication in Mosiah 15, insight and inspiration will come. Over time we can come to treasure this monumental chapter within the Book of Mormon.

We begin our study of this amazing chapter by acknowledging that the word "Father," as used in reference to God, has four definitions. First of all, Elohim is the Father of the spirits of all men and women, including Jesus Christ (see Hebrews 12:9; Numbers 16:22) and is thus the ultimate object of our worship (see 2 Nephi 25:16; Jacob 4:5). Elohim is our Father because He gave us life—provided a spirit birth for each of us.

Jesus Christ is also known by the title of "Father," particularly in Restoration scripture.[1] Understanding that Christ is sometimes known as Father will help clarify the beautiful but rather difficult scriptural passage contained in Mosiah 15—Abinadi's sermon concerning the Father and the Son. First of all, Jesus Christ is known as Father because of his role as *the Creator*. Acting under the direction of His Father, Jehovah was the Creator of worlds without end (see Ephesians 3:9; Colossians 1:16; Hebrews 1:1–2; Moses 1:32–33; 7:29–31). Because of this, Jehovah is appropriately known in the Book of Mormon as "the Father of heaven and earth, the Creator of all things from the beginning" (Mosiah 3:8; compare 2 Nephi 25:12; Alma 11:39; 3 Nephi 9:15).

Second, Christ is Father because of our *spiritual rebirth*. Those on earth who accept the gospel of Jesus Christ and the requisite covenants and ordinances are adopted into the family of Jesus Christ, take upon them the family name, and thus become inheritors of family obligations and family privileges. Even as one enters mortality through mortal birth, one qualifies for eternal life through spiritual rebirth, through being born again as to things of righteousness (see Mosiah 5:1–15; 15:11–12; 27:23–27; Alma 5:14; 3 Nephi 9:16–17; Ether 3:14; Moses 6:57–62).

The Master explained to a group in His Palestinian ministry, "I am come in my Father's name" (John 5:43). Our Lord acted and spoke on behalf of the Almighty Elohim and is therefore known as Father *by divine investiture of authority*, meaning that our Heavenly Father basically put His name upon the Son and authorized Him to speak for and on behalf of the Father, as though He were the Father. This principle is clearly seen in the accounts of prophets in the Pearl of Great Price (see Moses 1:4–6, 32–33; 6:51–52) as well as in the Doctrine and Covenants. In fact, in the latter book of scripture there are occasions in which the Lord chooses to speak as both Christ and Elohim in the same revelation (see Doctrine and Covenants 29:1, 42; 49:5, 28). There is perhaps no better way to establish firmly in the minds of the Saints that the words of Jehovah are the very same words of Elohim, that they have the same mind and thoughts,[2] that they are totally and completely one.

The Book of Mormon powerfully witnesses that Jesus Christ is Father because Elohim literally invests His Son with His own attributes and powers. The first five verses of Mosiah 15 are especially poignant. A number of key doctrinal matters are given in verses one through five:

1. God Himself—Jehovah, the God of ancient Israel—will come

to earth, take a physical body, and bring to pass redemption for all men and woman (verse 1).

2. Because Jesus Christ will have a physical body and dwell in the *flesh*—like every other mortal son and daughter of God—He will be known as the *Son* of God. On the other hand, because He will be conceived by the power of God and will thus have within Him the powers of the *Spirit*, He will be known as the *Father* (verses 2–3). This same doctrine is given in a modern revelation through the Prophet Joseph Smith: "I am the true light that lighteth every man that cometh into the world; and . . . I am in the Father, and the Father in me, and the Father and I are one—[I am] the Father because he [our Heavenly Father] gave me of his fulness, and [I am] the Son because I was in the world and made flesh my tabernacle, and dwelt among the sons of men" (Doctrine and Covenants 93:2–4).

3. The will of the Son is swallowed up in the will of the Father. That is, the *flesh* becomes subject to the *spirit*, the mortal is subject to the immortal (verse 5). "I seek not mine own will," Jesus explained, "but the will of the Father which hath sent me" (John 5:30; compare 6:38). In short, Jesus will do what the Father would have Him do.

4. Thus Christ is both the Father and the Son. He is called the Father because He was conceived by the power of God and inherited all of the divine endowments, particularly immortality, from His Father. He will be called the Son because of the flesh—His mortal inheritance from his mother, Mary. Therefore Christ, the Messiah, will be both *flesh* and *spirit*, both *man* and *God*, both *Son* and *Father* (verse 4). And they—the Son and the Father, the man and the God, the flesh and the spirit—are blended wondrously in one being, Jesus Christ, "the very Eternal Father of heaven and of earth."

The testimony of Abinadi is surely consistent with the message of the Apostle Paul—in Christ "dwelleth all the fulness of the Godhead bodily" (Colossians 2:9). Indeed, "great is the mystery of godliness" (1 Timothy 3:16; see also Doctrine and Covenants 19:10). Mysteries are things that can be understood only through the Spirit of God, but they *can* be understood if we search, ponder, and pray over the scriptures. "For thus saith the Lord—I, the Lord, am merciful and gracious unto those who fear me, and delight to honor those who serve me in righteousness and truth unto the end. Great shall be their reward and eternal shall be their glory. And to them will I reveal all mysteries, yea, all the hidden mysteries of my kingdom. . . . Yea, even the wonders of eternity shall they know" (Doctrine and Covenants 76:5–8).

CHAPTER 19

# Believe, Then Understand

MOSIAH 26

The Prophet Joseph Smith stated: "I told the brethren that the Book of Mormon was the most correct of any book on earth, and the keystone of our religion, and a man would get nearer to God by *abiding by its precepts,* than by any other book."[1] In browsing several dictionaries, I discovered that a *precept* is a rule, a law, a commandment, a mandate, a directive, an injunction, or a maxim. The Book of Mormon is filled with actual historical instances—experiences of real people in a real time—that symbolize universal spiritual truths, that focus on what each of us must do to be snatched, spared, sanctified, and saved. In other words, the Book of Mormon is filled with precepts.

The visitation of the Spirit leads to a softening of the heart, a malleability, a tenderness, an openness to the ways of the Master. We should be deeply grateful for a believing heart, for it is less and less common in today's world, a world ablaze with cynicism and skepticism. A woman who hears the servants of the Lord speak in general conference, for example, and who senses that what the leaders are saying represents the mind and will of the Almighty is in a blessed condition, especially in a day of compounding unbelief. "Blessed are they who humble themselves without being compelled to be humble," Alma explained, "or rather, in other words, blessed is he that believeth in the word of God . . . without being brought to know the word, or even compelled to know, before they will believe" (Alma 32:16). One of the first gifts of the Spirit listed in a modern revelation is the gift of believing. "To some it is given by the Holy Ghost to know that Jesus Christ is the Son of God, and that he was crucified for the sins of the world." Now look at what follows: "To others, it is given *to believe on their words, that they also might have eternal life if they continue faithful*" (Doctrine and Covenants 46:13–14; emphasis added).

Too many in our day are like the rising generation who lived many years after the time of King Benjamin. The people of this generation refused to believe the righteous traditions of their fathers. "They did not believe what had been said concerning the resurrection of the dead, neither did they believe concerning the coming of Christ." Now note these penetrating words: "And now *because of their unbelief they could not understand the word of God; and their hearts were hardened*" (Mosiah 26:1–3; emphasis added). There are some things that a skeptic will never make sense of. There are many things that a public doubter, a naysayer, will never understand. Hardened hearts must be softened, and in some cases broken, before spiritual progress can be made, before one can see things as they really are. The things that really matter in this life can only be understood and appreciated by the power of the Holy Spirit.

In a gospel sense, believing is seeing. A person who is growing spiritually believes the words of inspired spokespeople and receives their messages in a very personal way. Inquiries become more sincere (compare Alma 11:26–39 with 12:7–8). While an unrepentant woman or man is cynical, a reborn person is a believer. While a worldly man demands physical proof, the spiritual woman enjoys that measure of trust and divine patience that allows the Lord to do His own work in His own time. The Lord calls us not to gullibility but to openness. The earnest seeker of truth must be willing to suspend disbelief in order to have the truth confirmed in his or her heart. "Search diligently," the Redeemer implores in a modern revelation, "pray always, and be believing, and all things shall work together for your good, if ye walk uprightly and remember the covenant wherewith ye have covenanted one with another" (Doctrine and Covenants 90:24).

One group of people in the Book of Mormon spoke of their internal change as follows: "We, ourselves, . . . . through the infinite goodness of God, and the manifestations of his Spirit, have great views of that which is to come; and were it expedient, we could prophesy of all things" (Mosiah 5:3). Theirs was a view of the truth—of things as they are and as they were and as they are to come (see Doctrine and Covenants 93:24). Theirs was an elevated perspective, a glimpse of life and of the plan of God unfiltered through impure eyes or hearts. Cultivating the gift of the Holy Ghost in our lives allows us to gain a heightened sensitivity to things that matter. In writing of the person who is being changed by the power of the Spirit, Parley P. Pratt explained: "His mind is quickened, his intellectual faculties are aroused to intense activity. He is, as it were, illuminated. He learns more of divine truth in a few days, than he could have learned in a lifetime in the best merely human institutions in the world."[2]

For example, the Holy Ghost often works with members of the Church through their consciences, giving them a deeper sensitivity to right and wrong, greater manifestations of the gift of discernment, as well as more refined and educated desires. Maturing in the Spirit consists of gaining godly attributes and qualities and feeling a deeper compassion and empathy for those who mourn or suffer or reach out for succor. Such persons are less inclined to labor in secondary causes, and they have a consuming but patient passion to occupy themselves with that which brings light and life and love. They come to treasure the simple pleasures in life and rejoice in the goodness of their God. Joseph Smith taught that "the nearer man approaches perfection, the clearer are his views, and the greater his enjoyments, till he has overcome the evils of his life and lost every desire for sin."[3]

When a person chooses to be a believer rather than a cynic, over time the Spirit brings certitude and conviction and banishes the darkness of doubt. It is not that a person will never have questions or doubts again; rather, he or she knows for certain, by the power of the Holy Ghost, that the fundamental beliefs of the faith are true—that God is in His heaven; that the Church and kingdom of God have been restored to earth, with its keys and powers; and that those who have been chosen and anointed to lead the Church are divinely called. Questions and uncertainties may not immediately disappear, but they do not disturb. As the believer continues to cultivate an openness to truth, he or she gradually comes to understand matters that previously had been mysterious or seemed to be intellectually out of reach.

To have a believing heart is not to be gullible. It is to be open and teachable, willing to learn new things. It is to be humble. I once heard a university student make this comment to a friend: "I don't enjoy listening to [she then named an Apostle] at general conference. He lacks humility." His friend replied: "How do you know he is not humble?" The response: "Listen to him carefully when he speaks. He is bold. He is confident. He is filled with certitude." A strange assessment at best. Humility is the virtue of having a correct and accurate view of yourself, of knowing your strengths and your weaknesses. More important, it is knowing the source of your strength, the source of your power.

Maintaining a believing heart moves one closer and closer to certitude. President Gordon B. Hinckley declared: "Some time ago a journalist from a prominent national publication spoke in Salt Lake City. I did not hear him, but I read the newspaper reports of his remarks. He is quoted as having said, 'Certitude is the enemy of religion.' The words attributed to him have stirred within me much reflection. Certitude, which I define as complete and total assurance, is not the enemy of religion. It is of its very essence.

"Certitude is certainty. It is conviction. It is the power of faith that approaches knowledge—yes, that even becomes knowledge. It evokes enthusiasm, and there is no asset comparable to enthusiasm in overcoming opposition, prejudice, and indifference. Great buildings were never constructed on uncertain foundations. Great causes were never brought to success by vacillating leaders. The gospel was never expounded to the convincing of others without certainty. Faith, which is of the very essence of personal conviction, has always been and always must be at the root of religious practice and endeavor. . . .

"If the Latter-day Saints, as individuals, ever lose that certitude, the Church will dwindle as so many other churches have. But I have no fear of that. I am confident that an ever-enlarging membership will seek for and find that personal conviction which we call testimony, which comes by the power of the Holy Ghost, and which can weather the storms of adversity."[4]

Following Nephi's grand panoramic vision (see 1 Nephi 11–14), he returned to the tent of his father. There he found Laman and Lemuel "disputing one with another concerning the things which [Lehi] had spoken unto them." They had questions concerning the scattering and gathering of Israel, and so Nephi asked: "Have ye inquired of the Lord?" Their response is classic: "We have not; for the Lord maketh no such thing known unto us." Their refusal to believe was a roadblock to their understanding. Their unwillingness to exercise that "particle of faith" that Alma later described (Alma 32:27) prevented them from crossing the bridge that would have brought them precious insight. Nephi spoke boldly: "Do ye not remember the things which the Lord hath said?—*If ye will not harden your hearts*, and ask me in faith, *believing that ye shall receive*, with diligence in keeping my commandments, surely these things shall be made known unto you" (1 Nephi 15:1–11; emphasis added).

Clearly, the key to understanding any and all of the points of doctrine associated with the gospel of Jesus Christ is to put off one's pride and self-assurance and put on the mantle of belief, receptivity, openness, and eagerness to learn. No invitation from the Master is more often repeated than this: "Ask, and it shall be given you; seek, and ye shall find; knock, and it shall be opened unto you" (Matthew 7:7; 3 Nephi 14:7).

## CHAPTER 20

# "Bearing Down in Pure Testimony"

ALMA 4

We are engaged in the work of the Lord Jesus Christ. This is His Church. It administers His gospel and teaches His doctrine. It bears His priesthood and performs His ordinances. These are facts, and they are true. A knowledge, an inner certitude, a witness or conviction, of such things we call a testimony. "Your testimony is a most precious possession," Elder Gary E. Stevenson observed, "often associated with deep spiritual feelings. These feelings are usually communicated quietly and described as a 'still small voice' (1 Kings 19:12). It is your belief or knowledge of truth given as a spiritual witness through the influence of the Holy Ghost. Acquiring this witness will change what you say and how you act."[1]

We cannot progress in the kingdom without a witness of this work, without a testimony. We need a testimony of God as our Father, of Jesus as our Lord and Savior, of the restoration of the fullness of His gospel, of the truthfulness of the Book of Mormon and latter-day revelation, and of the fact that The Church of Jesus Christ of Latter-day Saints is divinely led by living apostles and prophets. A knowledge of such things comforts, motivates, and impels us to faithfulness in the face of opposition; such an assurance helps us know why we continue to do what we do.

To *bear* has at least two meanings. It means, first of all, to possess, in the sense that a man or woman possesses or bears responsibility or burdens. Second, it means to express, convey, or declare to others. Spiritual things can be *known*. We need not apologize for things we know by the power of the Spirit, for they are as real (if not more so) than the things we perceive in the physical world through the five senses. "*I know with a witness that is more powerful than sight*," President Harold B. Lee said to Brigham Young University students just three months before his death. "Sometime, if the spirit prompts me, I may feel free to tell you more, but may I say to you that *I know as though I had seen*, that He lives, that He is real, that God the Father and his Son are living realities, personalities with bodies, parts, and passions—glorified beings. If you believe that, then you are safe. If you don't believe it, then struggle for that witness, and all will be well with you."[2]

An episode in the book of Alma illustrates the potential power of testimony. A little more than eighty years before the coming of Christ, Alma the Younger, the chief judge or governor, seeing that wickedness was spreading among the Nephites, even to members of the Church, felt the need to resign from his role in government and devote himself full-time to ministry (Alma 9–18). "Now this he did," Mormon wrote, "that he himself might go forth among his people, or among the people of Nephi, *that he might preach the word of God unto them, to stir them up in remembrance of their duty*, and that he might pull down, by the word of God, all the pride and craftiness and all the contentions which were among his people, seeing no way that he might reclaim them save it were in *bearing down in pure testimony against them*" (Alma 4:19; emphasis added).

This very significant verse is a companion with another of Mormon's comments that, again, attests the power of the word of God. In recounting the story of Alma and his missionary companions as they were about to teach the gospel to the Zoramites, Mormon taught: "And now, as the preaching of the word had a great tendency to lead the people to do that which was just—yea, it had had more powerful effect upon the minds of the people than the sword, or anything else, which had happened unto them—therefore Alma thought it was expedient that they should try the virtue of the word of God" (Alma 31:5). To "try the virtue of the word of God" is to trust or have faith and confidence in the power of sound doctrinal teaching and solid testimony bearing. To those who wonder how they can bear testimony when they are not certain how much of a testimony they truly have, President Dallin H. Oaks said that "some testimonies are better gained on the feet bearing them than on the knees praying for them."[3]

Many years ago in one of my Book of Mormon classes at Brigham Young University, after I had finished a discussion of Alma 4:19 and the matter of bearing pure testimony, a student spoke to me after class. He said: "Brother Millet, I wanted so badly to bear my testimony in yesterday's fast and testimony meeting in my BYU ward, but I didn't have anything original to say. I didn't have a special message." His concern illustrates a problem we sometimes see in the Church: the presumption that one has to preach a sermon or make some original contribution to the meeting. The leaders of the Church have repeatedly stated that members of the Church are to be invited to bear brief, heartfelt testimonies and, where appropriate, share faith-promoting experiences. There really is no need for members of the Church to worry one-tenth of a second about coming up with something original to say or about giving a talk.

President Spencer W. Kimball counseled a group of young people gathered in a testimony meeting: "Do not exhort each other; that is not a testimony. Do not tell others how to live. *Just tell how you feel inside. That is the testimony. The moment you begin preaching to others, your testimony ended. Just tell us how you feel,* what your mind and heart and every fiber of your body tells you."[4] On another occasion, President Kimball said to a similar group: "Now, you are going to give your testimonies this afternoon. I hope that you'll just open your hearts and let us look inside. . . . A testimony is not an exhortation; a testimony is not a sermon; none of you are here to exhort the rest. You are here to bear your own witness."[5]

"Every missionary yearns for the power to persuade and convince," President Russell M. Nelson taught. "Nothing you will learn can ever match the power of pure testimony. Doctrines can be debated. Opinions can be argued. Interpretations can be challenged. But no one can dispute a testimony. It is uniquely unassailable."[6]

There's no question that when we have a genuine spiritual experience, we may be touched emotionally. Tears come easily for some of us, and there should never be the slightest embarrassment about such a thing. And yet we do ourselves and our youth a tremendous disservice if we begin to believe or imply that an emotional experience is always a spiritual experience. Tears may come, but they should never be manipulated or elicited. In the classroom, for example, there is plenty for the gospel teacher to do by way of study, prayer, preparation, organization, and presentation; he or she must not seek to usurp the role of the Holy Ghost. The Holy Ghost is the Comforter. He is the Revelator. He is the Converter. He is, in reality, the Teacher. We strive to be an instrument. We may seek and pray for an outpouring of the Spirit, but we must never attempt to manufacture one. President Howard W. Hunter, in speaking to Church Educational System personnel, said: "I think if we are not careful as professional teachers working in the classroom every day, we may begin to try to counterfeit the true influence of the Spirit of the Lord by unworthy and manipulative means. I get concerned when it appears that strong emotion of free-flowing tears are equated with the presence of the Spirit. Certainly the Spirit of the Lord can bring strong emotional feelings, including tears, but that outward manifestation ought not be confused with the presence of the Spirit itself.

"I have watched a great many of my brethren over the years and we have shared some rare and unspeakable spiritual experiences together. Those experiences have all been different, each special in its own way, and such sacred moments may or may not be accompanied by tears. Very often they are, but sometimes they are accompanied by total silence. Always they are accompanied by a great manifestation of the truth, of revelation to the heart.

"Give your students gospel truth powerfully taught; that is the way to give them a spiritual experience. Let it come naturally and as it will, perhaps with the shedding of tears, but perhaps not. If what you say is the truth, and you say it purely and with honest conviction, those students will feel the spirit of truth being taught them and will recognize that inspiration and revelation has come into their hearts. That is how we build faith. That is how we strengthen testimonies—with the power of the word of God taught in purity and with conviction."[7]

The Apostle Paul wrote to the Saints in Rome: "For whosoever shall call upon the name of the Lord shall be saved. How then shall they call on him in whom they have not believed? And how shall they believe in him of whom they have not heard? And how shall they hear without a preacher? . . . So then faith cometh by hearing, and hearing by the word of God" (Romans 10:13–14, 17). The Prophet Joseph Smith put it this way: "Faith comes by hearing the word of God, through the testimony of the servants of God; that testimony is always attended by the spirit of prophecy and revelation."[8]

There is no way, given our limited perspective in this life, that we can measure the eternal influence of pure testimony. Perhaps only when we are able to look back on the whole of our existence, able to see things as they really were and are, from God Almighty's point of view, will we be able to sense and feel the powerful coalescence of circumstances, the divinely contrived orchestration of people and events. Maybe then we will be in a position to measure how the power of pure human testimony has made a difference in our own lives.

CHAPTER 21

# God Grants unto All Nations

ALMA 29

I am fully persuaded that Jesus Christ, who is the embodiment of love and mercy and every Godly attribute in perfection, will do all that is appropriate to inspire, lift, edify, and encourage individuals, families, communities, and whole nations. Jehovah spoke on this matter to Nephi: "Know ye not that there are more nations than one? Know ye not that I, the Lord your God, have created all men, and that I remember those who are upon the isles of the sea; and that I rule in the heavens above and in the earth beneath; and *I bring forth my word unto the children of men, yea, even upon all the nations of the earth*?" (2 Nephi 29:7; emphasis added.)

Alma explained that "the Lord doth grant unto all nations, of their own nation and tongue, to teach his word, yea, in wisdom, all that he seeth fit that they should have" (Alma 29:8). In 1978, the First Presidency (Spencer W. Kimball, N. Eldon Tanner, and Marion G. Romney) called upon the Saints to broaden their perspective on our brothers and sisters of other faiths, and particularly their leaders. The First Presidency issued an official statement, a portion of which reads: "The great religious leaders of the world such as Mohammed, Confucius, and the Reformers, as well as philosophers including Socrates, Plato, and others, received a portion of God's light. Moral truths were given to them by God to enlighten whole nations and to bring a higher level of understanding to individuals."[1]

It is therefore reasonable that elements of truth—pieces of a much larger mosaic—should be found throughout the world in varying cultures and among diverse religious groups. Further, though the world has passed through phases of apostasy and restoration, relics of revealed doctrine have remained, albeit often in altered or convoluted forms. Persons who lack spiritual insight and the faith that derives from a knowledge of Christ's eternal plan of salvation may cast doubt on the true gospel; they may point to legends and traditions of creation epics or flood stories that presumably predate the Pentateuch; they may eagerly note similarities between ordinances of the temple and practices in pagan cultures; and thus they may suggest that Christianity has but copied from more ancient sources.

President Joseph F. Smith, a nephew of the Prophet Joseph, had much to say to those who seek to upstage Christianity. The Savior, he taught, "being the fountain of truth, is no imitator. He taught the truth first; it was his before it was given to man." Further, "if we find truth in broken fragments through the ages, it may be set down as an incontrovertible fact that it originated at the fountain, and was given to philosophers, inventors, patriots, reformers, and prophets by the inspiration of God. It came from him through his Son Jesus Christ and the Holy Ghost, in the first place, and from no other source. It is eternal." In summary, President Smith pointed out that "men are mere repeaters of what he has taught them. He has voiced no thought originating with man."[2]

Knowing what we know concerning God our Father, and knowing that many of the ancients also had this understanding, should we be surprised to find legends and myths about gods who have divine power but human attributes and passions? If Adam and Seth and Enos and Cainan and Mahalaleel and others of the antediluvians spoke of the coming of a Messiah who would come to earth as a man but be possessed of the powers of a God, is it not likely that they also knew that he would be born of a virgin? Then should we be surprised to find pagan traditions of virgin births and divine humans?

Adam heard a heavenly voice saying: "I am God; I made the world, and *men before they were in the flesh*" (Moses 6:51; emphasis added). That is, men and women in the earliest ages knew of a first estate, a premortal existence. Therefore, is it any wonder that several religious traditions are wedded to an idea of past lives? Points of doctrine such as rebirth, regeneration, resurrection, and the immortality of the soul were taught to Adam and his posterity, so why should we flinch when we discover beliefs in reincarnation or transmigration of souls in traditions like Hinduism, Jainism, and Sikhism, or when we encounter a people like the ancient Egyptians who were almost obsessed with life after death?

What is true of sacred practices and beliefs throughout the ancient non-Christian world is also true in today's modern Christian world. We believe that divine priesthood authority was withdrawn by God and that many plain and precious truths were taken away or kept back following the deaths of the meridian Apostles (see 1 Nephi 13:20–40). This does not mean, however, that Protestants or Catholics or Eastern Orthodox believers have no truth or that any scriptural interpretation from them is automatically suspect, incorrect, or corrupt. As noted earlier, elements of enlightenment, remnants of truth, and aspects of the faith of the former-day Saints may be found in modern Christianity. The Lord loves His children, all of them, and He delights to "honor those who serve [Him] in righteousness and in truth unto the end" (Doctrine and Covenants 76:5). "Have the Presbyterians any truth?" Joseph the Prophet asked in 1843. "Yes. Have the Baptists, Methodists, etc., any truth? Yes, they all have a little truth mixed with error. We should gather all the good and true principles in the world and treasure them up, or we shall not come out pure Mormons."[3]

Everyone has access to some measure of light and truth from the Almighty—what Latter-day Saints know as the Light of Christ or Spirit of Jesus Christ (see Doctrine and Covenants 84:44–48; 88:6–13;

Moroni 7:12–19). This is similar if not the same as what the Protestant or Catholic world calls "general revelation," and "common grace" is the fruits and divine assistance that flow from this light. President Brigham Young thus declared that there has never been "a man or woman upon the face of the earth, from the days of Adam to this day, who has not been enlightened, instructed, and taught by the revelations of Jesus Christ."[4]

On another occasion President Young pointed out that God "gives his Spirit when and to whom he pleases. . . . I never passed John Wesley's church in London without stopping to look at it. Was he a good man? Yes; I suppose him to have been, by all accounts, as good as ever walked on this earth, according to his knowledge." And then, speaking of Wesley in the postmortal spirit world, Brother Brigham asked: "Has he obtained a rest? Yes, and greater than ever entered his mind to expect; and so have thousands of others of the various religious denominations."[5]

A renowned Methodist itinerant preacher named Peter Cartwright recorded a memorable exchange between him and Joseph Smith in Nauvoo: "He [Joseph] believed that among all the Churches in the world the Methodists was the nearest right. But they had stopped short by not claiming the gift of tongues, of prophecy, and of miracles, and then quoted a batch of Scriptures to prove his position correct. . . . 'Indeed,' said Joe, 'if the Methodists would only advance a step or two further, they would take the world. We Latter-day Saints are Methodists, as far as they have gone, only have advanced further."[6]

The Prophet Joseph Smith demonstrated his elevated prophetic perspective, coupled with his breadth of soul, when he asked: "If I esteem mankind to be in error, shall I bear them down? No; I will lift them up, and in their own way too if I cannot persuade them my way is better; and I will not seek to compel any man to believe as I do, only by the force of reasoning; for truth will cut its own way."[7]

The prophets teach that if people will be true to the light and understanding they have, they will be led to greater and higher light, both here and hereafter. "And the Spirit giveth light to every man that cometh into the world; and the Spirit enlighteneth every man through the world, that hearkeneth to the voice of the Spirit" (Doctrine and Covenants 84:46).[8] The longer I live and the more God-fearing people I encounter, the more clearly I see God working through noble people throughout the earth.

Gaining a broader perspective on God's tender regard for all His children has changed my life. After more than three decades of interfaith endeavors; after reading scores of books and articles to better understand colleagues and associates of various Christian denominations; after spending hundreds of hours in intensive, probing conversations on doctrinal matters ranging from Adam to Zion—after all this, I have never been more committed to the restored Church than I am right now. The fruits of the Restoration have never been sweeter to my taste. At the same time, I feel a deep sense of love, admiration, and respect for marvelous women and men whose beliefs are somewhat different than mine but whose desire to seek out truth and gain deeper understanding is akin to my own.

In addition, I have been blessed to see and experience the love of God for all of His children; I have sensed that the Almighty is working through men and women of various religious persuasions to bring to pass the marvelous work and a wonder foreseen by Isaiah. I cannot count the number of times that after having multiday discussions and listening to dear friends offering their closing remarks, I have felt the reality of the Savior's words to His Apostles that "where two or three are gathered together in my name, there am I in the midst of them" (Matthew 18:20).

CHAPTER 22

# The Experiment of Faith

ALMA 32–34

As I have read and studied the Book of Mormon over the last half century, I've observed that there are certain words that are basically synonyms for faith in Jesus Christ, the first principle of the gospel (see Articles of Faith 1:4). They are *trust*, *confidence*, and *reliance*. To *trust* the Lord is to know that He is who the prophets have said He is and that He will always do His part to move me along the path toward eternal life. To paraphrase the words of a familiar hymn, I've "proved him in days that are past."[1] To have *confidence* in the Savior is to know that there is nothing lacking in His character, His might and majesty and power, or His capacity to do all that He says He can do to lift and liberate me. To *rely* upon Jesus is to lean on Him, to depend on Him, and to acknowledge Him as my mainstay. Nephi teaches that we must learn to "rely wholly" upon Him who is mighty to save (2 Nephi 31:19), while Moroni challenges us to "rely alone" upon the merits of Him who is mighty to save (Moroni 6:4).

The first principle of the gospel is faith in the Lord Jesus Christ. The gospel is the grand news, the glad tidings, that through exercising faith in Christ and His Atonement, coupled with repentance that flows therefrom, we may be forgiven of our sins and justified, or made right, with God. Our standing before the Almighty is thereby changed—we go from being tainted by sin to receiving heavenly favor and acceptance;

we travel the path from death to life (see Romans 5:9–10). "Therefore being justified by faith, we have peace with God through our Lord Jesus Christ" (Romans 5:1). The Apostle Peter taught: "Humble yourselves therefore under the mighty hand of God, that he may exalt you in due time: *casting all your care upon him: for he careth for you*" (1 Peter 5:6–7; emphasis added).

We can manifest our faith in the Savior during difficult, trying times when we feel helpless or incapable and then sense the need to lay our burdens at the feet of our Lord. Surely, as Peter taught, we can cast our burdens upon the Lord because He cares for us—because He loves us. But perhaps Peter intended more in this passage. We can give to Him who is the Balm of Gilead our worries, our anxieties, our fretting, and our awful anticipations because He will care for us and, in a way, *do the caring for us*. It is as though Peter had counseled us: "Quit worrying. Don't be so anxious. Stop wringing your hands. Let Jesus bear the burden while you receive and enjoy the peace."

This is what C. S. Lewis meant when he observed that maturing Christians despair of doing anything on their own and "leave it to God." True disciples of Christ leave it to God when they put all their trust in Christ and thereby allow the Savior to make up for their deficiencies. But saving the human soul is a joint effort—God and human working together. And so while we learn to leave the burdens of life at the altar of Christ, we continue to do our very best to keep the commandments. "Thus if you have really handed yourself over to Him," Lewis added, "it must follow that you are trying to obey Him. But *trying in a new way, a less worried way*."[2]

Alma calls upon the Zoramites and, by extension, each of us to try the experiment of faith, to plant the seed. And what is the seed that we are to plant? A careful reading of Alma 32–34 teaches that it is the knowledge that Jesus Christ is the Son of God, our Redeemer and Savior, and that He can, if we allow Him, make us into faithful and faith-filled disciples (Alma 33:21–23; 34:1–6). We begin with a rather weak hope that there is indeed a Savior. We thereby exercise "a particle of faith" and thus "desire to believe" (Alma 32:27). Alma goes on to explain that there are very discernible ways to know that the seed—a desire to believe that Jesus is our Lord and Redeemer—is a true seed, a good seed. He explains that if we plant the seed and do not reject the truth that we have a Savior, the seed "will begin to swell within [our] breasts." In addition, if the doctrine of Christ is true, then "it beginneth to enlarge [our] soul"; it will enlighten our understanding (Alma 32:28).

From my perspective, one of the most important verses in Alma 32 is verse 31: "And now, behold, are ye sure that this is a good seed? I say unto you, Yea; for *every seed bringeth forth unto its own likeness*" (emphasis added). What does this mean? I believe Alma is teaching us that as we allow the knowledge of the Savior to remain in our minds and our hearts, and as we ponder and pray earnestly about our need for redemption and the reality that Christ is the only means by which we can be redeemed, then that seed will ripen within us in the form of *our becoming more Christlike*—more eager to learn the will of God and carry it out, more patient and forgiving toward others, more loving and kind, more sensitive to the needs of others, more attentive to the pains and stresses of those about us, more eager to extend our hand in love, more willing to be inconvenienced. The seed will have thus brought forth fruit in the form of a person who is beginning to "have the mind of Christ" (1 Corinthians 2:16) and to be in harmony with Him and His will, a person who embodies what the Apostle Paul called "the fruit of the Spirit" (Galatians 5:22–25).

We begin the road to faith by hoping that the Only Begotten Son of the Father was indeed sent to earth on a grand mission of mercy and grace. As time passes, and as we strive to have our minds single to God, the simple hope with which we began the experiment ripens into a higher level of hope. "And what is it that ye shall hope for?" Mormon asks. "Behold I say unto you that ye shall have hope through the atonement of Christ and the power of his resurrection, *to be raised unto life eternal*, and this because of your faith in him according to the promise"

(Moroni 7:41; emphasis added). Our hope has matured and become anticipation, expectation, and the assurance of life eternal.

President M. Russell Ballard bore witness that "as we follow Jesus Christ with footsteps of faith, there is hope. There is hope in the Lord Jesus Christ. There is hope for all in this life. There is hope to overcome our mistakes, our sorrows, our struggles, and our trials and our troubles. There is hope in repentance and being forgiven and in forgiving others. I testify that there is hope and peace in Christ. He can carry us today through difficult times."[3]

There are many things that faith *is not.* Faith is not an event. Faith is not gullibility or falling for anything. Faith is not weakness or ignorance. Faith is not the absence of knowledge. Faith is not blind; in fact, for those with faith, believing is seeing. Faith is not the absence of certitude. Faith is not the power of positive thinking, nor is it the power to will something into existence. Once again, to have faith in the Lord Jesus Christ is to totally trust Him, to have complete confidence in Him, and to readily rely upon Him. And I testify that He is in every way worthy of our faith, and many of the blessings that flow from that faith are beyond mortal comprehension.

CHAPTER 23

# "This Life Is the Time"

ALMA 34

My wife, Shauna, and I often discuss the fact that, as we grow older, the years seem to fly by. Of course, time—24 hours a day, 7 days a week, 30 or so days a month, 365 days a year—hasn't changed at all. Time is time. But how very real it is that as time goes by, we find ourselves either ignoring or forgetting to do those things that we had intended to do, things that really need to be done. Things such as spending more time on my knees in prayer and listening; beginning and completing my personal history and getting serious about my family history responsibilities; studying the scriptures with greater intent; or becoming a more effective, responsive, and attentive Church minister.

Things that are important but neglected cause discomfort in our hearts and painful consciences. Why? Because we have the opportunity to live a mortal life only once. I am reminded of the occasion in Alma 60 when Captain Moroni complains and scolds Pahoran, the chief judge, for not sending more men, food, and supplies to strengthen the weak, discouraged soldiers in the field. In verse 5 we read: "Great has been the slaughter among our people; yea, thousands have fallen by the sword, while *it might have otherwise been* if ye had rendered unto our armies sufficient strength and succor for them" (emphasis added).

In speaking to the Zoramties, Alma explained that "now is the time and the day of your salvation; and therefore, if ye will repent and harden not your hearts, *immediately shall the great plan of redemption be brought about unto you*" (Alma 34:31; emphasis added). It is of real interest to me that Alma taught that making things right with God once again need not take forever; instead, once we begin the process of repentance, the Savior's Atonement and the redemption of a wayward soul are put into effect *immediately*. Thus putting off repentance until a later time is ignoring a precious opportunity to once again enjoy the Spirit of the Lord and rejoice in the peace that comes from being clean. That is tragic. Why? Because "*this life is the time for men to prepare to meet God*; yea, behold the day of this life is the day for men to perform their labors" (Alma 34:32; emphasis added). Mortality, earth life, here and now—this is the time to get ready to see God and declare to Him how I have spent my life, whether I took advantage of or neglected precious invitations to get up, dust myself off, and become better than I am. Amulek stressed that "if we do not improve our time while in this life"—that is, if we do not make wise use of our time—"then cometh the night of darkness wherein there can be no labor performed" (Alma 34:33).

What, exactly did Amulek mean when he spoke of this "night of darkness" wherein labor cannot be performed? My colleague and associate at BYU, Larry E. Dahl, explained that the "night of darkness" is "that point in time when one's probationary opportunities come to an end and the inevitable consequences of previous choices and behavior ensue. . . . Both Alma and Amulek clearly seem to have been warning their hearers not to procrastinate repentance until they leave their mortal probation through death. Both also associated this 'night of darkness,' this 'awful crisis,' and the point at which 'there can be no labor performed' with the time of resurrection." Brother Dahl added, "The night of darkness occurs for sons of perdition when they commit the unpardonable sin, the sin against the Holy Ghost. The devil enters into them and takes 'possession of their house' (Alma 40:13), having power also to 'possess [their] body in that eternal world' [Alma 34:34]. The devil seals them his permanently and has all power over them.

"Those who do not sin to the point of becoming sons of perdition but who procrastinate repentance until mortal death also experience a night of darkness 'wherein there can be no labor performed.' Nothing can be done to avoid the consequences of their earthly wickedness (Alma 34:33). Yet, this night of darkness is not permanent. By virtue of the atonement of Christ, 'the dead who repent will be redeemed, through obedience to the ordinances of the house of God. And after they have paid the penalty of their transgressions, and are washed clean, shall receive a reward according to their works, for they are heirs of salvation' (Doctrine and Covenants 138:58–59)."[1]

The Prophet Joseph Smith stated that "the infidel will grasp at every straw for help until death stares him in the face, and then his infidelity takes its flight, for the realities of the eternal world are resting upon him in mighty power. . . . Let this, then, prove as a warning to all, not to procrastinate repentance, or wait till a deathbed; for it is the will of God that man should repent, and serve him in health, and in the strength, and power of his mind, in order to secure his blessing; and not wait until he is called to die."[2] A beloved hymn instructs us to

*Improve the shining moments;*
*Don't let them pass you by.*
*Work while the sun is radiant;*
*Work, for the night draws nigh.*
*We cannot bid the sunbeams*
*To lengthen out their stay,*
*Nor can we ask the shadow*
*To ever stay away.*

*Time flies on wings of lightning;*
*We cannot call it back.*
*It comes, then passes forward*
*Along its onward track.*

*And if we are not mindful,*
*The chance will fade away,*
*For life is quick in passing.*
*'Tis as a single day.*[3]

"One of the most cruel games anyone can play with self," Elder Neal A. Maxwell declared in a general conference address, "is the 'not yet' game—hoping to sin just a bit more before ceasing; to enjoy the praise of the world a little longer before turning away from the applause; to win just once more in the wearying sweepstakes of materialism; to be chaste, but not yet; to be good neighbors, but not now. . . .

"The truth is that 'not yet' usually means 'never.' Trying to run away from the responsibility to decide about Christ is childish. Pilate sought to refuse responsibility for deciding about Christ, but Pilate's hands were never dirtier than just after he had washed them.

"The past of each of us is now inflexible. We need to concentrate on what has been called 'the holy present,' for now is sacred; we never really live in the future. The holy gift of life always takes the form of now. Besides, God asks us now to give up only those things which, if clung to, will destroy us!

"And when we tear ourselves free from the entanglements of the world, are we promised a religion of repose or an Eden of ease? No! We are promised tears and trials and toil! But we are also promised final triumph, the mere contemplation of which tingles the soul."[4]

Now, having sounded the voice of warning, with the prophets beckoning to us not to delay the day and time to pull ourselves together, we must also reflect on the comfort and reassurance we have received. "However late you think you are," Elder Jeffrey R. Holland declared, "however many chances you think you have missed, however many mistakes you feel you have made or talents you think you don't have, or however far from home and family and God you feel you have traveled, I testify that you have not traveled beyond the reach of divine love. It is not possible for you to sink lower than the infinite light of Christ's Atonement shines. . . . It is *never* too late so long as the Master of the vineyard says there is time. Please listen to the prompting of the Holy Spirit telling you right now, this very moment, that you should accept the atoning gift of the Lord Jesus Christ and enjoy the fellowship of His labor. Don't delay."[5]

CHAPTER 24

# Alma's Conversion: A Reason for Hope

MOSIAH 27; ALMA 36

Alma and the sons of Mosiah were stopped in their tracks, as it were, then turned about and redirected. Alma underwent a major spiritual transformation; he was born again—changed from a carnal and fallen state to a state of righteousness (see Mosiah 27:25). The sons of Mosiah—Ammon, Aaron, Omner, and Himni—underwent a similar transformation (see Mosiah 27:34–37). Thereafter the five of them devoted themselves wholly to the work of the Lord and were directly involved in converting thousands of souls to the gospel of Jesus Christ.

Their conversion could not repair every damage they had caused or retrieve every apostate word they had spoken. There are simply some things that we have broken that *we* cannot fix, some pain that we may have caused that *we* cannot remove. In such moments, when we feel helpless and are prone to look down, we should, as Elder Neil L. Andersen has written, "look up. If all you can manage is to simply lift your eyes to Him, you have done something in an effort to return to Him. You will come to know that He 'reaches your reaching.' You may have a long climb, a steep climb, even a daunting climb, but looking up is an important step in your journey forward. . . . More important than where you are is the direction you face, and especially Whom you face."[1]

And so it was that Alma and the sons of Mosiah transferred their burden to God and yielded themselves to the work of the Master. They "labored without ceasing, that [they] might bring souls unto repentance; that [they] might bring them to taste of the exceeding joy of which [they] did taste; that they might also be born of God, and be filled with the Holy Ghost" (Alma 36:24).

This conversion is a remarkable story, an inspiring narrative that spawns significant lessons that span the chasm of time. For example, we learn from their story that no one is beyond spiritual recovery. As mentioned in the last chapter, "all are within the reach of pardoning mercy, who have not committed the unpardonable sin."[2] God can recognize goodness and potential within each of us, as He did with Saul of Tarsus, the infamous persecutor of the Christians. When Ananias hesitated to assist this enemy of the faith after Saul had been struck down on the road to Damascus, the Lord said boldly: "Go thy way: for he is a chosen vessel unto me, to bear my name before the Gentiles, and kings, and the children of Israel" (Acts 9:15).

Parents may find especial comfort in Alma's conversion story, particularly parents whose children have wandered from the fold. It is so very difficult to keep going, to do all the right things, to keep one's head up and one's courage intact. It is extremely tough to stay at the wheel when those we love the most forsake the faith and way of life to which we have consecrated ourselves. And yet we have the promises that "the effectual fervent prayer of a righteous man [or woman] availeth much" (James 5:16) and that, both in time and eternity, our God will wipe away all tears (see Isaiah 25:8; Revelation 7:17; 21:4). Parents should thus continue to hope, pray, and trust in the power of the gospel covenant to restore, renew, and rekindle the flame of faith in the hearts of their children.

These assurances are indeed soothing and settling. There is, however, an aspect of Alma's story that may prove a bit unsettling for some, a dimension of his conversion that may cause unrest. Some questions arise: Why would an angel come to Alma, who had done so much wrong? Why should he be so privileged? Is that the way most of us are "turned around"? Where is the fairness in this system? Why should the bulk of humankind be asked to wait and yearn and suffer until something much less dramatic (if anything at all) comes to pass?

First, if all rebellious souls were struck down by an angel who confirmed the reality of God, the truthfulness of the gospel, and the certainty of a life beyond, there would be little need for faith on anyone's part. If every time I were about to take a backward step or to stray from the covenant path, my effort was blocked by a caring but conspicuous ministering angel, I would never be left to myself to choose good over evil and therefore would never grow into that spiritual maturity that derives from overcoming the world.

Second, if such appearances by angels were frequent, we might be tempted to obtain a testimony through negative behavior rather than through quiet and consistent gospel living. Young people could, for example, become fascinated with the possibility of seeing an angel. And what would be required? Simply to misbehave. Since few among the faithful are accorded the privilege of seeing angels, it would be a strange system of salvation that freely granted such a privilege to the wayward.

Third, it is possible that an appreciable number of people have indeed been ministered to by angels but rejected the divine counsel and chose to continue in their waywardness. We would undoubtedly be left without a record of such instances, except perhaps by believers who knew about them. The coming of an angel does not ensure change. We know, for example, that Laman and Lemuel were chastened by an angel but that his words were ignored. "Ye are swift to do iniquity," Nephi said to his older brothers, "but slow to remember the Lord your God. Ye have seen an angel, and he spake unto you; yea, ye have heard his voice from time to time; and he hath spoken unto you in a still small voice, but ye were past feeling, that ye could not feel his words; wherefore, he has spoken unto you like unto the voice of thunder, which did cause the earth to shake as if it were to divide asunder" (1 Nephi 17:45).

Fourth, the Savior explained that those who reject the testimony of scripture and living prophets are not more prone to accept the testimony of angels. In the parable of the rich man and Lazarus, the rich man, now in the postmortal spirit world and sensing finally that he has sealed his doom because he ignored the pleadings of the needy on earth, begs that words of warning be sent to his living kindred. "Then he said, I pray thee therefore, father [Abraham], that thou wouldst send him [Lazarus, who is now in paradise] to my father's house: for I have five brethren; that he may testify unto them, lest they also come into this place of torment. Abraham saith unto him, They have Moses and the prophets; let them hear them. And he said, Nay, father Abraham: but if one went unto them from the dead, they will repent. And he said unto him, *If they hear not Moses and the prophets, neither will they be persuaded, though one rose from the dead*" (Luke 16:27–31; emphasis added).

Fifth, the Apostle Paul offered the following sobering counsel: "Let brotherly love continue. Be not forgetful to entertain strangers: for thereby *some have entertained angels unawares*" (Hebrews 13:1–2; emphasis added). In other words, sometimes we are like the two disciples on the road to Emmaus—our eyes are holden or restrained (see Luke 24:16) so that we are not able to see who it is that walks among us, teaches us, lifts us up, and points or repoints us toward the abundant life. It is possible that unseen angels whisper or testify or warn in ways that we cannot now perceive but which will be obvious to us one day. In speaking of angels, Mormon affirmed that "the office of their ministry is to call men unto repentance, and to fulfil and to do the work of the covenants of the Father, which he hath made unto the children of men, to prepare the way among the children of men, by declaring the word of Christ unto the chosen vessels of the Lord, that they may bear testimony of him. And by so doing, the Lord God prepareth the way that the residue of men may have faith in Christ, that the Holy Ghost may have place in their hearts" (Moroni 7:31–32).

Finally, it should be remembered that the Lord, who can manifest His power in a variety of ways, is hardly limited to angelic ministrations or visions when He wants to communicate to His children. Many have had conversion experiences that offered a spiritual impact equal to that experienced by Alma and the sons of Mosiah—life-changing experiences that were the result of a coalescence of divinely contrived circumstances. These experiences may have involved such things as a confrontation with death; an inspired sermon; a scriptural passage that seemed to leap off the page; a caring and sensitive parent, relative, or friend; or a concerned and persistent priesthood or Relief Society minister.

Although our Heavenly Father will force no man or woman to heaven, He *will* do everything He can to attract and entice us toward the fullness of gospel blessings. A zealous but misdirected Saul of Tarsus was redirected by the Lord Jesus Himself. Alma's wayward course was interrupted by an angel, and his personal life and the Nephite narrative were never the same thereafter. Many of us are touched, stopped, redirected, and strengthened by angels, angels that may and do come in many forms. I have come to appreciate President Spencer W. Kimball's insight that "God does notice us, and he watches over us. But it is usually through another mortal that he meets our needs."[3]

"From the beginning down through the dispensations, God has used angels as His emissaries in conveying love and concern for His children," Elder Jeffrey R. Holland stated. "The scriptures and our own latter-day history . . . are so filled with accounts of angels ministering to those on earth"—"rich doctrine and rich history indeed.

"Usually such beings are *not* seen. Sometimes they are. But seen or unseen, they are always near. Sometimes their assignments are very grand and have significance for the whole world. Sometimes the messages are more private. Occasionally the angelic purpose is to warn. But most often it is to comfort, to provide some form of merciful attention, guidance in difficult times. . . .

"I have spoken here of heavenly help, of angels dispatched to bless us in time of need. But when we speak of those who are instruments in the hands of God, we are reminded that not all angels are from the other side of the veil. Some of them we walk with and talk with—here, now, every day. Some of them reside in their own neighborhoods. Some of them gave birth to us, and in my case, one of them consented to marry me. Indeed heaven never seems closer than when we see the love of God manifested in the kindness and devotion of people so good and so pure that *angelic* is the only word that comes to mind."[4]

CHAPTER 25

# Doctrinal Counsel to Corianton: Repentance and Forgiveness

ALMA 39

Alma learned, to his painful dismay, that his youngest son, Corianton, had yielded to temptation and violated the law of chastity while serving as a missionary. He had become involved with a woman named Isabel, who is described as a harlot who had contributed to the downfall of many men. Alma suggests that Corianton became caught in Isabel's web for a number of reasons:

1. He had become haughty. He had given in to feelings of self-sufficiency. In the words of Alma, Corianton had begun to boast in his own strength (Alma 39:2), to rely less and less on the arm of the Lord and more and more on the arm of flesh. If Corianton had lived in our day, he might have put it this way: "I can handle it!" Corianton learned through a painful experience that no woman or man has sufficient personal strength to resist Satan's pull toward sin. Alma had pleaded a number of years earlier as he taught the Zoramites: "Cast off your sins, and [do] not procrastinate the day of your repentance; but . . . humble yourselves before the Lord, and call on his holy name, and watch and pray continually, that ye may not be tempted above that which ye can bear" (Alma 13:27–28).

2. Corianton had forsaken the ministry (Alma 39:3): he had left his duty station. He was not where he had been assigned to be. One who sings, "I'll go where you want me to go, dear Lord," must not then

be guilty of desertion, negligence, or waywardness when the assignment comes. "No man," the Savior taught, "having put his hand to the plough, and looking back, is fit for the kingdom of God" (Luke 9:62).

3. He had been associating with the wrong people; he eventually surrendered to the allurements and pressures to conform to the ways of the worldly. Because others gave in to sin, however, was no reason for him to do the same. "This was no excuse for thee, my son. Thou shouldest have tended to the ministry wherewith thou wast entrusted" (Alma 39:3–4).

Alma then stresses the seriousness of Corianton's particular sin by placing things in perspective: he explained that only two sins were more serious in the sight of God: (1) the sin against the Holy Ghost and (2) murder or the shedding of innocent blood. In modern revelation, we learn that the sin against the Holy Ghost (or becoming a son of perdition) can only be committed by one who knows God's power and has been a partaker of the same, who denies the faith and defies God's power. In the words of Joseph Smith, such a person "must receive the Holy Ghost, have the heavens opened unto him, and know God, and then sin against him. . . . He has got to say that the sun does not shine while he sees it; he has got to deny Jesus Christ when the heavens have been opened unto him, and to deny the plan of salvation with his eyes open to it."[1]

These persons are "vessels of wrath, doomed to suffer the wrath of God, with the devil and his angels in eternity; concerning who [Jesus Christ has] said there is no forgiveness in this world nor in the world to come." They deny the Son of God, "having crucified him unto themselves and put him to an open shame" (Doctrine and Covenants 76:33–35; compare 132:27). This sin is known as the *unpardonable* sin because it is not covered by the Atonement of Christ, and no amount of personal suffering can bring about forgiveness. The sons of perdition who received a physical body will be raised in the Second or Last Resurrection but will not receive a kingdom of glory (Doctrine and Covenants 88:32). These are the ones who suffer the final spiritual death, the ultimate separation from God and things pertaining to righteousness.

Of the second most serious sin, Alma points out that "whosoever murdereth against the light and knowledge of God, it is not easy for him to obtain forgiveness" (Alma 39:6). This offense, known as the *unforgivable* sin, seems to refer to those who have accepted the fullness of the gospel, including all of its covenants and ordinances, but who then are guilty of what we would describe today as premeditated, first-degree murder. The Prophet Joseph Smith stated that "a murderer, for instance, one that sheds innocent blood, cannot have forgiveness."[2] By combining what we learn about evildoers in the vision of the glories (see Doctrine and Covenants 76:103–6) with what John the Beloved wrote (see Revelation 21:8; 22:15), we understand that murderers will inherit the telestial kingdom.

Alma explains that sexual immorality ranks third in order of serious offenses before God. The sin against the Holy Ghost results in spiritual death, and the sin of murder results in physical death. When we sin against the law of chastity, we are tampering with the fountains of life, the giving of physical birth. At the October 1998 general conference, Elder Jeffrey R. Holland taught: "By assigning such seriousness to a physical appetite so universally bestowed, what is God trying to tell us about its place in His plan for all men and women? I submit to you He is doing precisely that—commenting about the very plan of life itself. Clearly among His greatest concerns regarding mortality are how one gets into this world and how one gets out of it. He has set very strict limits in these matters. . . .

"Fortunately, in the case of how life is terminated, most seem to be quite responsible. But in the significance of *giving* life, we sometimes find near-criminal irresponsibility." Elder Holland pointed out that "human intimacy is reserved for a married couple because it is the ultimate symbol of total union, a totality and a union ordained and defined by God. . . . Can you see the moral schizophrenia that comes from *pretending* you are one, pretending you have made solemn promises before God, sharing the physical symbols and the physical intimacy of your counterfeit union but then fleeing, retreating, severing all such other aspects of what was meant to be a total obligation? . . .

"If some few of you are carrying such wounds—and I know that you are—to you is extended the peace and renewal of repentance available through the atoning sacrifice of the Lord Jesus Christ. In such serious matters the path of repentance is not easily begun nor painlessly traveled. But the Savior of the world will walk that essential journey with you. He will strengthen you when you waver. He will be your light when it seems most dark. He will take your hand and be your hope when hope seems all you have left. His compassion and mercy, with all their cleansing and healing power, are freely given to all who truly wish complete forgiveness and will take the steps that lead to it."[3]

Much of Corianton's problem was apparently borne of doctrinal ignorance and misunderstanding, particularly concerning justice and punishment for sin (see Alma 41). It is fitting, then, that Alma should instruct his son about repentance and point the way back to the path of peace and happiness. Having stressed the seriousness of Corianton's offense, Alma then begins to deal with whether Corianton was experiencing godly sorrow for sin, the kind of sorrow that is an essential element of true repentance. In other words, Alma wants his son to experience appropriate guilt—to suffer no more than is requisite but no less than is needful to bring about change. Alma observes: "I would to God that ye had not been guilty of so great a crime. I would not dwell upon your crimes, to harrow up your soul, if it were not for your good" (Alma 39:7).

Alma knew, only too well, the awful agony associated with grievous sin; on the other hand, he understood as few others do, how exquisite pain can be transformed into consummate joy, how suffering can make saints out of sinners. Appropriate, godly sorrow for sin can and does have a sanctifying effect: it alerts offenders to the spiritual chasm between themselves and their maker and motivates them thereafter to pursue a godly walk.

"Now my son," Alma continues, "I would that ye should repent and forsake your sins, and go no more after the lusts of your eyes, but cross yourself in all these things" (Alma 39:9). For Corianton to "cross himself" was for him to turn away from evil inclinations and to take up his cross. In other words, he was to deny himself of ungodliness and every worldly lust (see JST, Matthew 16:26; 3 Nephi 12:30), to work at cross purposes to the natural man, to forsake worldly paths, and to chart and navigate a course of righteousness.

By his unwise and sinful actions, Alma's youngest son hindered the work of the Lord among the Zoramites (see Alma 39:11) and caused deep pain and sorrow for those who knew and loved him. But his sinful actions were neither unpardonable nor unforgivable. The Savior's sweet promise in the Book of Mormon is that "as often as my people repent will I forgive them their trespasses against me" (Mosiah 26:30). A similar invitation is extended by that same Lord in a modern revelation: "I the Lord cannot look upon sin with the least degree of allowance; nevertheless, he that repents and does the commandments of the Lord shall be forgiven" (Doctrine and Covenants 1:31–32).

We have every reason to believe that Corianton's repentance was genuine and his spiritual rehabilitation complete and that he qualified to return to the ministry and to full fellowship within the household of faith. We read of Corianton's labors a year or so later: "Thus ended the nineteenth year of the reign of the judges over the people of Nephi." Mormon points out that there was peace and prosperity among the Saints because of "their heed and diligence which . . . they gave unto the word of God, which was declared unto them by Helaman, and Shiblon, and *Corianton*, and Ammon and his brethren" (Alma 49:29–30; emphasis added). Truly, "salvation is free" (2 Nephi 2:4). It is freely available, and the Lord's hand is extended to all such that "whosoever will come may come and partake of the waters of life freely" (Alma 42:27; compare Isaiah 55:1–2).

CHAPTER 26

# Doctrinal Counsel to Corianton: Life Hereafter; Justice and Mercy

ALMA 40–42

The prophet Alma, recognizing that the Resurrection—the inseparable union of both spirit and body—does not immediately follow death, inquires of the Lord about the state of the soul (that is, the spirit) between death and the Resurrection. An angel taught Alma about the nature of the world that comes after this mortal sphere, and through Alma's explanation of these things to Corianton, we too have an understanding of these sacred and exciting matters.

Alma explains that, according to what he had been taught by an angel, "the spirits of all men, whether they be good or evil, are taken home to that God who gave them life" (Alma 40:11). "Then shall the dust return to the earth as it was," said the Preacher, "and the spirit shall return unto God who gave it" (Ecclesiastes 12:7). Both of these scriptural preachers are speaking in broad terms, and their words should not be interpreted to mean that the spirit, at the time of death, goes into the immediate presence of the Lord. Elder Orson Pratt stated that to go into the presence of God is not to be "placed within a few yards or rods, or within a short distance of his person."[1] President George Q. Cannon explained: "Alma, when he says that 'the spirits of all men, as soon as they are departed from this mortal body, . . . and is taken home to that God who gave them life,' has the idea, doubtless, in his mind that our God is omnipresent—not in his own personality but through

His minister, the Holy Spirit. He does not intend to convey the idea that they are immediately ushered into the personal presence of God. He evidently uses that phrase in a qualified sense."[2]

The transition from time into eternity is immediate. As the physical self breathes its last breath, the spirit self passes through a veil that separates this world from the next. At this point, the spirit experiences what might be called a "partial judgment."[3] Those who have been true and faithful to their trust in mortality, Alma explains, are received into paradise, "a state of rest, a state of peace, where they shall rest from all their troubles and from all care, and sorrow" (Alma 40:12). Those things which burden the obedient—the worldly cares and struggles, the vicissitudes of life—are shed with the physical body. Paradise is a place where the spirit is free to think and act with a renewed capacity and with the vigor and enthusiasm that characterized individuals in their prime. In paradise a person does not "rest" per se from the work associated with the plan of salvation, but they are delivered from those cares and worries associated with a fallen world and a corrupt body.

Those, however, who have been wicked on earth—who gave themselves up to the lusts and lasciviousness of the flesh—are received into that portion of the spirit world called variously hell (2 Nephi 9:10–12), spirit prison (1 Peter 3:19), or, as Alma refers to it, "outer darkness," a place of "weeping, and wailing, and gnashing of teeth, and this because of their own iniquity, being led captive by the will of the devil" (Alma 40:13). The Prophet Joseph Smith explained: "The great misery of departed spirits in the world of spirits, where they go after death, is to know that they come short of the glory that others enjoy and that they might have enjoyed themselves, and they are their own accusers."[4] On another occasion, the Prophet taught that "a man is his own tormentor and his own condemner. Hence the saying, They shall go into the lake that burns with fire and brimstone. The torment of disappointment in the mind of man is as exquisite as a lake burning with fire and brimstone. I say, so is the torment of man."[5] Hell or outer darkness is both a place (a part of the world of spirits where suffering and sorrow and repentance take place) and a state (a condition of the mind associated with remorseful realization). The righteous remain in paradise and the wicked in hell until the time of their resurrection (see Alma 40:14).

Many in the Christian world believe that at the time of death a person goes either into heaven or into hell and that this is the judgment that will prevail at the time of the Resurrection. This belief is linked to the idea that once a person has died, his or her judgment is set and that no one will change or repent or progress after death. The reasoning goes something like this: once you die, you go to heaven or hell, and eventually you will be resurrected. Attempting to correct this way of thinking, N. T. Wright, one of the most respected New Testament scholars in the world, wrote that the first-century Christian discussions about heaven or the Resurrection weren't "a way of talking about life after death. It was a way of talking about *a new bodily life after whatever state of existence one might enter immediately upon death*. It was, in other words, *life after life after death*."[6]

No doctrine provides more powerful assurance and comfort to the bereaved than the doctrine of resurrection—the grand truth that all who have taken physical bodies through birth will survive death and receive those bodies again in the Resurrection. "The soul [spirit] shall be restored to the body," Alma says to Corianton, "and the body to the soul; yea, and every limb and joint shall be restored to its body; yea, even a hair of the head shall not be lost; but all things shall be restored to their proper and perfect frame" (Alma 40:23; compare 11:43).

President Joseph F. Smith taught: "The body will come forth as it is laid to rest, for there is no growth or development in the grave. As it is laid down, so will it arise, and changes to perfection will come by the law of restitution. But the spirit will continue to expand and develop, and the body after the resurrection will develop to the full stature of man."[7] His son, Joseph Fielding Smith, explained: "President Smith was in full accord with Amulek and Alma. He taught that the body will be restored as stated in Alma 11:42–45 and 40:22–23. While he expresses the thought that the body will come forth as it is laid down, he also expresses the thought that it will take time to adjust the body from the condition of imperfections. This, of course, is reasonable, but at the same time the length of time to make these adjustments will not cover any appreciable extent of time. President Smith never intended to convey the thought that it would take weeks or months of time in order for the defects to be removed. These changes will come naturally, of course, but almost instantly. We cannot look upon it in any other way."[8]

From Abinadi's, Amulek's, and Alma's perspective, we understand that the First Resurrection will comprise the righteous dead—that is, "an innumerable company of the spirits of the just" (Doctrine and Covenants 138:12), from Adam to Christ. With information revealed to Joseph Smith, we know that the First Resurrection will resume at the time of the Second Coming of the Savior; the Lord will bring with Him the hosts of the righteous from the days of Jesus and the Apostles to the time of His coming to earth in power and glory. The Second or Last Resurrection—the resurrection of those who are telestial and the ones who are guilty of the unpardonable sin—will be at the end of the Millennium. A simple but marvelous summary is found in the Doctrine and Covenants: "The spirit and the body are the soul of man. And the resurrection from the dead is the redemption of the soul" (88:15–16).

The Resurrection, Alma explains, is but a part of a larger system of restoration: not only will spirit and body be inseparably united, but all things will be restored to the way they were here on earth. In short, our station and reward hereafter will be directly related to the manner in which we managed our time and spiritual resources while in this life. It is therefore ludicrous for one to hope for a glorious resurrection and transcendent reward hereafter when her or his thoughts and actions in this life were shoddy and superficial. What was to the Apostle Paul the law of the harvest (Galatians 6:7) was to Alma the law of restoration. "The plan of restoration," Alma observes, "is requisite with the justice of God . . . that men should be judged according to their works; and if their works were good in this life, *and the desires of their hearts were good*, that they should also, at the last day, be restored unto that which is good," what we know as eternal life and exaltation in the highest degree of the celestial kingdom. "And if their works are evil they shall restored unto them for evil" (Alma 41:2–4; emphasis added).

Wickedness can never be happiness here or hereafter. Carnality never was and never will be spirituality here or hereafter. Charting a course contrary to God and His plan of salvation in this life can never lead to spiritual union and joy with Him in the life to come. Truly, "wickedness never was happiness" (Alma 41:10). In summary, "that which ye do send out [the life we live and the deeds we do] shall return unto you again, and be restored; therefore the word restoration more fully condemneth the sinner, and justifieth him not at all" (Alma 41:15).

To emphasize the importance of justice and to show that there are always consequences for our transgressions, Alma recounts the story of the Fall of Adam and Eve. The Fall brought on the justice of God and resulted in spiritual and physical death, both of which are necessary in the eternal plan of the Father. Centuries earlier, Jacob taught that "death hath passed upon all men, to fulfill the merciful plan of the great Creator" (2 Nephi 9:6). The justice of God must be meted out so that the mercy of God can be extended to us; as the Fall is the ancestor of the Lord's Atonement, so justice paves the way for mercy (see Alma 42:1–13).

The balance of justice and mercy is achieved only through a God, only in and through a being in whom there is a perfect balance, only through Him who is both infinitely just and merciful. The balance is achieved only by Him who is sinless and upon whom justice has no claim, through Him who has no need of divine pardoning mercy. The scriptures affirm that "there is one God, and one mediator between God and men, the man Christ Jesus" (1 Timothy 2:5). Mercy comes because of the Atonement of the Lord Jesus Christ. Mercy is extended to the penitent (see Alma 42:23). Those who accept Christ as their Benefactor and pursue the path of godly sorrow for sin, repentance, and forgiveness are delivered from the demands of justice and come to know that quality and kind of peace available only through Him who is the Way, the Truth, and the Life (see John 14:6).

CHAPTER 27

# Remember, Remember

HELAMAN 5

One of the most repeated words in scripture, both ancient and modern, is the divine charge for the Saints of God to *remember*. In the Book of Mormon, it is stunning how often the older generation pleads with the younger members of the Church to remember. Here are a few examples:

> Nephi: "Wherefore, I, Nephi did exhort them [his brothers] to give heed unto the word of the Lord . . . and *remember* to keep his commandments always in all things." (1 Nephi 15:25; emphasis added)
>
> Lehi to his son Joseph: "*Remember* the words of thy dying father." (2 Nephi 3:25; emphasis added)
>
> Jacob: "O, my beloved brethren, *remember* the awfulness in transgressing against that holy God, and also the awfulness of yielding to the enticings of that cunning one. . . . *Remember* the greatness of the Holy One of Israel." (2 Nephi 9:39–40; emphasis added)
>
> King Benjamin: "If ye do not watch yourselves, and your thoughts, and your words, and your deeds, and observe the commandments of God, and continue in the faith of what ye have heard concerning the coming of our Lord, even unto the

end of your lives, ye must perish. And now, O man, *remember*, and perish not." (Mosiah 4:30; emphasis added)

Alma the Younger: "I say unto you, my brethren, . . . have you sufficiently *retained in remembrance* the captivity of your fathers? Yea, and have you sufficiently *retained in remembrance* his mercy and long-suffering towards them? And moreover, have ye sufficiently *retained in remembrance* that he has delivered their souls from hell? Behold, he changed their hearts; yea, he awakened them out of a deep sleep, and they awoke unto God." (Alma 5:6–7; emphasis added)

Mormon: "And thus we see that except the Lord doth chasten his people with many afflictions, yea, except he doth visit them with death and with terror, and with famine and with all manner of pestilence, they will not *remember* him." (Helaman 12:3; emphasis added)

Samuel the Lamanite: "And in the days of your poverty ye shall cry unto the Lord; and in vain ye shall cry, for your desolation is already come upon you, and your destruction is made sure; and then shall ye weep and howl in that day . . . : O that I had repented and had not killed the prophets, and stoned them, and cast them out. . . . O that we had *remembered* the Lord our God in the day that he gave us our riches." (Helaman 13:32–33; emphasis added)

Moroni: "And I exhort you to *remember* these things; for the time speedily cometh that ye shall know that I lie not, for ye shall see me at the bar of God; and the Lord God will say unto you: Did I not declare my words unto you, which were written by this man, like as one crying from the dead, yea, even as one speaking out of the dust?" (Moroni 10:27; emphasis added)

We remember to prevent ourselves from making the same mistakes in the future that we made in the past. We remember spiritual experiences of the past so that in those moments of testing and trial that inevitably come to all of us, we do not suffer from spiritual amnesia—a disease that seems to be spreading in our day. "I wish to encourage every one of us," Elder Jeffrey R. Holland pleaded with Brigham Young University students, "regarding the opposition that so often comes after enlightened decisions have been made, after moments of revelation and conviction have given us a peace and an assurance we thought we would never lose. . . . Don't lose your confidence. *Don't forget how you once felt. Don't distrust the experience you had.* . . . Once there has been illumination [once you have received revelation regarding the truthfulness of a matter], *beware the temptation to retreat from a good thing. If it was right when you prayed about it and trusted it and lived for it, it is right now.*"[1]

Perhaps the most well-*remembered* verse in the Book of Mormon about the importance of remembering was spoken by Helaman, the son of Helaman, to his sons Nephi and Lehi: "And now, my sons, *remember, remember, that it is upon the rock of our Redeemer, who is Christ, the Son of God, that ye must build your foundation*; that when the devil shall send forth his mighty winds, yea, his shafts [spears or darts] in the whirlwind, yea, when all his hail and his mighty storm shall beat upon you, it shall have no power over you to drag you down to the gulf of misery and endless wo, because of *the rock upon which ye are built*, which *is a sure foundation*, a foundation whereon if men build they cannot fall" (Helaman 5:12; emphasis added).

Every person, whether he or she knows it, builds a house of faith of some kind. Even those who claim to be atheists—who profess that they do not believe in God or a supreme power—have faith in something, even if it is in their nonbelief or lack of faith. Some seek to build upon financial success, while others build upon innate talents and charisma. Some build their house of faith on the power of their intellect or their impressive capacity to come to conclusions through rational thinking or discourse. Others put their trust in social values, in the tenets of the shifting sands of secularity.

So what did Helaman mean when he charged his two remarkable sons to build their foundation upon the rock of their Redeemer? For one thing, they were to have faith in Him: to place their total trust, their complete confidence, and their ready reliance upon the Savior. He is the one person (as is His Father) in whom we can depend absolutely. We never need to doubt that He will come through, that He will do what He said He would do, or that He can make us into the best version of ourselves, something far greater than we could come to on our own.

*Trust*, *confidence*, and *reliance*—these are the synonyms for faith. What does it mean to say that I trust my wife, Shauna? I trust her in the sense that because I know she loves me, I know that she knows me well enough to understand my heart, my deepest desires and longings. I trust her because although she knows, only too well, my weaknesses and my inclination to be less than I should be, she displays regularly patience and long-suffering, which is so often required on her part. I trust her because she is ever ready and willing to forgive me. I trust her in that I know I can share my heaviest burdens, my darkest moments, my lingering doubts, and I know that she will think no less of me. Finally, I trust Shauna because I know that ours is a winning team and that our companionship blesses and elevates my life and makes me so much more, so much better than I would be on my own. Further, I have confidence in her in the sense that I know she will always come through. And heaven only knows how much I rely on her wisdom and judgment, her discernment, and her unending devotion and loyalty.

Returning to our topic of being built upon the rock of our Redeemer, the Apostle Paul taught important truths. In his first letter to the Corinthians, the Apostle Paul wrote, "Moreover, brethren, I would not that ye should be ignorant, how that all our fathers were under the cloud [the holy cloud, what the Jews called the *Shekinah*], and all passed through the sea; and were all baptized unto Moses in the cloud and in the sea; and did all eat the same spiritual meat; and did all drink the same spiritual drink; for they drank of that spiritual Rock that followed them: and *that Rock was Christ*" (1 Corinthians 10:1–4; emphasis added).

Nephi, son of Lehi, wrote: "We talk of Christ, we rejoice in Christ, we preach of Christ, we prophesy of Christ, . . . that [we and] our children may know to what source [we] may look for a remission of [our] sins" (2 Nephi 25:26). Whenever we step off the covenant path and surrender to sin—and each one of us does—we desperately need to know how to have our hands made clean and our hearts made pure. In order to undergo that purifying process, our focus must be upon Jesus Christ, upon Him whose atoning sacrifice has made spiritual recovery possible and salvation available. "Without the power of God working miracles in our life," Elder Neil L. Andersen explained, "going through a perfunctory list of things to do to repent, or asking the bishop what we must do to right our life, will rarely have the staying power to sustain us in a continuing commitment to keep the commandments of God."[2]

Elder Kevin W. Pearson of the Seventy spoke of the importance of building on a solid foundation. "If our spiritual foundation is shallow or superficial," he stated, "we might be inclined to base our willingness [to focus on Christ] on a social cost-benefit analysis or a personal inconvenience index. And if we embrace the narrative that the Church consists primarily of outdated or politically incorrect social policies, unrealistic personal restrictions, and time commitments, then our conclusions about willingness will be flawed. *We should not expect the principle of willingness to trend positively with social media influencers or TikTok enthusiasts. The precepts of man rarely align with divine truth.*

"The Church is a gathering place for imperfect individuals who love God and are willing to follow the Lord Jesus Christ. That willingness is rooted in the reality that Jesus is the Christ, the Son of the living God. This divine truth can only be known by the power of the Holy Ghost. Therefore, *our willingness is directly proportionate to the amount of time we commit to be in holy places where the influence of the Holy Ghost is present.*"[3]

We build our houses of faith on the foundation of Christ as we take upon us His name and act in that name. "Wherefore, God also hath highly exalted him [Jesus], and given him a name which is above every name: that at the name of Jesus every knee should bow, of things in heaven, and things in earth, and things under the earth; and that every tongue should confess that Jesus Christ is Lord, to the glory of God the Father" (Philippians 2:9–11). As God has placed His name upon His Beloved Son, so has the Son placed His holy name upon those who come into His Church, join His family, and bear His name with dignity and fidelity and devotion for the remainder of their mortal lives. To act in the name of the Lord is a sacred trust, deserving of solemn and ponderous thought. I wonder if we would not preach more gospel doctrine and bear more fervent testimonies if we had fixed in our minds the weighty fact that the words spoken are not ours alone but are, in fact, the words of Him whom we represent, Him from whom we have received a heavenly authorization.

My prayer for each one of us is that we will always, *always* remember the source of our blessings, what it cost Jesus Christ and the Father to win our souls with love, and what we can do to more frequently express our love and undying gratitude for what our Savior and Redeemer did and continues to do for us. May we always, *always* remember Him and build our house upon the only sure foundation, the foundation of Jesus the Messiah.

CHAPTER 28

# The Resurrected Christ Appears and Teaches

3 NEPHI 11

In 3 Nephi 8, we read that the tempests, earthquakes, fires, and massive upheavals—all of which signaled the death of the Savior of the world—took place "in the thirty and fourth year, in the first month, on the fourth day of the month" (verse 5). At the end of 3 Nephi 10, we read these words from Mormon, the great compiler and editor of the gold plates: "And it came to pass that *in the ending of the thirty and fourth year*, behold, I will show unto you that the people of Nephi who were spared, and also those who had been called Lamanites, who had been spared, did have great favors shown unto them, and great blessings poured out upon their heads, insomuch that soon after the ascension of Christ into heaven he did truly manifest himself unto them" (3 Nephi 10:18; emphasis added). Now, if I read the text correctly, that means that it was several months after the destruction in ancient America that Jesus appeared to His American Hebrews at the temple in Bountiful.

As He descends from heaven, the risen Lord introduces Himself and speaks of the atoning mission He had recently carried out: "Behold, I am Jesus Christ, whom the prophets testified shall come into the world. And behold, I am the life and the light of the world; and *I have drunk out of that bitter cup which the Father hath given me*, and have glorified the Father in taking upon me the sins of the world, in the which I have suffered the will of the Father in all things from the beginning" (3 Nephi 11:10–11; emphasis added). The bitter cup was the Savior's suffering in the Garden of Gethsemane and on the cross of Calvary, where His Father's comforting, sustaining Spirit was withdrawn during our Lord's excruciating ordeal.[1]

The resurrected Savior invites Nephi to come forward out of the crowd of 2,500. Mormon writes tenderly that "Nephi arose and went forth, and bowed himself before the Lord and did kiss his feet" (3 Nephi 11:19). Such a moment says a great deal about Nephi's love and adoration for the Savior. Like other prophet-leaders through the ages, he understood very clearly that he merely walked in the shadow of the Light of the world. I am reminded of the final conference address delivered by Elder Bruce R. McConkie, only days before his death. Having spoken of the Creation, Fall, and Atonement of the Lord Jesus Christ, Elder McConkie bore what was, for thousands if not millions of Latter-day Saints throughout the world, one of the most moving and powerful testimonies of Christ given by an Apostle in this dispensation:

"And now, as pertaining to this perfect atonement, wrought by the shedding of the blood of God," Elder McConkie began, "I testify that it took place in Gethsemane and at Golgotha, and as pertaining to Jesus Christ, I testify that he is the Son of the Living God and was crucified for the sins of the world. He is our Lord, our God, and our King. This I know of myself independent of any other person." And then with much emotion, this remarkable special witness declared: "I am one of his witnesses, and *in a coming day I shall feel the nail marks in his hands and in his feet and shall wet his feet with my tears. But I shall not know any better then than I know now that he is God's Almighty Son, that he is our Savior and Redeemer, and that salvation comes in and through his atoning blood and in no other way.*"[2] I was there in the Salt Lake Tabernacle when he spoke those tender but penetrating words. I, for one, was never the same.

When Nephi arises from the ground, the Lord says to him: "I give unto you power that ye shall baptize this people when I am again ascended into heaven" (3 Nephi 11:21). We might ask: Why would

Christ need to give Nephi the power to baptize? Didn't the Nephites already have this power? We may recall that when Samuel the Lamanite had finished his call to repentance, many people believed what was said, and "they went away unto Nephi to be baptized." Remember that the Nephi referred to in 3 Nephi 11 is Nephi, the son of Nephi. The elder Nephi, with his brother Lehi, had enjoyed phenomenal success among the Lamanites, leading some eight thousand people to the waters of baptism (see Helaman 5:19). This earlier Nephi had, in fact, heard these words of the Lord: "Behold, *I give unto you power, that whatsoever ye shall seal on earth shall be sealed in heaven*; and whatsoever ye shall loose on earth shall be loosed in heaven; and thus shall ye have power among this people" (Helaman 10:7). Clearly the Melchizedek Priesthood, including the sealing power, was held by the Nephites; they had the proper authority.

And so we re-ask the question: Why would the risen Jesus need to reordain Nephi and the other Nephite Apostles? While the Book of Mormon text does not provide an answer, let's consider this matter. Up to this time, the Nephites had been a part of what might be called the Mosaic dispensation; Moses was one of seven dispensation heads (Adam, Enoch, Noah, Abraham, Moses, Jesus Christ, and Joseph Smith). When Jehovah came to the Nephites in AD 34, the Lord essentially began a new dispensation among the descendants of Lehi—the dispensation of Jesus Christ.

In our dispensation, the Church that was organized on April 6, 1830, was called the Church of Christ. While the Saints were in Kirtland, Ohio, the Church began to be known as the Church of the Latter-day Saints. (That name is found on the front of the Kirtland Temple to this day.) On April 26, 1838, in Far West, Missouri, the Lord directed that the name of the restored Church should be The Church of Jesus Christ of Latter-day Saints (Doctrine and Covenants 115:4). A modern prophet, President Russell M. Nelson, reinforced the use of that proper name again and again, indicating that if we called the Church by its correct name, we as a people would enjoy many great blessings.[3]

A related point of doctrine that I have pondered on for some time is that to do something—and more specifically, to perform the saving and exalting ordinances—in the name of Jesus Christ is to do it in the name of the Father, the Son, and the Holy Ghost—the entire Godhead. Note the following words of Jesus: "Verily I say unto you, that whoso repenteth of his sins through your words [the words of the Nephite Apostles], and desireth to be baptized *in my name*, on this wise shall ye baptize them—Behold, ye shall go down and stand in the water, and *in my name* shall ye baptize them." He then provides the words to be used in performing the ordinance of baptism: "Having authority given me of Jesus Christ, I baptize you *in the name of the Father, and of the Son, and of the Holy Ghost.* Amen. . . . For behold, verily I say unto you, that the Father, and the Son, and the Holy Ghost are one" (3 Nephi 11:23–27; emphasis added).

We encounter something very similar earlier in the Book of Mormon. The scriptures are very clear that the Father delegated to the Son the role of judge (see John 3:35; 5:22; Acts 17:31; 2 Nephi 9:41; Mosiah 3:10). In preaching repentance to the wicked people of Ammonihah, Amulek speaks powerfully about the Lord's atoning work, including His making resurrection available to every child of God. "Now, this restoration [the reuniting of the body and the spirit] shall come to all, both old and young, both bond and free, both male and female, both the wicked and the righteous; and even there shall not so much as a hair of their heads be lost; but every thing shall be restored to its perfect frame, as it is now, or in the body, and shall be brought and *be arraigned before the bar of Christ the Son, and God the Father, and the Holy Spirit, which is one eternal God* [one perfectly united Godhead], *to be judged according to their works, whether they be good or whether they be evil*" (Alma 11:44; emphasis added). The Apostle Paul thus wrote that "it pleased the Father that in [Christ] should all fulness dwell. . . . For in him dwelleth all the fulness of the Godhead bodily" (Colossians 1:19; 2:9).

Only a few verses later in 3 Nephi 11, the Lord cautions His disciples against disputations or arguments over the ordinance of baptism. "For verily, verily I say unto you, he that hath the spirit of contention is not of me, but is of the devil, who is the father of contention, and he stirreth up the hearts of men to contend with anger, one with another." Therefore Jesus directed that "such things should be done away" (verses 29–30). As a young missionary in the Eastern States Mission in the late 1960s, my companions and I frequently encountered Evangelical Christians and Jehovah's Witnesses, both of whom were eager to confront "the Mormon Elders," to attack our doctrine with arguments in what became known as "scripture bashes." I never had a good experience when we debated over what this or that passage of scripture meant; in fact, my companion and I would inevitably feel a sense of spiritual discomfort as we walked away from such occasions. If we had been more serious students of the Book of Mormon at the time, we would have recognized that the Spirit of the Lord did not abide in that kind of climate.

I am reminded of a seldom-discussed incident in the first chapter of Alma that took place some 130 years earlier in Nephite history. Mormon mentions that following the nefarious efforts and eventual execution of Nehor, the anti-Christ, arguments and vocal attacks began to take place between the members of the Church and those who did not belong to the Church. Mormon mentions that there were "many among them [the members of the Church] who *began to be proud, and began to contend warmly with their adversaries, even unto blows*; yea, they would smite one another with their fists."

These displays of anger and verbal attacks were "the cause of much trial with the church." Then comes a poignant and powerful warning against such antics: "*For the hearts of many*" members of the Church of Jesus Christ "*were hardened, and their names were blotted out*, that they were remembered no more among the people of God. And also many withdrew themselves from among them" (Alma 1:19–24; emphasis added). Here is a significant lesson: Even when what you believe and teach is true, and you are right, if you allow yourself to be drawn into a contentious situation, you are wrong, and you will lose the Spirit of the Lord; the Spirit cannot remain in the midst of contention. When dealing with what is often called "anti-Mormon literature," we must be extremely careful that we do not become anti-antis; the spiritual cost is too high.

In our current time, we see arguments, debates, name-calling, pigeonholing, and perpetual division, even in U.S. politics, where party loyalty seems to be valued much more than what is best for the people of the country. The two main political parties purposely seek to block every proposal made by the other party, no matter its value. Compromising and working together to make progress are rare. "The widespread deterioration of civil discourse is . . . a concern," Elder Quentin L. Cook taught. "The eternal principle of agency requires that we respect many choices with which we do not agree. Conflict and contention now often breach 'the boundaries of common decency.'"[4]

Jesus declares His doctrine by reminding the people of the significance of the first principles of the gospel—faith in Jesus Christ, repentance from sin, baptism by water for the remission of sins, and the baptism of fire that comes through the gift of the Holy Ghost. "This is my doctrine," Christ declared (3 Nephi 11:32–36). In other words, the doctrine of Christ is the gospel of Jesus Christ. A few verses later we find these fascinating words: "And again I say unto you, ye must repent, and become as a little child, and be baptized in my name, or ye can in nowise receive these things. And again I say unto you, ye must repent, and be baptized in my name, and become as a little child, or ye can in nowise inherit the kingdom of God" (3 Nephi 11:37–38).

Was the Savior here simply being repetitious to emphasize the importance of a specific teaching? That certainly could have been the case. I am prone to believe, however, that our Lord was attempting to teach something far more profound. We must repent and become as little children in order to enter into the Lord's kingdom, in order to come into His Church through baptism and confirmation. But then, after baptism and for the rest of our lives, we should strive to be as childlike as possible—"submissive, meek, humble, patient, full of love, willing to submit to all things which the Lord seeth fit to inflict upon [us], even as a child doth submit to his father" (Mosiah 3:19). Jesus made the following comment to His Apostles in the Old World: "Except ye be converted and become as little children, ye shall not enter into the kingdom of heaven" (Matthew 18:3).

The resurrected Christ then says to the faithful descendants of Lehi gathered at the temple in Bountiful: "Verily, verily, I say unto you, that this is my doctrine, and whoso buildeth upon this buildeth upon my rock, and the gates of hell shall not prevail against them." Now attend to what follows: "*And whoso shall declare more or less than this, and establish it for my doctrine, the same cometh of evil, and is not built upon my rock*; but he buildeth upon a sandy foundation, and the gates of hell stand open to receive such when the floods come and the winds beat upon them" (3 Nephi 11:39–40; emphasis added). My late friend and colleague Joseph Fielding McConkie referred to the above as "the doctrine of more than and less than."

The restored gospel of Jesus Christ does not need supplementation from the rank-and-file members of the Church. We do not need extra truths, additional commandments, or added practices. If the Lord should decide that such additions are needed, they will come to the body of the Church through the proper channel—prophets, seers, and revelators. There always seems to be a member of the Church somewhere, possibly well-meaning but usually ill-advised, who insists that it is sinful to eat white bread or chocolate; or that he or she has discovered the specific day and time of the Lord's Second Coming; or that anyone who wants to have more frequent and grander spiritual experiences, including having regular visits from the Savior Himself, needs to read this book or attend that special workshop. All of these examples and many more constitute what the leaders of the Church used to refer to as "gospel hobbies."[5]

One sign of our spiritual maturity is steadiness, our capacity to navigate the strait and narrow path in a stable and fairly consistent manner, to work with zeal but patient maturity, to stay in the mainstream of the Church. God does not expect us to work ourselves into spiritual, emotional, or physical oblivion, nor does He desire that the members of the true Church be truer than true. There is little virtue in excess, even in gospel excess. In fact, as members of the Church exceed the bounds of propriety and go beyond the established mark, they open themselves to deception and ultimately spiritual destruction. Imbalance leads to instability. If Satan cannot cause us to lie or steal or be immoral, he just may try to turn our strength—our zeal for goodness and righteousness—into a weakness. He will encourage excess, for surely any virtue, when taken to the extreme, becomes a vice.

On the other hand, there are members of the Church who tend to believe in something "less than" the doctrine of Christ. There are those who have concluded that it is not necessary for us to believe that the Book of Mormon is an actual historical record; that the Prophet Joseph did not really "translate" the gold plates; that the President of the Church has no right to speak on matters other than spiritual ones; or that it is not necessary to attend church on Sunday, since one can get just as close to God by climbing a mountain or paddling a canoe. The fear I have for the "less than" crowd is that, if they are less careful in the future than they were in the past, their quest for peace here and for eternal life hereafter may result in them receiving less than the celestial kingdom.

What a transcendent experience it must have been for the faithful to whom the risen Lord appeared at Bountiful following His death and Resurrection! To listen intently as the gospel of Jesus Christ was taught and expounded upon by Jesus Christ Himself must have been an indescribable experience. Reading and reflecting on this supernal time in Nephite history causes me to long for the day when that same King of kings and Lord of lords will once again, on a paradisiacal earth, preach His gospel and expound all the scriptures in one (see 3 Nephi 23:6, 14; 24:1).

## CHAPTER 29

# Called to a Higher Righteousness

3 NEPHI 12–14

The Savior's Sermon on the Mount (Matthew 5–7) was delivered in Galilee primarily to His Twelve Apostles to prepare them for their ministry. (We could perhaps view the occasion as a type of ancient Missionary Training Center.) Others were in attendance, and His teachings would have been very beneficial to any who made the effort to listen intently. The sermon in Bountiful in ancient America, on the other hand, was delivered to "a great multitude gathered together" (3 Nephi 11:1), and a careful study of the sermon shows that some instructions were given to both the Nephite Apostles and the others in attendance.[1]

The portion of the sermon in Matthew 5 begins with what we have come to know as the Beatitudes, a list of ways in which the faithful may be blessed. These are also in the Bountiful sermon, with a few occasional differences. Stated in a slightly different way, Jesus seems to be saying, "Fortunate are those who . . ." The Savior delivers the Beatitudes—the beautiful attitudes—for such persons are blessed or fortunate. These include the poor in spirit (the humble); those who mourn; those who are meek (who are humble and also demonstrate poise under provocation); those who hunger and thirst after righteousness; those who are merciful; those who are pure in heart; those who are peacemakers; those who are persecuted because they have chosen to follow Christ; and those who are reviled and persecuted (see 3 Nephi 12:3–12). The sermon at Bountiful contains a couple of additional Beatitudes, found in verses 1 and 2 of 3 Nephi 12: "*Blessed are ye if ye shall give heed unto the words of these twelve* whom I have chosen from among you to minister unto you, and to be your servants; and unto them I have given power that they may baptize you with water; and after that ye are baptized with water, behold I will baptize you with fire and with the Holy Ghost. . . . Yea, *blessed are they who shall believe in your words, and come down into the depths of humility and be baptized,* for they shall be visited with fire and with the Holy Ghost, and shall receive a remission of their sins."

I view both the sermon in Galilee and the sermon in Bountiful as a call from Jesus Christ to His followers to ascend to a higher righteousness. President Harold B. Lee once taught that "blessedness is defined as being higher than happiness." Then, quoting from *Dummelow's Bible Commentary*, President Lee continued: "Happiness comes from without and depends upon circumstances; blessedness is an outward fountain of joy in the soul itself, which no outward circumstances can seriously affect." And then President Lee, the eleventh President of the Church, said simply but profoundly, that the Beatitudes "embody. . . the constitution for a perfect life."[2] If you and I want to better understand the character of Jesus and what virtues and qualities we need to seek after to become more like our Master, we would do well to read often and study carefully the Beatitudes.

In Matthew 5 and 3 Nephi 12, Jesus speaks of commandments and instructions that were given anciently in the law of Moses and then calls His listeners (and those who thereafter read and obey the teachings of the Old Testament or the brass plates) to live a higher law. For example:

- In addition to not killing another person, we should avoid anger (see 3 Nephi 12:21–22).
- In addition to not committing adultery, we should avoid lustful thoughts (12:27–30).

- Instead of swearing oaths, our word should be our bond. If we say yes, we mean yes; if we say no, we mean no (12:33–37).
- Instead of reacting to violence with more violence, we should turn the other cheek (12:38–39).
- Instead of hating our enemies, we should strive to love them (12:43–45).

Many scholars over the years have felt that in this sermon Jesus was essentially "fencing the Torah." Instead of coming as close as we can to the fire without being burned, we instead should use wisdom and stay as far away from the flame as we can. John Hilton III has written: "I use the term *fence laws* broadly to describe rules, practices, and guidelines that protect us from breaking *core laws*. Core laws include love of God and neighbor, the Ten Commandments, and commandments relating to our temple recommends. Some fence laws come directly from God and should be followed. At times the Spirit of the Lord inspires us to do or avoid something that is beyond a written commandment. In those cases it is vital for us to obey those promptings. Fence laws can include both dos and don'ts: for example, 'Don't go to bars' (fence law to protect me from breaking the Word of Wisdom), or 'Do write down a tender mercy each day' (fence law to help me love God with all my heart). Fence laws exist around many commandments and come from a variety of sources, including teachers, family, culture, prophets, and the Holy Ghost."[3]

In 3 Nephi 13 (and Matthew 6), we see our Savior once again calling each of us to a higher level of righteousness. Life in Christ is more than correct behavior, more than appropriate actions, more than what we *do*. It is being. It is what we *are*. True disciples seek that sanctifying influence that derives from the Holy Spirit, so that they come to do the right things for the right reasons. Life in Christ is characterized by pure attitudes, motives, and desires. Thus in chapter 13 of 3 Nephi, we see the Lord Jesus challenging His disciples to give to the poor without worrying about how such a deed is seen by other people (verses 1–4); to pray sincerely, to be heard of God regardless of what others may think of their prayers (verses 5–8); and to fast with a pure heart, a heart that desires to draw closer to God and also to care for the poor, rather than spending one second wondering whether others are impressed (verses 16–18).

Doing a good deed for the right reason brings peace and spiritual satisfaction, while those who seek to put on airs, to impress, or to make people think highly of them will eventually make points with the crowd but not with the heavens. Or, as Jesus said, such people "have their reward" (3 Nephi 13:2). Dietrich Bonhoeffer, a German theologian and pastor once asked how we are to resolve a paradox in Christ's teachings—letting our light shine while, at the same time, not seeking the applause of others. "How is this paradox to be resolved? The first question to ask is: From whom are we to hide the visibility of our discipleship? Certainly not from other men, for we are told to let them see our light. No, *we are to hide it from ourselves*. Our task is simply to keep on following, looking only to our leader who goes on before, *taking no notice of ourselves or what we are doing. We must be unaware of our own righteousness*, and see it only insofar as we look unto Jesus; then it will seem not extraordinary, but quite ordinary and natural. . . . The Christian is a light unto the world, not because of any quality of his own, but only because he follows Christ and looks solely to him."[4]

Put another way, we need to keep *an eye single to the glory of God*. In modern revelation, we are told that those who do so have a promise: "And if your eye be single to my glory, your whole bodies shall be filled with light, and there shall be no darkness in you; and that body which is filled with light comprehendeth all things" (Doctrine and Covenants 88:67–68; see also 3 Nephi 13:22; Matthew 6:22).

In chapter 14 (and Matthew 7), Jesus continues His call to a higher level of Christian discipleship as He charges His followers to judge righteously (verses 1–5; see also JST, Matthew 7:1–2); avoid dispensing sacred truths to those who would merely scoff, find fault, or make them an offender for a word (verse 6); do unto others as they hope would be done unto them (verse 12); enter in at the strait gate, fully understanding that the Christian way is narrow, requiring the disciple to discard those things that simply will not make it through celestial customs (verses 13–14); discern true prophets from false ones by their fruits, the product and outcome of what they teach (verses 15–20); and, finally, remember that the highest heaven hereafter is reserved only for those who (1) have kept God's commandments and performed righteous deeds while on earth and (2) have come to know Christ (not just know about Him) and to be known by Him (verses 21–23). The Savior closes His Sermon at Bountiful by adding that "whoso heareth these sayings of mine and doeth them, I will liken him unto a wise man, who built his house upon a rock—and the rain descended and the floods came, and the winds blew, and beat upon that house; and it fell not, for it was founded upon a rock" (verses 24–25).

In a revelation given in March of 1833, Jesus Christ spoke very similar words through the man called to initiate and lead the dispensation of the fullness of times: "Verily I say unto you, the keys of this kingdom shall never be taken from you, while thou art in the world, neither in the world to come; nevertheless, *through you shall the oracles [the revelations of God] be given* to another, yea, even to the church. And all they who receive the oracles of God"—meaning both the Lord's prophets and the words that come through those prophets—"*let them beware how they hold [receive] them lest they are accounted as a light thing, and are brought under condemnation thereby*, and stumble and fall when the storms descend, and the winds blow, and the rains descend, and beat upon their house" (Doctrine and Covenants 90:3–5; emphasis added).

## CHAPTER 30

# The Praying Savior

### 3 NEPHI 17, 19

There is a great deal to learn about prayer from the Book of Mormon. In addition to what the prophets teach about prayer, Jesus teaches us all to pray by praying. He is our model, our pattern, our prototype. Note in 3 Nephi 17:13–14: "And it came to pass that when they had all been brought, and Jesus stood in the midst, he commanded the multitude"—at this point there are 2,500 men, women, and children present—"that they should kneel down upon the ground. And it came to pass that when they had knelt upon the ground, Jesus groaned within himself, and said: Father, I am troubled because of the wickedness of the people of the house of Israel." Here we see the sublime sensitivity and omniscient awareness of our Master. He knows perfectly well that "the wicked are like the troubled sea, when it cannot rest, whose waters cast up mire and dirt. There is no peace, saith my God, to the wicked" (Isaiah 57:20–21; compare 48:22).

"And when he had said these words, he himself also knelt upon the earth; and behold he prayed unto the Father, and *the things which he prayed cannot be written*, and the multitude did bear record who heard him. And after this manner do they bear record: The eye hath never seen, neither hath the ear heard, before, so great and marvelous things as we saw and heard Jesus speak unto the Father; and *no tongue can speak, neither can there be written by any man, neither can the hearts of men conceive so great and marvelous things as we both saw and heard Jesus speak; and no one can conceive of the joy which filled our souls at the time we heard him pray for us unto the Father*" (3 Nephi 17:15–17; emphasis added).

Why could these things not be written? Some spiritual experiences are so time-and-place specific, so reserved for the ears and eyes and hearts of those who experience them, that it is divinely inappropriate to try to replicate them, to speak openly of them, or to try to rehearse or record them. In addition, some matters are ineffable, literally unspeakable or unrecordable. Mere words fail us. Telestial or even terrestrial expressions cannot do justice to celestial language or experiences.

I have reflected for many years upon the notion that the people's hearts were filled with joy as they heard and saw Jesus pray unto the Father for them. How would it be to hear my Redeemer importune the Father for me? Listen to the Savior's words to Peter at the Last Supper: "Simon, Simon, behold, Satan hath desired to have you, that he may sift you as wheat." Then He says this most unusual phrase: "But *I have prayed for thee*, that thy faith fail not: and when thou art converted, strengthen thy brethren" (Luke 22:31–32; emphasis added). I have wondered what that senior Apostle must have felt to know that Jesus, the Lord of the universe, had been praying for him.

In the October 2001 general conference, only a matter of days after the horrors of September 11, 2001, President Gordon B. Hinckley closed the conference with a message of hope and encouragement, reminding the people of the covenant that if they would only turn to God, they would be empowered to stand in holy places, poised and unafraid, even amid wars and rumors of wars. "And now as we close this conference," he said, "even though we shall have a benediction, I should like to offer a brief prayer in these circumstances." The fifteenth President of The Church of Jesus Christ of Latter-day Saints, the man prepared and called to stand in the shoes of the Prophet Joseph Smith, then petitioned the heavens:

"O God, our Eternal Father, Thou great Judge of the Nations, Thou who art the governor of the universe, Thou who art our Father and our God, whose children we are, we look to thee in faith in this dark and solemn time. Please, dear Father, bless us with faith. Bless us with love. Bless us with charity in our hearts. Bless us with a spirit of perseverance to root out the terrible evils that are in this world. Give protection and guidance to those who are engaged actively in carrying forth the things of battle. Bless them; preserve their lives; save them from harm and evil. Hear the prayers of their loved ones for their safety. We pray for the great democracies of the earth which Thou hast overseen in creating their governments, where peace and liberty and democratic processes obtain.

"O Father, look with mercy upon this, our own nation, and its friends in this time of need. Spare us and help us to walk with faith ever in Thee and ever in Thy Beloved Son, on whose mercy we count and to whom we look as our Savior and our Lord. Bless the cause of peace and bring it quickly to us again, we humbly plead with Thee, asking that Thou wilt forgive our arrogance, pass by our sins, be kind and gracious to us, and cause our hearts to turn with love toward Thee. We humbly pray in the name of Him who loves us all, even the Lord Jesus Christ, our Redeemer and our Savior, amen."[1]

As I heard these words from the Lord's prophet, mine was a feeling unlike anything I had ever experienced before. I felt a deeper closeness to my Heavenly Father, a stillness and peace within my soul, an assurance that the Almighty was not far away, and a love for my family and friends, for my city and nation, and for the world—even for those who had chosen to do this horrid and despicable thing. About midway through President Hinckley's prayer, my mind reverted to the scene in 3 Nephi 17, and I realized that I too could not fully express the inexpressible, that I was woefully inadequate in forming my poor and puny words into sentences that would convey the meaning of what we were *feeling and seeing*. I felt and I saw something divinely remarkable. I saw things with new eyes. I saw that the power of a righteous Saint's effectual, fervent prayer avails much (see James 5:16). I witnessed the simplicity but the profundity of mighty prayer. Perhaps what I felt was something akin to what the Nephites experienced. I thought of the Nephites and also the two disciples on the road to Emmaus. I wanted to ask my wife, "Did not our hearts burn within us as we heard him pray unto the Father for us?" (see Luke 24:32).

The praying Savior then called the little children unto Him, one by one, blessed them, and prayed for them (3 Nephi 17:21–24). Jesus was overcome by the experience and wept. Only one who has looked deeply into the eyes of little children can grasp why. Only one who has sensed how near to the heavens, how close to the angels, and how innocent and worthy of our respect, admiration, and awe these little ones are can understand why the Purest of the pure wept as He associated with the purest among the Nephites. Angels came down and ministered personally to the children, an actual event that bespeaks a mighty truth, one that the Lord taught in the Old World: "Take heed that ye despise not one of these little ones; for I say unto you, That in heaven their angels [premortal spirits] do always behold the face of my Father which is in heaven" (Matthew 18:10). Indeed, how we feel toward little children, how we treat them, how we speak to them—these are fairly good measures of how much like the Master we are.

As remarkable as the Savior's prayers were, some may wonder, Why did Jesus need to pray? During His mortal ministry Jesus set aside much of the power and glory He had enjoyed before He came into the world (see John 17:5; Philippians 2:7–8). By choice, Jesus did not turn stones to bread, although He certainly possessed the power to do so (Luke 4:3–4). By choice, Jesus did not cast Himself down from the pinnacle of the temple and anticipate divine deliverance, although He had the power to do so (Luke 4:9–12). By choice, our Lord did not call down legions of angels to deliver Him in the Garden of Gethsemane, although He indeed could have done so (Matthew 26:53–54). And by choice, the Master of ocean and earth and skies did not come down from the cross and bring an end to the pain, suffering, ignominy, and irony of His Crucifixion and death, although the power to do just that was within his grasp (Matthew 27:39–40; Luke 23:39).

By setting aside power and glory, He was able to know mortality in its fullness, to know by experience what it felt like to be hungry, thirsty, tired, snubbed, ridiculed, and excluded; in short, He chose to endure the throes and toils of this estate so that He would be in a position to succor His people (see Alma 7:11–13; Doctrine and Covenants 62:1). Thus when He felt the need for reassurance, He prayed to His Father in Heaven. When He needed answers or perspective, He prayed. When He needed the sacred, sustaining influence of the Father in His darkest hours, He prayed earnestly (see Luke 22:44). Because of the Spirit, which conveys the mind of God (see 1 Corinthians 2:16),[2] He was in the Father, as the Father was in Him. They were one.

But then why did the risen Lord among the Nephites need to pray? Why would a glorified, immortal, and resurrected being, now possessing the fullness of the glory and power of the Father (see Matthew 28:18; Doctrine and Covenants 93:16), spend so much of His time in prayer among the Nephites? Was there some truth He did not know, some godly attribute He did not possess, some energy or strength He lacked? Was there some approval of the Father, some encouragement or permission He needed? I rather think not. When the Savior appeared, the descendants of Lehi might have cried out *Emmanuel*, meaning "God is with us." Jesus prayed frequently as an example to the Saints and to all men and women of the need to communicate with God—often, regularly, consistently, intensely, and reverently.

Building on these truths, there are perhaps other purposes of prayer, both in time and eternity. Jesus prayed to the Father because He loved the Father. Jesus prayed to the Father because it was a reverential way of speaking to His Father, who is forever worthy of the reverence of His children. Jesus prayed to the Father because They enjoyed communion. The word *communion* is especially meaningful and worth much reflection. Jesus possessed perfect spirituality because He had overcome the world (see John 16:33) and because He enjoyed perfect communion with the Father. The Savior's example is a call to you and me to live our lives in such a manner that we increasingly cultivate the cleansing and revelatory benefits of the Spirit.

All of this also points us to the ordinal relationship between the Father and the Son, the fact that even though Jesus possessed the same divinity and the fullness of the glory and power of the Father, He still looked to the Father as His superior. It would never seem appropriate, for example, for the Father to pray to the Son or the Holy Ghost. It is "the province of the Father," Joseph Smith taught, "to preside as the Chief or President, Jesus as the Mediator, and the Holy Ghost as the Testator or Witness."[3]

Finally, another scene in 3 Nephi provides an unspeakable promise to each of us. As the disciples continued to pray, "*his countenance did smile upon them, and the light of his countenance did shine upon them, and behold they were as white as the countenance and also the garments of Jesus*; and behold the whiteness thereof did exceed all the whiteness, yea, even there could be nothing upon earth so white as the whiteness thereof." The Savior then dropped to the ground and uttered thanks to the Father for purifying His chosen Twelve. Much as He had done in His great Intercessory or High Priestly Prayer only moments before the Roman soldiers came to arrest Him, Jesus prayed for the Twelve and those who would give heed to their words and expressed His desire for them to be unified with one another and the Godhead (3 Nephi 19:25–30; see also John 17). In likening this passage to ourselves, we can conclude that when we pray, God is pleased. He smiles upon us. We bring light and divine glory into our countenances and our conduct. We are sanctified—made pure and holy—and renewed in mind and body. Prayer prepares us for His presence.

Jesus Christ is truly the Light we hold up to one another and to all the world (see 3 Nephi 18:24). Mortals are but dim reflections of that light—mere lamps in comparison to the light of the Son. In prayer, as in all facets of our lives, we look to our Model and Master: "And as I have prayed among you even so shall ye pray in my church. . . . Behold, I am the light; I have set an example for you" (3 Nephi 18:16).

## CHAPTER 31

# "This Is My Gospel"

### 3 NEPHI 27

There is a phrase, an expression, that most of us have heard hundreds, if not thousands, of times. We hear it as a member of the Church closes his or her sacrament meeting address, and we especially hear it in our monthly fast and testimony meetings. Many a Saint begins bearing testimony with "I know the gospel is true" or "I know *this* gospel is true." We'll come back to that shortly. If we seek a definition of "the gospel," we eventually come to "good news" or "glad tidings." But what is the good news? What are the glad tidings?

Some of the most important doctrinal messages delivered by the Savior to the Nephites (and to us) during His ministry in ancient America are contained within 3 Nephi 27. Here we find one of the most comprehensive but clearly understandable definitions of the gospel. "Behold I have given unto you my gospel," the resurrected Redeemer began, "and *this is the gospel* which I have given unto you—*that I came into the world to do the will of my Father, because my Father sent me. And my Father sent me that I might be lifted up upon the cross, that I might draw all men unto me,* that as I have been lifted up by men even so should men be lifted up by the Father, to stand before me, to be judged of their works, whether they be good or whether they be evil—and for this cause have I been lifted up; therefore, according to the power of the Father I will draw all men unto me, that they may be judged according to their works" (3 Nephi 27:13–15; emphasis added).

Good news is always more appreciated when we know what the bad news was or might have been. The bad news is that because of the Fall of Adam and Eve, each one of us is subject to both spiritual and physical death, and there is no way whatsoever that we can solve these painful dilemmas by ourselves. It requires the intervention of a God, a divine being who avoided spiritual death by keeping all the commandments of His Father and never sinned; consequently, He owed no debt to the justice of God. Further, this divine being overcame physical death when He was raised from the dead by the power of our Heavenly Father (see 2 Corinthians 13:4; Mormon 7:5). This is the good news. This is the gospel.

Notice how the gospel is defined in the revelation that unfolds to us the vision of the degrees of glory: "And this is the gospel, the glad tidings, which the voice out of the heavens bore record unto us—that *he came into the world, even Jesus, to be crucified for the world, and to bear the sins of the world, and to sanctify the world*, and to cleanse it from all unrighteousness; that through him all might be saved whom the Father had put into his power and made by him" (Doctrine and Covenants 76:40–42; emphasis added). In short, the gospel of Jesus Christ is the good news of the Atonement of Jesus Christ, including, as its capstone, His and our resurrection from the dead (see 1 Corinthians 15:21–22).

After reading verses 13–15 of 3 Nephi 27, a typical Latter-day Saint might ask: "What about the Garden of Gethsemane? Wasn't the Lord's Atonement worked out there?" Yes, Christ's redeeming suffering began in the Garden of Gethsemane and was completed on the cross. "Cross" was a word often used by the Apostle Paul in his epistles to describe the whole of the redeeming work of Jesus Christ (see, for example, 1 Corinthians 1:17, 18; Galatians 6:14; Ephesians 2:16; Philippians 3:18; Hebrews 12:2).

Let's look more carefully at these words: "And my Father sent me that I might be lifted up upon the cross, . . . *that I might draw all men unto me,* that as I have been lifted up by men even so should men be lifted up by the Father, to stand before me, to be judged of their works, whether they be good or whether they be evil" (3 Nephi 27:14). We've spoken elsewhere of this concept—that in the Book of Mormon, resurrection and eternal judgment are companion points of doctrine. The Resurrection and Judgment make it possible for every single person on earth to overcome, at least for a brief time, spiritual death, since everyone will be raised from the dead and returned to the presence of the Lord to stand before God to be judged.

Now, there is another way "the gospel" is defined in holy scripture. The gospel is the means by which we can appropriate the powers and blessings of the Lord's Atonement. Notice the following: "And no unclean thing can enter into his kingdom; therefore nothing entereth into his rest save it be those who have washed their garments in my blood, because of their faith, and the repentance of all their sins, and their faithfulness unto the end. Now this is the commandment: Repent, all ye ends of the earth, and come unto me and be baptized in my name, that ye may be sanctified by the reception of the Holy Ghost, that ye may stand spotless before me at the last day. Verily, verily, I say unto you, *this is my gospel*" (3 Nephi 27:19–21; emphasis added).

And from modern revelation: "Repent and be baptized, every one of you, for a remission of your sins; yea, be baptized even by water, and then cometh the baptism of fire and of the Holy Ghost. Behold, verily, verily, I say unto you, *this is my gospel*" (Doctrine and Covenants 33:11–12).

"And verily, verily, I say unto you, he that receiveth my gospel receiveth me; and he that receiveth not my gospel receiveth not me. And *this is the gospel*—repentance and baptism by water, and then cometh the baptism of fire and the Holy Ghost, even the Comforter, which showeth all things, and teacheth the peaceable things of the kingdom" (Doctrine and Covenants 39:5–6; emphasis added).

Do we see the message? In these passages, the gospel is the

process by which we appropriate and take full advantage of the Savior's Atonement; it is the first principles and ordinances of the gospel—faith, repentance, baptism by immersion, and laying on of hands for the gift of the Holy Ghost. Joseph the Prophet spoke of these principles and ordinances as "the articles of adoption,"[1] the process by which we are born again and adopted into the family of the Lord Jesus Christ, becoming His sons and daughters (Mosiah 5:6–7; 27:25–26).

It is especially interesting to read through the Prophet Joseph Smith's translation of the early chapters of Genesis. What we have just described as the gospel of Jesus Christ is set forth in sacred insights first delivered to Adam and Eve: "Therefore I give unto you a commandment, to teach these things freely unto your children, saying: That by reason of transgression cometh the fall, which fall bringeth death, and inasmuch as ye were born into the world by water, and blood, and the spirit, which I have made, and so became of dust a living soul, even so *ye must be born again into the kingdom of heaven, of water, and of the Spirit, and be cleansed by blood, even the blood of mine Only Begotten*; that ye might be sanctified from all sin, and enjoy the words of eternal life in this world, and eternal life in the world to come, even immortal glory; for *by the water ye keep the commandment; by the Spirit ye are justified, and by the blood ye are sanctified*. . . . And now, behold, I say unto you, *This is the plan of salvation unto all men*" (Moses 6:58–60, 62; emphasis added).

Let's return to where we began. Even if we do not realize it, when we declare that "I know the gospel is true," we are bearing witness of the efficacy of the atoning work of Jesus Christ. We are saying that we know that the Savior's Atonement is real and that it really works. When a person testifies that "the Church is true," he or she means a number of things: (1) that the restored Church is in fact the Lord's Church; (2) that what is taught in the Church—the doctrine of the faith—is true; and (3) that this Church is, in the language of God, "the only true and living church upon the face of the whole earth" (Doctrine and Covenants 1:30), the only authority-bearing religious institution on the planet. We do not, of course, bear this kind of testimony in order to hurt or offend those of other faiths, for there is a great deal of truth and goodness to be found throughout the world. Instead, we testify that The Church of Jesus Christ of Latter-day Saints is the restoration of the first-century Christian Church and is now the custodian of the fullness of the gospel of Jesus Christ.

CHAPTER 32

# The Mission of the Three Nephites

3 NEPHI 28

We do not know if, during Jesus's time among the Nephites, He was with them just during the days or if He returned to be with and bless them in the evenings. The most information we get about how long the Savior stayed with them is found in verse 13 of chapter 26: "Therefore, I would that ye should behold that the Lord truly did teach the people, for the space of three days; and after that he did show himself unto them oft, and did break bread oft, and bless it, and give it unto them."

Chapter 28 begins with the detail that "he spake unto his [twelve] disciples, one by one, saying unto them: What is it that ye desire of me, after that I am gone to the Father?" Can you imagine being this close to the Son of God and Him asking you what He could do for you? What would you ask for? What things would you really like but dare not ask for? (It's a fascinating scenario to contemplate, and my response to His question might well reveal more about me than I would want to be known!) This question from the second member of the Godhead causes us to reflect on what things matter most in our lives, what things would truly bless us individually and our families.

Nine of the Nephite Apostles ask for the same thing: "We desire that after we have lived unto the age of man, that our ministry, wherein thou hast called us, may have an end, that we may speedily come unto thee in thy kingdom" (3 Nephi 28:2). Elder Jeffrey R. Holland wrote that these nine "asked for the privilege of a sure and swift return to the Savior's side after their earthly ministries were complete. This the Master granted at the close of their designated term of mortality—seventy-two years." I am in complete agreement with what Elder Holland next explained: "The other three disciples held back, reluctant to express their desires. After all, who would not like to be in the Savior's presence as soon—and as long—as possible? To desire anything to the contrary could surely be misunderstood by the Lord Himself. But Jesus perceived their thoughts and granted them their wish—to remain on the earth in a translated state to further the work of the ministry until the Savior's second coming."[1]

Jesus explained to the three Apostles that their request was the same as that which John the Beloved had made in the Old World. John had requested of the Savior: "Lord, give unto me power over death, that I may live and bring souls unto thee. And the Lord said unto me: Verily, verily, I say unto thee, because thou desirest this thou shalt tarry until I come in my glory, and shalt prophesy before nations, kindreds, tongues, and people" (Doctrine and Covenants 7:1–3; see also John 21:20–22).

What does it mean to say that the Three Nephites were *translated*? It means that the Lord caused a change to come upon their bodies, such that they were "sanctified in the flesh," no longer subject to sin, pain, bodily decay, and death (see 3 Nephi 28:7–9, 39). Under the divine superintendence of our God, who knows perfectly well when and under what circumstances to send His servants to earth, the Lord has chosen occasionally to translate His children.

Translated beings are still mortal, but their bodies have been transformed from a telestial to a terrestrial order.[2] They are given great power and are able to appear and disappear as they choose (see 3 Nephi 28:27–30). The nature of their activities is determined and governed by the Lord, and their whereabouts are known only to Him. The Three Nephites "did go forth upon the face of the land, and did minister unto all the people, uniting as many to the church as would believe in their preaching; baptizing them, and as many as were baptized did receive the Holy Ghost" (3 Nephi 28:18). They will remain in this condition until the Second Coming of Christ in glory, at which time they will undergo a change equivalent to death and be transformed instantaneously from mortality to resurrected and glorified immortality (see 3 Nephi 28:7–8, 39–40). Indeed, as the Prophet Joseph Smith explained, "Translated beings cannot enter into rest until they have undergone a change equivalent to death."[3]

Persons in scripture who have been translated include Enoch and his city (Genesis 5:21–24; Doctrine and Covenants 107:48–49; Moses 7:68–69); Melchizedek and the city of Salem (JST, Genesis 14:25–40); Moses (Alma 45:19); Elijah (2 Kings 2; Doctrine and Covenants 110:13); Alma the Younger (Alma 45:18–19); Nephi the son of Helaman (3 Nephi 1:2–3; 2:9); John the Beloved (John 21:20–23; Doctrine and Covenants 7); and the three Nephite Apostles (3 Nephi 28). Those who were translated before the Resurrection of Christ—Enoch, Melchizedek, Moses, Elijah, Alma, and Nephi—were resurrected at the time of that first resurrection, following Jesus's rise from the tomb (see Doctrine and Covenants 133:54–55).

Those who have been translated since the Resurrection of Christ—John the Beloved and the Three Nephites—will remain in their translated condition until the Second Coming of the Savior (see 3 Nephi 28:37–40). In addition, in a revelation given to the Shakers (the United Society of Believers in Christ's Second Appearing), the Lord spoke: "Wherefore, I will that all men shall repent, for all are under sin, except those which I have reserved unto myself, *holy men that ye know not of*" (Doctrine and Covenants 49:8; emphasis added). Of this particular verse, President Joseph Fielding Smith explained that "'holy men that you know not of,' who were without sin, and reserved unto the Lord, are translated persons such as John the Revelator and the Three Nephites, who do not belong to this generation and yet are in the flesh in the earth performing a special ministry until the coming of Jesus Christ."[4]

Mormon's account continues: "And it came to pass that when Jesus had spoken these words, he touched every one of them with his finger save it were the three who were to tarry, and then he departed." We are told that at this time "the heavens were opened, and they [the three] were caught up into heaven, and saw and heard unspeakable things. And it was forbidden them that they should utter; neither was it given unto them power that they could utter the things which they saw and heard; and whether they were in the body or out of the body, they could not tell; for it did seem unto them like a transfiguration of them, that they were changed from this body of flesh into an immortal state, that they could behold the things of God" (3 Nephi 28:12–15).

This experience parallels what the Apostle Paul described (2 Corinthians 12:1–4), as well as what, to some degree at least, Joseph Smith experienced in his vision of the celestial kingdom in January of 1837 (Doctrine and Covenants 137:1). Mormon's comment that the Three Nephites seemed to be *transfigured* is accurate. To be transfigured is to be raised to a higher spiritual level for a temporary period so that a person may see and experience things that cannot take place in one's natural, unaided condition. The Three Nephites, however, were not actually "changed from this body of flesh into an immortal state" (3 Nephi 28:15; see also verse 17), since one can become immortal only after he or she has passed through death and is resurrected. Mormon later learned more details about the condition of the Three Nephites: "There must needs be a change wrought upon their bodies, or else it must needs be that they must taste of death. . . . Now this change was not equal to what shall take place at the last day" (3 Nephi 28:37–39)—when the Savior will return to earth and the three Apostles will be resurrected instantaneously "in the twinkling of an eye" (3 Nephi 28:8)—"but there was a change wrought upon them insomuch that Satan could have no power over them, that he could not tempt them;

and they were sanctified in the flesh, that they were holy, and that the powers of the earth could not hold them" (3 Nephi 28:39).

And what kind of work were they to do throughout the earth? Mormon explains that "they will be among the Gentiles, and the Gentiles shall know them not. They will also be among the Jews, and the Jews shall know them not. And it shall come to pass, when the Lord seeth fit in his wisdom that they shall minister to all the scattered tribes of Israel, and unto all nations, kindreds, tongues, and people, and shall bring out of them unto Jesus many souls, that their desire may be fulfilled, and also because of the convincing power of God which is in them. And they are as the angels of God, and if they shall pray unto the Father in the name of Jesus they can show themselves unto whatsoever man it seemeth them good" (3 Nephi 28:27–30).

(As a rather light aside, whenever I taught the Book of Mormon to college students, one of the questions I put on an exam was the following: "True or False: the names of the Three Nephites are contained in the Book of Mormon." Almost every student responded with "false" because of what is said in verse 25 of this chapter: Mormon thought he might give their names, but the Lord forbade it. However, the names of each of the Twelve are given in verse 4 of chapter 19, and so their names are in fact contained within the Book of Mormon.)

When I was a boy, I heard many stories of unusual appearances and miraculous deeds, many of which were attributed to the Three Nephites. In recent decades I have heard fewer and fewer of these. Clearly, not everything that is good or productive or unusual that takes place throughout the world ought to be attributed to the work of the Three Nephites. I am persuaded, however, that we ought not to be cynical and absolutely unbelieving, even in some cases poking fun at such stories. Why? Because our Heavenly Father and His Son, Jesus Christ, love the people throughout our world and wish to ease their burdens, settle their souls, and inspire them in whatever ways They can, including occasionally by sending special representatives. Let's not be closed to that possibility.

In that spirit, Moroni warned against denying revelation, spiritual gifts, and miracles: "Behold I say unto you, *he that denieth these things knoweth not the gospel of Christ*; yea, *he has not read the scriptures; if so, he does not understand them*. . . . But behold, *I will show unto you a God of miracles*, even the God of Abraham, and the God of Isaac, and the God of Jacob; and it is that same God who created the heavens and the earth, and all things that in them are" (Mormon 9:7–8, 11; emphasis added).

# CHAPTER 33

# The Nephite Mini-Millennium

## 4 NEPHI

The Book of Mormon is a timely and timeless book, a scriptural record that can provide inspiration and direction in any decade and any century. President Ezra Taft Benson stated that "a major portion of the book centers on the few decades just prior to Christ's coming to America. By careful study of that time period, we can determine why some were destroyed during the terrible judgments that preceded His coming and what brought others to stand at the temple in the land of Bountiful and thrust their hands into the wounds of His hands and feet."[1] Similarly, there is marvelous insight to be gained regarding the great day of peace and rest that lies ahead of us—the Millennium. While 3 Nephi 1–7 gives us a prophetic glimpse into the chaos and wickedness that will grip the earth before Jesus Christ returns in glory, 4 Nephi provides a prophetic perspective on what life will be like in that day when war and dissension and violence and immorality are done away. Sadly, it also helps us better understand the circumstances in which the Millennium will be brought to a close.

Within two years after the Lord's appearance in Bountiful, "the people were all converted unto the Lord, upon all the face of the land, both Nephites and Lamanites, and there were no contentions and disputations among them, and every man did deal justly one with another" (4 Nephi 1:2). Every person who will survive the cleansing of the Second Coming—those persons who have lived either a celestial or a terrestrial life—will, as the Apostle Paul taught, "confess that Jesus Christ is Lord, to the glory of God the Father" (Philippians 2:11). President Brigham Young was emphatic about the fact that during the Millennium, especially the first part of that thousand-year period, not everyone will be a member of The Church of Jesus Christ of Latter-day Saints. "If the Latter-day Saints think, when the kingdom of God is established on the earth, that all the inhabitants of the earth will join the church called Latter-day Saints, they are egregiously mistaken. I presume there will be as many sects and parties then as now."[2] On another occasion President Young said: "When Jesus comes to rule and reign as King of Nations as he now does King of Saints, the veil of the covering will be taken from all nations, that *all flesh may see his glory together, but that will not make them all Saints.* Seeing the Lord does not make a man a Saint, seeing an Angel does not make a man a Saint by any means."[3]

Later in 4 Nephi we read that "there was no contention in the land, because of the love of God which did dwell in the hearts of the people. And there were no envyings, nor strifes, nor tumults, nor whoredoms, nor lyings, nor murders, nor any manner of lasciviousness; and surely there could not be a happier people among all the people who had been created by the hand of God" (4 Nephi 1:15–16). And so it will be in that grand day when the Savior dwells once again among His people. Isaiah spoke of a time when "the wolf also shall dwell with the lamb, and the leopard shall lie down with the kid; and the calf and the young lion and the fatling together; and a little child shall lead them. . . . They shall not hurt nor destroy in all my holy mountain: for the earth shall be full of the knowledge of the Lord, as the waters cover the sea" (Isaiah 11:6, 9).

"What is the key to this breakthrough in contented, happy living?" Elder Jeffrey R. Holland inquired. "It is embedded there in the text in one sentence: 'The love of God . . . did dwell in the hearts of the people' [4 Nephi 1:15]. When the love of God sets the tone for our own lives, for our relationships to each other and ultimately our feeling for all humankind, then *old distinctions, limiting labels, and artificial divisions begin to pass away, and peace increases.* That is precisely what happened in our Book of Mormon example. . . . The people had taken on just one transcendent identity. They were all, it says, to be known as 'the children of Christ' [4 Nephi 1:17]."[4]

When people truly love one another after the manner in which the Savior loves us, they will inevitably begin to see to the needs of their loved ones and neighbors. Some three millennia before the Lord's ministry in ancient America, a previously slow-of-speech and self-conscious Enoch loved and labored among a people until the Lord called his people "Zion, because they were of one heart and one mind, and dwelt in righteousness; and there was no poor among them" (Moses 7:18). And as it was with the city of Enoch, so it was with the Nephites following the personal visit of the Savior: "And many of them saw and heard unspeakable things, which are not lawful to be written. And they taught, and *did minister one to another; and they had all things common among them, every man dealing justly, one with another*" (3 Nephi 26:18–19; emphasis added; compare Acts 4:32–35). And of course these same principles were delivered to Joseph Smith by revelation. These sacred principles and practices are known as the law of consecration and stewardship.

We learn in verse 10 of 4 Nephi 1 that "the people of Nephi did wax strong, and did multiply exceedingly fast, and became an exceedingly fair and delightsome people. And *they were married, and given in marriage, and were blessed according to the multitude of the promises which the Lord had made unto them*" (4 Nephi 1:10–11; emphasis added). I believe these two verses are speaking about the new and everlasting covenant of marriage. When a person enters into an eternal marriage, marriage in the temple of the Lord, he or she enters into the patriarchal order of the Melchizedek Priesthood (see Doctrine and Covenants 131:1–2). Through their faithfulness, they open themselves to the "promises made to the fathers" anciently (Doctrine and Covenants

2:2)—that is, the blessings of Abraham, Isaac, and Jacob, which are the blessings of the Abrahamic Covenant (see Abraham 2:8–11).

Mormon, the prophet-editor of the Book of Mormon, explains that the people "did not walk any more after the performances and ordinances of the Law of Moses; but they did walk after the commandments they had received from their Lord and their God" (4 Nephi 1:12). The atoning sacrifice of Jesus Christ brought an end to the law of Moses and all that appertained to it. The law was fulfilled in Christ because the sacrifice of Christ was the fulfillment and the realization of all of the Messianic prophecies and sacrificial offerings that had pointed to the great and last sacrifice of the Son of God (see Alma 34:13–14).

Following the destruction that took place after Jesus had been put to death, the voice of the Lord instructed: "And ye shall offer up unto me no more the shedding of blood; yea, your sacrifices and your burnt offerings shall be done away, for I will accept none of your sacrifices and your burnt offerings. And ye shall offer for a sacrifice unto me a broken heart and a contrite spirit. And whoso cometh unto me with a broken heart and a contrite spirit, him [or her] will I baptize with fire and with the Holy Ghost" (3 Nephi 9:19–20; compare Psalm 51:17; Doctrine and Covenants 59:8).

And so what was it that brought the nearly two-hundred-year era of peace and righteousness to an end? We are told that Nephi delivered the Nephite record to his son Amos and that Amos "kept it eighty and four years, and there was still peace in the land, save it were *a small part of the people who had revolted from the church and taken upon them the name of Lamanites*; therefore there began to be Lamanites again in the land" (4 Nephi 1:19–20; emphasis added). This observation is subtle, but it is also tragic and stunningly current. Those who had "revolted" from the Church decided that it was no longer sufficient to be called the children of God or the children of Christ, not enough to be called Christians or members of the Church of Jesus Christ. Instead, they demanded that they be called Lamanites. Their label, their identifying mark, their moniker, their title, mattered more than being known as "the peaceable followers of Christ" (Moroni 7:3). It was a blatant demonstration of the sin that is behind practically every other sin, pride—what President Ezra Taft Benson called "the universal sin, the great vice," the "great stumbling block to Zion."[5]

Only three verses later, we read that "the people had multiplied, insomuch that they were spread upon all the face of the land, and . . . they had become exceedingly rich, because of their prosperity in Christ." Mormon adds that the people began to be prideful and to be obsessed with "the wearing of costly apparel, and all manner of fine pearls, and of the fine things of the world." And then comes a haunting verse: "And *from that time forth they did have their goods and their substance no more common among them*" (4 Nephi 1:23–25; emphasis added).

President George Q. Cannon once declared that this is exactly what will bring the thousand-year Millennium to an end: "After the thousand years [Satan] will regain some of his present power. *It will be as it was among the Nephites. . . . Men will arise who will object to working for the benefit of others; class distinctions will once more make themselves apparent.*"[6] On another occasion he explained that "when Satan is loosed again for a little while, when the thousand years shall be ended, it will be through mankind departing from the practice of those principles which God has revealed, and this Order of Enoch probably among the rest. He can, in no better way, obtain power over the hearts of the children of men, than by appealing to their cupidity, avarice, and low, selfish desires."[7]

Despite this sobering warning, the book of 4 Nephi offers us sweet anticipation of a time when evil will be banished and the love of God will dwell in every heart, when Christ the Redeemer will rule and reign on earth among His people. It also cautions us of the need to look to God and give thanks to Him and to acknowledge His hand in all things (see Doctrine and Covenants 59:7, 21) that thereby we can avoid the great stumbling block of Zion.

CHAPTER 34

# Mormon's Distillation of the Book of Mormon

MORMON 7

In the last several years of my father's life, he suffered the disastrous effects of diabetes, including irreparable damage to both his kidneys and his liver. He phoned me (I was living in Orem, Utah, and he was in Louisiana) in quite a good mood. He said: "I suppose you'd better arrange to come down for a visit. My doctor tells me that I only have a few days to live." He hadn't completely lost his sense of humor, for he then added: "I'm told I'm dying of a drinking man's disease, cirrhosis of the liver, but I've never enjoyed the benefits!" (Dad had never broken the Word of Wisdom.) I caught the soonest flight I could and arrived at Mom and Dad's home at 10:00 the next night.

Dad and I talked together for a couple of hours. He wanted to know all about Shauna and the children, my job, my Church calling, and my health. By about midnight he grew weaker, and we helped him into bed. I kissed him and started to leave the room so that he could get some rest. He said to me: "Stop. Come back and sit with me a few more minutes." I began talking about the many things Dad had accomplished through the years—his employment, his many years of service in the Church, and how much so many people loved him. After allowing me to speak for a couple of minutes, he cut me off and said, "I don't want to talk about me. I want to talk about you and your wife and your children." He looked me in the eyes, and the tears began to make their way down his face. He said, "You do know how very proud of you that I am, don't you?" I was also very emotional and unable to speak; I nodded my head.

Dad then began to talk about how much he loved my wife; in fact, he said with a smile on his face, "I think I love Shauna more than you!" I replied that he was very wise. He then talked about each of our six children and basically gave me a charge to love them with all my heart, more than anything else on earth. Again, I nodded. We embraced for the last time. He went into the hospital early in the morning and into a coma by about 2:00 p.m. He passed away at 11:30 that night.

I've taken the time to share these thoughts with you because they illustrate what I want to emphasize: as most of us face death, we will want to think and talk about the things of greatest worth in our lives—faith, family, and friends. So it was with the prophet-editor Mormon. Chapter 7 of Mormon seems to be among his final words, addressed principally to people in the future.

As I have read and reflected many, many times on Mormon 7, it has seemed to me as though Mormon is delivering his "last lecture." The chapter is basically a distillation of some of the most important doctrinal points made throughout the Book of Mormon. It's as if Mormon is speaking the following to you and me: "In case you haven't picked up on these things as you have read this sacred record, let me remind you of some of the most important truths." For example:

*"Know ye that ye are of the house of Israel"* (verse 2). Mormon wants us to know who we are, what we were sent to earth to do, and what kind of influence for good we should have on earth. When we know who we are—children of God the Eternal Father; children of our earthly parents; sons and daughters of the Lord Jesus Christ; and children of Abraham, Isaac, and Jacob—we will act accordingly. As such, we are entitled to the blessings of the Abrahamic Covenant: the gospel of Jesus Christ, the Holy Priesthood, and an eternal family unit (see Abraham 2:8–11). We are of Israel.

*"Know ye that ye must come unto repentance, or ye cannot be saved"*

(verse 3). Over and over in the Book of Mormon we read that no unclean thing can enter into the presence of God. Repentance is a daily task and a daily responsibility. It is a sweet privilege that is made available to us through our Heavenly Father's plan of salvation, or great plan of happiness. Thank God that we can repent, that we can change and strive to overcome, and that we can improve and do the works of righteousness (see Doctrine and Covenants 1:31–32). If there was no repentance, we would, as Jacob taught, become subject to the devil at the time of our death (2 Nephi 9:8–9).

*"Know ye that ye must lay down your weapons of war, and delight no more in the shedding of blood"* (verse 4). War is antithetical to all that is good and of God. Jesus Christ is the Prince of Peace, and he has called us to be peacemakers (see 3 Nephi 12:9). The Savior has charged us to love our enemies, while war generally requires that we hate our enemies. According to the teachings of the Book of Mormon (especially Alma 43–62), there are times when it is permissible to *enter* war when God commands us to do so, but we must never initiate it (see Alma 43:46; 48:14; 3 Nephi 3:20–21). While we may be required to go to war to protect our home, family, liberties, and religion, we should seek to end war as soon as possible and then lift an ensign of peace.

*"Know ye that ye must come to the knowledge of your fathers, and repent of all your sins and iniquities, and believe in Jesus Christ, that he is the Son of God, and that he was slain by the Jews, and by the power of the Father he has risen again, whereby he hath gained the victory over the grave." By and through the Resurrection, "man must be raised to stand before his judgement-seat"* (verses 5–6). Here we are called to look to Jesus Christ for redemption from death and hell, made available through His atoning blood and Resurrection.

*"Lay hold upon the gospel of Christ which shall be set before you, not only in this record [the Book of Mormon] but also in the record which shall come unto the Gentiles from the Jews, which record shall come from the Gentiles unto you [the Bible]."* Mormon continues: "For behold, this [the Book of Mormon] is written for the intent that ye may believe that

[the Bible]; and if ye will believe that [the Bible] ye will believe this [the Book of Mormon] also" (verses 8–9). We discussed this topic in greater detail in chapter 3.

"Love for [His] other sheep brought the resurrected Lord to them here on the American hemisphere," President Russell M. Nelson explained. "He taught the gospel to them. Here He established His Church. He charged them with the responsibility of keeping records of His ministry among them. This precious record we received from them as the Book of Mormon is the great clarifying scripture. It is the great missionary scripture. It is another testament of Jesus Christ. Its four major writers—Nephi, Jacob, Mormon, and Moroni—were all eyewitnesses of the Son of God. No wonder this sacred text has become our great and valuable friend as we teach and testify of the Lord."[1]

Chapter 7 of Mormon is a good outline for studying the remarkable scriptural record known as the Book of Mormon. Indeed, searching out and reflecting deeply on the items that Mormon addresses briefly in this chapter will build one's understanding and appreciation for the Nephite-Jaredite record. Such searching, such study, and such spiritual investment will also plant in our hearts the precepts that will, as the Prophet Joseph Smith declared, bring us nearer to God than any other book.[2]

# CHAPTER 35

## "Never Have I Shown Myself"

ETHER 3

The book of Ether is Moroni's abridgment of the twenty-four gold plates. These plates were discovered by the people of King Limhi about 120 years before the birth of Christ and translated by King Mosiah (see Mosiah 8:9; 21:25–27; 28:11–17). In Mormon's words, these twenty-four plates "gave an account of the people who were destroyed [the Jaredites], from the time that they were destroyed back to the building of the great tower, at the time the Lord confounded the language of the people and they were scattered abroad upon the face of all the earth, yea, and even from that time back until the creation of Adam" (Mosiah 28:17; see also Ether 1:3). On the title page of the Book of Mormon, Moroni adds the interesting detail that "the Lord confounded the language of the people when *they were building a tower to get to heaven*" (emphasis added).

As the story begins, some 2,200 years before the birth of the Savior, two men—Jared and his brother—are directed to take their family and friends and leave the area, being assured that the Lord would bring them to a promised land, "a land which is choice above all the lands of the earth" (Ether 1:42). It is interesting that the name of the brother of Jared is not given in the scriptural text. Daniel H. Ludlow suggested three possibilities for why his name is not given: (1) the brother of Jared may himself, out of modesty, have purposely omitted his name from the record, in a similar manner to John the Beloved in his Gospel; (2) the final writer on the plates of Ether, a descendant of Jared (see Ether 1:6, 32), perhaps emphasized the name of his progenitor; or (3) Moroni may have found the name too difficult to translate adequately into the Nephite language.[1]

The name of the brother of Jared was revealed to the Prophet Joseph Smith. Elder George Reynolds recorded: "While residing in Kirtland, Elder Reynolds Cahoon had a son born to him. One day when President Joseph Smith was passing his door, he called the Prophet in and asked him to bless and name their baby. Joseph did so and gave the name of Mahonri Moriancumer. When he had finished the blessing, he laid the child on the bed, and turning to Elder Cahoon he said, the name I have given your son is the name of the Brother of Jared; the Lord has just shown [or revealed] it to me. Elder William F. Cahoon, who was standing near, heard the Prophet make this statement to his father; and this was the first time the name of the brother of Jared was known in the Church in this dispensation."[2]

Looking to the brother of Jared as their spiritual leader and spokesman, Jared and his family petition him to ask the Lord that their language not be confounded. Because of the brother of Jared's faith, the Lord honored his request. Neither the Bible (see Genesis 11:1–8) nor the Book of Mormon fully explain what Moroni meant when he recorded that the Lord "did not confound the language of Jared" (Ether 1:35). We are left to wonder if they retained their previous language (presumably the Adamic language) or if their or their friends' language was changed but that they then all still spoke the same language and were therefore not "confounded."

From Moroni's narrative of the Jaredites, we know that they built large boats or barges to cross the ocean. The brother of Jared faced two significant challenges in building these boats. First, the matter of ventilation: how would he and his people breathe when the boats, perhaps submarine-like, were under the water? Architecturally speaking, this seemed to be beyond the brother of Jared's comprehension or abilities, and so the Lord Jehovah gave specific instructions for how to deal with the first problem (see Ether 2:19–21). The second challenge was how they would have light within the vessels when they were submerged.

Elder Bruce R. McConkie explained that "the Brother of Jared—having confidence because he was talking to the Lord, because he was communing and getting answers—asked another question: he asked for a solution to a problem he should have figured out himself and not taken up with the Lord. He said, 'What will we do for light in the vessels?'. . . And the Lord talked to him about it a little, and then [the Lord] said this: 'What will ye that I should do that ye may have light in your vessels?' (Ether 2:23.) . . . In other words, 'Moriancumer, this is your problem. Why are you troubling me? I've given you your agency; you are endowed with capacity and ability. Get out and solve the problem.'

"Well, the brother of Jared got the message. He went up into a mount called Shelem, and the record says he 'did molten out of a rock sixteen small stones; and they were white and clear, even as transparent glass.' (Ether 3:1.) . . . Moriancumer said to the Lord: 'Touch these stones, O Lord, with thy finger, and prepare them that they may shine forth in darkness."

Elder McConkie then taught a great principle of this story: "There is a fine balance between agency and inspiration. We are expected to do everything in our power and then to seek an answer from the Lord, a confirming seal that we have reached the right conclusion; and sometimes, happily, in addition, we get added truths and knowledge that we hadn't even supposed."[3]

The account in Ether continues by explaining that "the Lord stretched forth his hand and touched the stones one by one with his finger. And the veil was taken from off the eyes of the brother of Jared, and he saw the finger of the Lord; and it was as the finger of a man, like unto flesh and blood; and the brother of Jared fell down before the Lord, for he was struck with fear" (Ether 3:6). Moriancumer explains that he fell to the earth for fear "lest he should smite me; for I knew not that the Lord had flesh and blood." Jehovah then declares: "Thou hast seen that I shall take upon me flesh and blood; and never has man come before me with such exceeding faith as thou hast." The Lord asks Moriancumer if he had seen more than his finger, and in a beautiful, childlike manner Mahonri replies: "Nay; Lord, show thyself unto me." As a kind of preassessment, the Lord asks: "Believest thou the words which I shall speak?" (Ether 3:7–11). What an interesting situation: the Lord wants to know, not if the brother of Jared believes *all that the Lord has said in the past,* but rather if he will believe *what will yet be spoken.* Faith looks to the future, as well as the past.

At this point, Jehovah reveals Himself completely to the brother of Jared. Among other things, the Lord says: "I am Jesus Christ. I am the Father and the Son. In me shall all mankind have life, and that eternally, even they who shall believe on my name; and they shall become my sons and my daughters." Jehovah then makes a statement that has proven difficult for many Latter-day Saints to understand: "And *never have I showed myself unto man whom I have created, for never has man believed in me as thou hast*" (Ether 3:14–15; emphasis added). Given that we have scriptural support for God appearing to such prophets as Adam, Enoch, and Noah, what did the Lord mean when He stated that He had never revealed Himself to man? Here are a few possible answers to this question:

First, this may well be the first time chronologically when *Jehovah* manifested Himself and identified Himself specifically as Jesus Christ, *the Son* (see verse 14).

Second, perhaps He did not reveal himself to "man" in the sense of unbelieving, unredeemed, or unsaved man, and certainly not to natural men.[4]

Third, the Lord may have never revealed Himself in such a total and complete manner. President Joseph Fielding Smith suggested that "the Savior stood before the brother of Jared plainly, distinctly, and showed him his whole body."[5]

Fourth, President Harold B. Lee suggested that the uniqueness of

Moriancumer's experience lay in the fact that he saw the Lord Jesus as He would be—that is, he saw a vision of Christ as His body would be during His mortal ministry in some two thousand years. President Lee stated that the brother of Jared "was amazed because he said he saw not only the finger of a spiritual being, but his faith was so great that he saw the kind of body that he would have when he came down to the earth. It was of flesh and blood—flesh, blood, and bones. And the Master said, 'No man has had this kind of faith.'"[6]

Fifth, the Lord might essentially have been saying, "No man has had the kind and depth of faith that you have," a faith that was of such magnitude that "he could not be kept from within the veil," and the Lord "could not withhold anything from him" (Ether 3:20, 26).[7]

Sixth, perhaps the matter is simpler than we suppose. Could it be that the pronouncement is a relative statement, that it pertains only to the Jaredites? That is, maybe Jehovah was explaining that "Never before have I showed myself to anyone in your dispensation, the Jaredite dispensation."

Of course these six possibilities are not mutually exclusive—that is, more than one or all of them could be true.

I long for the day when we may be allowed to see the whole of the story of the Jaredite nation and to learn more about the brother of Jared and the depth of his faith. In speaking to Moroni, the Savior declared that "in that day that [men and women] shall exercise faith in me, . . . even as the brother of Jared did, that they may become sanctified in me, then will I manifest unto them the things which the brother of Jared saw, even to the unfolding unto them all my revelations" (Ether 4:7). What a promise! What a motivation to live in such a manner that we might enjoy the constant companionship of the Spirit and thereby qualify to see such grand visions in a future day.

# CHAPTER 36

## "My Grace Is Sufficient"

ETHER 12

In reading and studying the Book of Mormon, we are aided immeasurably by those occasions when the writer or compiler inserts himself into the narrative. In fact, some of the most profound precepts of the Book of Mormon come in the form of "And thus we see" or "And thus we can plainly discern." We are blessed particularly by the comments and commentary that Moroni offers in chapter 12 of the book of Ether, a book that he abridged.

This chapter begins with a brief introduction to the prophet Ether, who during the reign of King Coriantumr, testified, prophesied, and warned the Jaredites of impending disaster if they did not repent of their sins. Of Ether, Moroni writes that "he could not be restrained because of the Spirit of the Lord which was in him. For he did cry from the morning, even unto the going down of the sun, exhorting the people to believe in God unto repentance lest they should be destroyed, saying unto them that by faith all things are fulfilled—wherefore, whoso believeth in God might with surety hope for a better world, yea, even a place at the right hand of God." We are told that Ether uttered many prophecies that the people would not believe "because they saw them [the sobering scenes of destruction] not." Moroni then adds a grand principle or precept—that "faith is things which are hoped for and not seen; wherefore, dispute not because ye see not, for *ye receive no witness until after the trial of your faith*" (Ether 12:2–6; emphasis added).

What does it mean to have one's faith "tried"? The word *tried* is of course related to the word *trial.* Men and women go through trials, for example, when they find themselves in conditions that are uncomfortable, dangerous, painful, or frightening. In one sense, then, people undergo a trial of their faith when their faith is tested, when under frightful or even life-threatening conditions, they have to choose to hold fast to that which they believe and know in their hearts. Earlier in the Book of Mormon, the prophet Abinadi was murdered because of his unwillingness to recant his condemnation of King Noah and his wicked priests (see Mosiah 17). Alma and Amulek were thrown into prison for what they believed and taught. They were even required to witness many of the faithful believers being burned to death because of the people's faith (see Alma 14). The two thousand stripling warriors—sons of converted Lamanites who had forsaken warfare and buried their weapons deep in the earth—went to battle under the direction of Helaman, fought courageously, and were spared miraculously. Why? Because of their deep commitment to what they had been taught by their mothers—that if they did not doubt, God would deliver them (see Alma 56:45–48; 57:19–21). And we could go on and on in relating instance after instance in the Book of Mormon and the Bible where women and men stood true and faithful to their beliefs, had their faith tested, and passed the tests.

Another less dramatic but important way that you and I may undergo a trial of our faith is by obeying a command or following the direction of Church leaders when we cannot look into the future and see the outcome or immediately enjoy heaven's blessings for doing so. A simple example would be the payment of tithing; we do not pay tithing with money, but rather *with faith*. We come to know that paying tithing and offerings is the right thing to do by paying them. We gain a testimony of the gospel of Jesus Christ by bearing it. We come to know the blessings associated with living the Word of Wisdom—both temporal and spiritual—by following the divine counsel found in section 89 of the Doctrine and Covenants. Sometimes we are required to "walk to the edge of the light, and perhaps a few steps into the darkness, and [then] find that the light will appear and move ahead of [us]."[1] Jesus said: "If any man will do his [the Father's] will, he shall know of the doctrine, whether it be of God, or whether I speak of myself" (John 7:17). As we discussed in the very first chapter of this book, first we *do*, and then we come to *know*.

There is another grand precept found in chapter 12 of the book of Ether. Moroni seems to become self-conscious about the fact that he and his Nephite associates are much more powerful speakers than writers. "Lord, the Gentiles will mock at these things [the writing within the Book of Mormon], because of our weakness in writing; for Lord thou hast made us mighty in word [speaking] by faith, but thou hast not made us mighty in writing." A few verses later, we read the words of the Lord Jesus Christ to Moroni: "And if men come unto me I will show unto them their weakness. I give unto men weakness that they may be humble; and my grace is sufficient for all men that humble themselves before me; for if they humble themselves before me, and have faith in me, then will I make weak things become strong unto them" (Ether 12:23, 27).

Over the last several years, I have heard some form of the following statements many times: "I don't know why God would give me cancer" or "I cannot understand why God would force me to struggle with diabetes" or "I see no purpose in God cursing me with depression." While there may be times when our Father in Heaven causes a person to suffer to accomplish some divine purpose, I am prone to believe that such instances are rare. When I have expressed my views on this matter, I have occasionally had someone respond quickly with, "But what about the Lord's words in Ether 12:27?" First of all, notice that the word is *weakness*, singular, not *weaknesses*. Yes, if you and I pray to our Father in Heaven to reveal our weaknesses, those places where we fall short or are in need of repentance, He will certainly do so. From my study of the gospel, however, I have concluded that the "weakness" spoken of here is mortality, a fallen, telestial existence. God "gives unto us weakness" in the sense that He places us in a world where we are confronted with our ever-present limitations and circumstances that are tough, painful, distressing, and even tragic.

Challenges, difficulties, or trials are, of themselves, neither good nor bad for us. The key issue is what we choose to do with those painful events in our lives. If we choose to be bitter and antagonistic or to scorn or curse God for "what He has done to me," the result will probably be sad, unfortunate, and spiritually counterproductive. On the other hand, if you and I seek the Lord's comfort and strength always, in good times and in bad, He will make known unto us our weakness, meaning our absolute need for divine assistance, our need for His grace. And when we confess to God our inabilities, our limitations, and our utter ineptitude, as well as our total trust in and absolute dependence upon Him, He will gradually transform weakness into strength. When the Apostle Paul pleaded with God to remove his "thorn in the flesh," the Lord said unto him, "My grace is sufficient for thee: for my strength is made perfect in weakness. Most gladly therefore will I rather glory in my infirmities [my weakness], that the power of Christ may rest upon me. . . . For when I am weak, then am I strong" (2 Corinthians 12:7, 9–10).

To believe and teach that God always gives us our problems and challenges could eventually lead us to believe He is responsible for wars, natural disasters, physical and sexual abuses, murders, terrorist attacks, and holocausts. As Latter-day Saints, however, we don't believe that the sovereignty of God means that He is responsible for everything that takes place on earth, including traumas and disasters.

Christ's remark to Moroni that *His grace is sufficient* seems closely related to Nephi's teachings that the followers of our Lord must *rely "wholly upon the merits of him who is mighty to save"* (2 Nephi 31:19; emphasis added). This is also similar to what Moroni wrote concerning persons who had accepted the gospel and come into the Church of

Jesus Christ: "And after they had been received unto baptism, and were wrought upon and cleansed by the power of the Holy Ghost, they were numbered among the people of the church of Christ; and their names were taken, that they might be remembered and nourished by the good word of God, to keep them in the right way, to keep them continually watchful unto prayer, *relying alone upon the merits of Christ, who was the author and the finisher of their faith*" (Moroni 6:4; emphasis added).

Some years ago, I became acquainted with a wonderful Christian gentleman, the late Professor J. I. Packer, a British scholar who was one of the great theological minds in Evangelical Christianity. Dr. Packer wrote that "in many respects, and certainly in spiritual matters, we are all weak and inadequate, and we need to face it. . . . We need to be aware of our limitations and to let this awareness work in us humility . . . and a realization of our helplessness on our own. Thus we may learn our need to depend on Christ, our Savior and Lord, at every turn of the road, to practice that dependence as one of the constant habits of our heart, and thereby to discover what Paul discovered before us: 'when I am weak, then am I strong' (2 Corinthians 12:10)."[2]

Stephen Robinson and I were once invited to meet with three leaders of the Southern Baptist Convention for a doctrinal discussion in Kansas City. For the first couple of hours, the conversation was pleasant and productive in terms of coming to better understand one another. We had been discussing the Atonement of Jesus Christ for a while when one of them said, rather harshly, "The problem with you folks [Latter-day Saints] is that you have no concept of grace. You think you can save yourselves if you work hard enough!" Steve had, of course, authored the bestselling book *Believing Christ*, and I had written a couple of books on the same subject. We looked at each other quizzically and began to explain what we do believe regarding the goodness and mercy and grace of the Lord. One of them then responded with: "Yes, you have a rather strange concept of grace; you believe in the 'Christ of the gaps'; you believe that what you should do is to work yourselves into glory and, if you should fall short of the requirements of heaven, Jesus will step up and cover the difference. He is the Christ of the gaps."

We spent about a half hour attempting to disabuse our new friends of their misunderstanding of what the scriptures of The Church of Jesus Christ of Latter-day Saints actually teach. We left on fairly good terms and made our way to the airport. All the way to the airport and on much of the way home, we discussed this "Christ of the gaps" notion and wondered how we or other Latter-day Saints might have led others to think we believe in this false idea. We read passage after passage in the Book of Mormon about the grace of God and, of course, could find nothing in that sacred volume that would give such an impression.

We also came away with a strong desire to teach the Atonement of Jesus Christ and the powerful and burden-lifting doctrine of the grace of God in a more effective way. Persons of other faiths who listen to us or read what we write need to know what we really do believe—that salvation or eternal life is free, the greatest of all the gifts of God (see 2 Nephi 2:4; 26:23–27; Doctrine and Covenants 6:13; 14:7); that our good works are a necessary but an insufficient condition for salvation; and that we keep the commandments of God in an effort to express our love and our undying gratitude for all that the Father, Son, and Holy Ghost have done for us.[3] Members of our Church, as well as other followers of Jesus, must know that we have faith in the Lord Jesus Christ—that is, we trust Him totally. We have complete confidence in Him. And we rely wholly upon Him. Indeed, His grace is sufficient for us.

# CHAPTER 37

# "Search Diligently in the Light of Christ"

## MORONI 7

The prophet Mormon spoke in a synagogue, a place of worship, on faith, hope, and charity, and his son Moroni shares his father's marvelous teachings with us in chapter 7 of Moroni. Mormon begins by addressing himself to the members of the Church of Jesus Christ "that are the peaceable followers of Christ, and that have obtained a sufficient hope by which ye can enter into the rest of the Lord, from this time henceforth until ye shall rest with him in heaven" (Moroni 7:1, 3). Here Mormon refers to the "rest of God." This expression is used in two different ways.

First, there is the rest enjoyed by those who have received the gift of the Holy Ghost and are striving to walk in the light of the Lord. In speaking to the Saints and the world about "overcoming the world," President Russell M. Nelson pleaded with us to "find rest from the intensity, uncertainty, and anguish of this world by *overcoming* the world through your covenants with God. Let Him know through your prayers and your actions that you are serious about overcoming the world. Ask Him to enlighten your mind and send the help you need. Each day, record the thoughts that come to you as you pray, then follow through diligently. Spend more time in the temple, and seek to understand how the temple teaches you to rise above this fallen world."[1]

Notice in verse 3 of Moroni 7 that Mormon also speaks of a time when we "shall rest with him in heaven." At the time of death, the faithful enter into paradise, the abode of righteous spirits, in "a state of happiness, . . . a state of peace, where they shall rest from all their troubles and from all care, and sorrow" (Alma 40:13). There, they will "expand in wisdom" and "have respite from all their troubles, . . . where care and sorrow do not annoy."[2] In speaking of ancient Israel, a modern revelation states that they "hardened their hearts and could not endure [Jehovah's] presence; therefore, the Lord in his wrath, for his anger was kindled against them, swore that they should not enter into his rest while in the wilderness, *which rest is the fulness of his glory*" (Doctrine and Covenants 84:24; emphasis added). "I judge these things of you," Mormon adds, "because of your peaceable walk with the children of men" (Moroni 7:4). What a marvelous insight is here—entering into the rest of God will affect how we interact with our neighbors, how we see them and feel about them, how we yearn to assist them and strengthen them.

In Moroni 7:13, Mormon puts forward a simple principle that has profound and long-range implications: "That which is of God inviteth and enticeth to do good continually; wherefore everything which inviteth and enticeth to do good, and to love God, and to serve him, is inspired of God." This passage is basically speaking of what we know as spiritual discernment, which helps us to determine if a person or an enterprise is worthy of our time and attention or if it is a primary or a secondary concern. Verse 16 speaks of the "Spirit of Christ," what most of us know as the Light of Christ. This light is "given to every man [and woman], that [they] may know good from evil; wherefore, I show unto you the way to judge; for every thing which inviteth to do good, and to persuade to believe in Christ, is sent forth by the gift and power of Christ; wherefore ye may know with a perfect knowledge it is of God."

What exactly is this Light or Spirit of Jesus Christ? Elder Bruce R. McConkie wrote: "The light of Christ . . . is the agency of God's power and the law by which all things are governed. It is also the agency used by the Holy Ghost to manifest truth and dispense spiritual gifts to many people at one and the same time (Moroni 10:17). For instance, it is as though the Holy Ghost, who is a personage of spirit, was broadcasting all truth throughout the whole universe all the time, using the light of Christ as the agency by which the message is delivered. But only those who attune their souls to the Holy Spirit receive the available revelation. It is in this way that the person of the Holy Ghost makes his influence felt in the heart of every righteous person at one and the same time."

Elder McConkie also observed that the Light of Christ "has neither shape nor form nor personality. It is not an entity nor a person nor a personage. It has no agency, does not act independently, and exists not to act but to be acted upon. . . . It is the power of God who sitteth upon his throne. It may be that it is also priesthood and faith and omnipotence, for these too are the power of God."[3]

Stephen R. Covey once remarked in a Brigham Young University devotional: "I believe that what the scientist calls nature is the Spirit of Jesus Christ. I believe that what [many in the Christian world] call God is the Spirit of Jesus Christ. And perhaps this is what all religions call God. . . . I believe that what the humanist would call decency and what a man on the street would call common sense is the Spirit of Jesus Christ."[4]

Mormon continues: "Seeing that ye know the light by which ye may judge, which light is the light of Christ, see that ye do not judge wrongfully. . . . Wherefore, I beseech of you . . . that ye should *search diligently in the light of Christ* that ye may know good from evil" (Moroni 7:18–19; emphasis added). How, exactly, does one "search diligently in the light of Christ"? Perhaps among other things, Mormon is essentially encouraging the members of the Church of Jesus Christ to (1) rid themselves of distracting and destructive influences that might cloud their eternal perspective; (2) spend more time in prayer, meditation, and thoughtful reflection on things of greatest worth; (3) listen carefully and hearken to our consciences, being particularly attentive to that "inner voice" that is the Spirit of Jesus Christ; and (4) act according to what they feel and know to be the right and proper course.

In speaking of the blessings that can come to us as we "search diligently in the light of Christ," President Dieter F. Uchtdorf stated: "If you open your mind and heart to receive the Light of Christ and humbly follow the Savior, you will receive more light. Line upon line, here a little and there a little, you will gather more light and truth into your souls until darkness has been banished from your life. God will open your eyes. God will give you a new heart. God's love, light, and truth will cause dormant things to spring to life, and you will be reborn into a newness of life in Christ Jesus."[5]

In the latter part of Moroni 7, Mormon speaks of faith, hope, and charity. In the scriptures, to have faith in Christ is to have total trust in Him, complete confidence in Him, and a ready reliance upon Him; our faith is all about Jesus Christ. To have hope is to have an anticipation, an expectation, an assurance that through my faith in Christ I will gain eternal life (see Moroni 7:40–42); hope is about me and my standing before God. When we come to verses 45–47 of Moroni 7, we read words, beautiful words, that seem very familiar, words found in chapter 13 of 1 Corinthians. How do we explain these almost identical expressions about the gift of charity and the truly charitable person? In an address delivered just months before his death, Elder Bruce R. McConkie stated: "Both Paul and Mormon expounded with great inspiration about faith, hope, and charity, in many verses using the same words and phrases. . . . It does not take much insight to know that both Mormon and Paul had before them the writings of some Old Testament prophet on the same subjects."[6]

In verse 47 of Moroni 7, Mormon defines charity as "the pure love of Christ," possibly meaning (1) Christ's pure love for us, (2) our pure love of Christ, and (3) our pure love for others. Verse 48 teaches a profound principle: interestingly, we are not told to "pray with all the energy of heart" for charity so that we can then be motivated to love and serve others, as important as that is. Rather, Mormon counsels readers to "pray unto the Father with all the energy of heart, that ye may be filled with this love, which he hath bestowed upon all who are true followers of his Son, Jesus Christ." Notice that this love is a bestowal, a spiritual endowment, a gift. Now attend to what follows: "that ye may become the sons [and daughters] of God; that *when he [Jesus Christ] shall appear, we shall be like him*, for we shall see him as he is; that we may have this hope; that we may be purified even as he is pure" (emphasis added).

"The Savior asks us to learn of Him and do the things we have seen Him do," Sister J. Anette Dennis of the General Relief Society Presidency reminded us (see 3 Nephi 27:21–22). "He is the embodiment of charity, of pure love. *As we incrementally learn to do what He asks of us*—not out of duty or even for the blessings we might receive but purely out of love for Him and our Heavenly Father (see Matthew 22:37–39)—*His love will flow through us and make all that He asks not only possible but eventually much easier and lighter* (see Mosiah 24:15) *and more joyful than we could ever imagine.* It will take practice; it could take years, as it has for me, but as we even desire to have love be our motivating force, He can take that desire (see Alma 32:27), that seed, and eventually turn it into a beautiful tree, full of the sweetest fruit (see Alma 32:41)."[7] Charity, or the pure love of Christ, sanctifies our souls and makes us just like the Prototype of all saved beings—the Lord Jesus Christ.[8]

CHAPTER 38

# The Innocence of Little Children

MORONI 8

Without a proper understanding of the life and ministry of Jesus Christ or of the breadth and depth of His atoning sacrifice, there are many things that we will never understand. One of these matters is the status and worthiness of little children. Misunderstanding on this particular doctrine dates some 1,800 years before the Lord's birth. As Nephi is taught by an angel in 1 Nephi 13, many plain and precious truths and many covenants of the Lord were taken away or kept back from the Bible by evil and designing persons. The Joseph Smith Translation of the Bible (JST) restores a great many truths that were discarded or lost during the centuries of the Bible's transmission.

We learn some fascinating things from the JST of chapter 17 of Genesis. "And it came to pass, that Abram fell on his face, and called upon the name of the Lord. And God talked with him, saying, *My people have gone astray from my precepts, and have not kept mine ordinances*, which I gave unto their fathers; and they have not observed mine anointing, and the burial, or baptism wherewith I commanded them; but have turned from the commandment, and *taken unto themselves the washing of children, and the blood of sprinkling; and have said that the blood of righteous Abel was shed for sins; and have not known wherein they are accountable to me*" (JST, Genesis 17:3–7; emphasis added). What a fascinating restoration this is—an insight into an apostate practice and belief afloat in the days of Father Abraham. The people had begun to baptize children, which demonstrates that they were either ignorant or purposefully corrupt.

But what is this strange reference to Abel, the son of Adam and Eve? It seems that some people living in the days of Abraham had come to believe that the blood of Abel, shed by his brother Cain, had cleansing and redemptive powers. Clearly these people misunderstood the doctrine of the Savior's Atonement and the whole question of accountability. Understanding these matters helps us make sense of what is a rather enigmatic passage in the New Testament: "But ye are come unto mount Zion, and unto the city of the living God, the heavenly Jerusalem, and to an innumerable company of angels, to the general assembly and church of the firstborn, which are written in heaven and to God the judge of all, and to the spirits of just men made perfect." Now here is the odd verse: "And to Jesus the mediator of the new covenant, and to the blood of sprinkling, *that speaketh better things than that of Abel*" (Hebrews 12:22–24; emphasis added). In other words, the blood of Jesus Christ far transcends the blood of Abel when it comes to forgiveness, sanctification, and salvation.

The practice of infant baptism was introduced in Christianity in the second and third centuries AD. It arose because of another related misunderstanding—that because of the "original sin" of our first parents, humans inherit the effects of that original sin (this belief is what often leads to the doctrine of human depravity), and thus it is necessary to baptize children very early, even in infancy. Interestingly, in the New World, Mormon condemns infant baptism some time between AD 400 and 421. Note the sobering words Mormon uses in Moroni 8 to describe this false practice: gross error (verse 6); solemn mockery (verses 9, 23); perversion of the ways of the Lord (verse 16); awful wickedness (verse 19); denial of the mercies of Christ (verse 20); practice that avails nothing (verse 22). Mormon boldly states further: "Behold I say unto you, that *he that supposeth that little children need baptism is in the gall of bitterness and in the bonds of iniquity*; for he hath neither faith, hope, nor charity; wherefore, *should he be cut off while in the thought, he must go down to hell*" (verse 14; emphasis added).

Why such strong language? What is it about little children that makes the practice of infant baptism so corrupt? Note what is said by the Lord and by Mormon about children: the whole need no physician (verse 8); little children are whole and not capable of committing sin (verse 8); the curse of Adam is taken from them through Christ (verse 8); parents should humble themselves, as their little children (verse 10); little children do not need repentance or baptism (verse 11); all children are alive in Christ (verses 12, 19, 22); little children are all alike and partakers of salvation (verse 17).

The knowledge that there is no original sin, that Adam and Eve's transgression is not inherited by every person born on earth, was taught from the very beginning of time. The prophet Enoch wrote of a conversation between Father Adam and God. Adam inquired: "Why is it that men must repent and be baptized in water? And the Lord said unto Adam: Behold, *I have forgiven thee thy transgression in the Garden of Eden.* Hence came the saying abroad among the people, that *the Son of God hath atoned for original guilt, wherein the sins of the parents cannot be answered upon the heads of the children*, for they [children] are whole from the foundation of the world" (Moses 6:53–54; emphasis added).

The doctrine of the innocence of children was taught much earlier among the Nephites. In about 124 BC, after speaking of the condescension of Jesus Christ (what the Christian world calls the Incarnation), King Benjamin teaches powerfully about the Lord's atoning sacrifice, including that the Son of God would sweat blood from every pore, "so great shall be his anguish for the wickedness and the abominations of his people." King Benjamin goes on to explain that salvation comes through faith on the Lord Jesus Christ, although many of His day would consider Him to be a mere human "and say that he hath a devil, and shall scourge him, and shall crucify him." Benjamin continues to prophesy that Jesus would rise from the dead on the third day after His death and stand to judge the world (Mosiah 3:5–10). But note what King Benjamin says in verse 16: "And even if it were possible that little children could sin they could not be saved." Wait a minute. What are we missing? Why couldn't children be saved if they sinned? The verse could be repeated this way: "And even if it were possible that little children could sin, they could not be saved *if there was no Atonement of Christ.*" Benjamin helps clarify by saying, "But I say unto you they are blessed; for behold, *as in Adam, or by nature, they fall, even so the blood of Christ atoneth for their sins*" (emphasis added).

Benjamin is declaring that all people on earth, including children, are subject to the effects of the Fall of Adam and Eve. While you and I are not *responsible* for what happened in Eden and are not *accountable* for their partaking of the forbidden fruit, we certainly are affected by the Fall. We are affected physically, spiritually, mentally, and emotionally, but we are not accountable for or depraved because of the Fall. Benjamin is teaching here that little children are innocent. But why are they innocent? Is it because they are sweet and kind and unselfish or that they are ever willing to share their toys and never whine or pout? Are they innocent by nature? No, the Book of Mormon is very clear: little children are declared innocent as one of the unconditional benefits of the Savior's atoning sacrifice. They are innocent by virtue of Christ's redemption.

We might add here that the prophet Abinadi, in discussing the breadth and depth of Christ's redemption, speaks powerfully about the First Resurrection, the resurrection of the just, which will include "the resurrection of all the prophets, and all those that have believed in their words, or all those that have kept the commandments of God." Abinadi also adds to the list of those who will come forth in the First Resurrection: "And little children also have eternal life" (Mosiah 15:18–25).

The doctrine of the innocence of little children has come through loud and clear in the dispensation of the fullness of times, confirming what is taught in the Book of Mormon. In a revelation given through Joseph Smith the Prophet in June 1829, we read: "You must preach unto the world, saying: You must repent and be baptized, in the name of Jesus Christ; for all men must repent and be baptized, and not only men, but women, and *children who have arrived at the years of accountability*" (Doctrine and Covenants 18:41–42; emphasis added).

In a revelation received in September 1830, Christ spoke: "I say unto you, that little children are redeemed from the foundation of the world through mine Only Begotten; wherefore, *they cannot sin, for power is not given unto Satan to tempt little children, until they begin to become accountable before me*" (Doctrine and Covenants 29:46–47; emphasis added). Put simply, "Little children are holy, being sanctified through the atonement of Jesus Christ" (Doctrine and Covenants 74:7). And from Joseph Smith's vision of the celestial kingdom, we learn that "all children who die before they arrive at the years of accountability are saved in the celestial kingdom of heaven" (Doctrine and Covenants 137:10).

Some Nephite prophets saw the future (see Mormon 8:35; 9:30) and could sense that their words and teachings, particularly concerning the Savior's Atonement and the related concept of accountability, would prove extremely valuable to the followers of the Savior in the latter days. Because of their prescience, they included seminal teachings on the Atonement of our Lord and the reach of that Atonement to all of God's children, including and particularly, little children.

## CHAPTER 39

# Reflections on Moroni's Promise

MORONI 10

In the last chapter of the Book of Mormon, it seems as though Moroni, sensing that his work with the gold plates will soon be over, focuses on things that he feels matters most (as did his father in Mormon 7). In many ways, chapter 10 of Moroni summarizes some of the most crucial teachings in the Book of Mormon.

The words of verses 6 and 7 should sound familiar: "And whatsoever thing is good is just and true; wherefore, nothing that is good denieth the Christ, but acknowledgeth that he is." This passage is essentially a restatement of what Mormon taught in Moroni 7 (see verses 10–17). Moroni was taught well, and he learned well. I want to comment on something that I did not mention in our earlier discussion of chapter 7. Verse 16 of Moroni 7 has been particularly important to me as I have been involved in interfaith relations during the last thirty years. Let's restate the verse: "For behold, the Spirit of Christ [or the Light of Christ] is given to every man, that he may know good from evil; wherefore, I show unto you the way to judge; for *every thing which inviteth to do good, and to persuade to believe in Christ, is sent forth by the power and gift of Christ; wherefore ye may know with a perfect knowledge it is of God*" (emphasis added). Can we see what is being said here? I have no doubt whatsoever that The Church of Jesus Christ of Latter-day Saints is the custodian of the fullness of the gospel of Jesus

Christ; that the keys of the kingdom of God rest with those we sustain as prophets, seers and revelators; and that the Church is in very deed the restoration of first-century Christianity. My expression of testimony does not mean, however, that light and truth and goodness are not to be found in other Christian and non-Christian faiths.

Regarding this subject, Elder B. H. Roberts of the First Council of the Seventy, one of the great self-taught doctrinal minds in our history, made a very significant statement: "While the Church of Jesus Christ of Latter-day Saints is established for the instruction of men; and is one of God's instrumentalities for making known the truth, yet he is not limited to that institution for such purposes, neither in time nor place. *God raises up wise men . . . of their own tongue and nationality, speaking to them through means that they can comprehend; not always giving a fulness of truth such as may be found in the fulness of the gospel of Jesus Christ; but always giving that measure of truth that the people are prepared to receive.* . . . Wherever God finds a soul sufficiently enlightened and pure, one with whom his Spirit can communicate, lo! he makes of him a teacher of men."[1]

Similarly, Elder Orson F. Whitney of the Quorum of the Twelve Apostles, in speaking of persons not of our faith, stated: "Perhaps the Lord needs such men on the outside of His Church to help it along. They are among its auxiliaries, and can do more good for the cause where the Lord has placed them, than anywhere else. . . . Hence, some are drawn into the fold and receive a testimony of the truth, while others remain unconverted . . . , the beauties and glories of the [restored] gospel being veiled temporarily from their view, for a wise purpose. The Lord will open their eyes in His own due time." Elder Whitney then delivered this particularly poignant message: "God is using more than one people for the accomplishment of His great and marvelous work. The Latter-day Saints cannot do it all. It is too vast, too arduous for any one people. . . . We have no quarrel with [those of other faiths]. They are our partners in a certain sense."[2] These statements require us to broaden our scope and expand our minds to acknowledge that our

Heavenly Father loves all of His children and wants them to have as much light and truth as they are prepared to receive.

In verses 7–8 of Moroni 10, Moroni repeats a message that had been delivered by Lehite prophets for hundreds of years—a plea for women and men not to deny the power of God or the gifts of God. And then, to emphasize the importance of this plea, Moroni lists various spiritual gifts, gifts that are given by a gracious God for the benefit of individuals and to aid the growth and expansion of the Church of Jesus Christ. The gifts Moroni mentions include the gift of teaching both wisdom and knowledge (verses 9–10); the gift of faith and the gifts of healing and working mighty miracles (verses 11–12); the gift of prophecy (verse 13); the gift of the ministering of angels (verse 14); and the gift of tongues and the interpretation of tongues (verses 15–16). Moroni adds a significant point here: "And all these gifts come by the Spirit of Christ; and they come unto every man severally, according as he will" (verse 17).

Moroni next repeats some of what his father had taught about faith, hope, and charity. "And except ye have charity ye can in nowise be saved in the kingdom of God; neither can ye be saved in the kingdom of God if ye have not faith; neither can ye if ye have no hope." Moroni then adds this sobering principle: "And if ye have no hope ye must needs be in despair; and despair cometh because of iniquity. . . . And now I speak unto all the ends of the earth—that if the day cometh that the power and gifts of God shall be done away among you, it shall be because of unbelief," meaning a lack of faith (Moroni 10:21–22, 24).

Because of the great importance of verses 3–5 in Moroni 10, I have saved our discussion of them for the end of this chapter. These verses are among the most beloved and well-known passages in all of Latter-day Saint literature and serve as a kind of summary statement for the entire Book of Mormon. Thousands upon thousands of young full-time missionaries memorize these verses before they memorize anything else. Everyone who investigates the message of the Restoration is invited to read and ponder over these verses and to follow their instructions; these verses set forth how a person is to gain a testimony of the truthfulness of the Book the of Mormon.

In verse 2, Moroni indicates: "And I seal up these records [the gold plates], after I have spoken a few words by way of exhortation unto you." The exhortation he delivers has to do with the Book of Mormon and the ratifying power of God's Holy Spirit. "Behold, I would exhort you that when ye shall read these things, *if it be wisdom in God that ye should read them* . . ." Let's pause here. Why would it not be wisdom in God for everyone to receive these things? I believe this is Moroni's way of saying, "If the Lord orchestrates events such that you encounter the Book of Mormon and the Restoration," or "If the time comes that you have an opportunity to receive and read the Book of Mormon . . ." He goes on to exhort us that "when ye shall read these things, if it be wisdom in God that ye should read them, that ye would *remember how merciful the Lord hath been unto the children of men*, from the creation of Adam even down until the time that ye shall receive these things, and *ponder it in your hearts*" (verse 3; emphasis added). So what is it the reader is to ponder? We may be quick to reply, "The truthfulness of the Book of Mormon."

Well, that's certainly necessary for one to gain a testimony, but is that specifically what Moroni is exhorting us to ponder on? I sense that Moroni is instructing us to *remember how merciful God has been to His children.* If we reflect seriously and genuinely on how merciful our Father has been through the ages, how good and kind He is to His children, we will realize how merciful He is to us in placing in our hands "Another Testament of Jesus Christ" and how merciful and eager He is to answer our prayers concerning its truthfulness and its vital importance.

Then follows Moroni's instructions to ask God, in the name of our Savior, if the things that are taught within this book of books is true. What does it mean for the Book of Mormon to be true? It means, first, that it is an actual historical and religious history of a group of Israelites who left Jerusalem some six hundred years before the coming of Christ and came to ancient America. But it is much more than a history. "While it chronicles a people for a thousand and twenty-one years," President Boyd K. Packer explained, "and contains the record of an earlier people [the Jaredites], it is in fact not a history of a people. *It is the saga of a message, a testament.*"[3]

Second, for the book to be true, the people within it must be real, actual people from a real time. That is, there must have been a real person named Nephi or Abinadi or Alma or Captain Moroni or Samuel the Lamanite. Third, for the Book of Mormon to be true, Jesus the Christ, the living Son of the living God, resurrected and glorified, needs to have visited and taught and ordained this group of American Hebrews in the New World some months following His Crucifixion and Resurrection in the Old World. Fourth, for the Book of Mormon to be true, the sermons and writings within it must teach the truth.

Moroni promises any and all readers that "if ye shall ask with a sincere heart, with real intent, having faith in Christ, he will manifest the truth of it unto you, by the power of the Holy Ghost" (verse 4). Individuals who really want to know if the Book of Mormon is indeed holy scripture must be genuine, must be sincere. Very few people who test the Book of Mormon's truthfulness by doing everything possible to prove it untrue will gain a witness. A person must have what might be called "a willing suspension of disbelief" before the book's truth can be discerned. It is far more valuable to begin one's test of the Book of Mormon's truthfulness by asking questions like the following: Is it possible that this book is actually another testament of Jesus Christ? Could it be a companion to the Holy Bible? Could any man write this book?

Finally, let's spend a moment on verse 5: "And by the power of the Holy Ghost ye may know the truth of all things." I once heard a Sunday School teacher quote verse 5 and say, essentially, "If you want to know and understand the depth and breadth of chemistry or physics or astronomy, you can do so by the power of the Holy Ghost." Well, the Spirit can certainly assist us in our study of any subject, but is this what Moroni has in mind here? I don't think so. I believe Moroni is saying that, in the same way that you and I or any of God's children can come to know of the truthfulness of the Book of Mormon, we can know or discern or perceive the truthfulness or untruthfulness of any matter, written or unwritten, and whether it is worthy of our time and attention. We can, by the power of the Holy Spirit, discern whether this teaching or that practice is of God, of man, or of the devil. In this sense, we can "know the truth of all things."

CHAPTER 40

# "Come unto Christ and Be Perfected"

MORONI 10

On the last page of the Book of Mormon, Moroni delivers this invitation, charge, and assurance to any and all who read his words: "Yea, come unto Christ, and be perfected in him, and deny yourselves of all ungodliness; and if ye shall deny yourselves of all ungodliness, and love God with all your might, mind, and strength, then is his grace sufficient for you, that by his grace ye may be perfect in Christ; and if by the grace of God ye are perfect in Christ, ye can in nowise deny the power of God" (Moroni 10:32). This one verse teaches that we simply cannot perfect ourselves; perfection, wholeness, or integrity of character cannot be acquired through our own unaided labors, no matter how many good deeds we perform or how faithful we try to be. Perfection comes by and through Jesus the Christ, the only truly perfect person to walk the earth.

What does it mean to "come unto Christ"? It means to look to Him; recognize who He is and what He has done; turn to Him for forgiveness and comfort; lean on Him; and rely wholly upon Him—upon His merits, mercy, and grace (see 2 Nephi 2:8; 31:19). Coming unto Christ means to study His life and His teachings and to seek to apply the principles He taught to embody the righteousness of which He spoke. It means to strive to imitate Him and His life, to emulate Him, to move from admiration to adoration. It is to confess Him in private and in public as the Son of God, the Only Begotten of the Father. It means to make Him the only Lord and Master of our lives.

To deny yourself of all ungodliness is, to use Alma's unusual words to his son Corianton, to "cross yourself" (Alma 39:9)—to resist evil, to go against or defy the natural man or woman, to thwart your carnal nature, to resist the pull of the fallen man. Denying ourselves of ungodliness is to choose the path of obedience and faithfulness. It is to "take up [our] cross," as the Savior declared (Matthew 16:24). Elder Ulisses Soares of the Quorum of the Twelve Apostles taught, "We learn through the scriptures that those who wish to take their cross upon themselves love Jesus Christ in such a way that they deny themselves of all ungodliness and of every worldly lust and keep His commandments (see JST, Matthew 16:25–29). Our determination to cast off all that is contrary to God's will and to sacrifice all we are asked to give and to strive to follow His teachings will help us to endure in the path of Jesus Christ's gospel—even in the face of tribulation, the weakness of our souls, or the social pressure and worldly philosophies that oppose His teachings."[1]

Lasting and permanent change can come only by a miraculous intervention from God. "I can to some extent control my acts," C. S. Lewis pointed out, but "I have no direct control over my temperament. And if . . . what we are matters even more than what we do—if indeed, what we do matters chiefly as evidence of what we are—then it follows that the change which I most need to undergo is a change that my own direct, voluntary efforts cannot bring about. . . . I cannot, by direct moral effort, give myself new motives. After the first few steps in the Christian life we realize that everything which really needs to be done in our souls can be done only by God."[2]

Near the end of His powerful instructions to His Apostles in the upper room, only hours before His sufferings and death, Jesus said: "I am not alone, because the Father is with me. These things I have spoken unto you, that in me ye might have peace." Then comes this deeply consoling truth: "In the world ye shall have tribulation: but *be of good cheer; I have overcome the world*" (John 16:32–33; emphasis added). Indeed, Jesus overcame the tribulation, the trials, the taunts, and the turmoil. He faced head-on the insults, the insolence, and the profound injustice. President Russell M. Nelson testified that "because Jesus Christ overcame this fallen world, and because He atoned for each of us, you too can overcome this sin-saturated, self-centered, and often exhausting world. . . .

"You can overcome the spiritually and emotionally exhausting plagues of the world, including arrogance, pride, anger, immorality, hatred, greed, jealousy, and fear. Despite the distractions and distortions that swirl around us, you can find true *rest*—meaning relief and peace—even amid your most vexing problems. . . . What does it mean to overcome the world? It means overcoming the temptation to care more about the things of this world than the things of God. It means trusting the doctrine of Christ more than the philosophies of men. It means delighting in truth, denouncing deception, and becoming 'humble followers of Christ' [2 Nephi 28:14]. It means choosing to refrain from anything that drives the Spirit away. It means being willing to 'give away' even our favorite sins [Alma 22:18]. . . .

"Overcoming the world is not an event that happens in a day or two. It happens over a lifetime as we repeatedly embrace the doctrine of Christ. We cultivate faith in Jesus Christ by repenting daily and keeping covenants that endow us with power. We stay on the covenant path and are blessed with spiritual strength, personal revelation, increasing faith, and the ministering of angels. . . . As we strive to live the higher laws of Jesus Christ, our hearts and our very natures begin to change. The Savior *lifts* us above the pull of this fallen world by blessing us with greater charity, humility, generosity, kindness, self-discipline, peace, and *rest*."[3]

We take the sacrament each week and covenant that we will "always remember [the Savior], that [we] may have his Spirit to be with [us]" (Moroni 5:2; Doctrine and Covenants 20:79). In order to always remember Him, *we need to think about Him more often*—about who He is, what He taught, how He ministered to others, what He has done for us, and how very much He and His Eternal Father love us. Elder Jeffrey R. Holland declared: "Most people in trouble end up crying, 'What was I thinking?' Well, whatever they were thinking, *they weren't thinking of Christ.* . . . So *let us work a little harder at remembering Him*—especially that He has 'borne our griefs, and carried our sorrows . . . ; [that] he was bruised for our iniquities . . . ; and with his stripes we are healed' [Isaiah 53:4–5]. . . . If we do sin, however serious that sin may be, we can be rescued by that same majestic figure, He who bears the only name given under heaven whereby *any* man or woman can be saved [see Acts 4:12]."[4]

We are "made perfect" by and through Jesus Christ. That wholeness will come to us by trusting in Him and His promises. It will come to us through relying and drawing upon His infinite and eternal atoning sacrifice. During His final meal with His beloved Apostles, Jesus taught: "I am the way, the truth, and the life: no man cometh unto the Father, but by me" (John 14:6). The Son of God does not merely point the way; He is the Way! Jesus does not simply tell us the truth; He is the Truth! Our Lord not only extends to us His life; He is the Life! Even in the midst of a darkening world, at a time when wickedness abounds on every side, we must have hope. We must rejoice. We must never believe the lies that issue forth from the father of lies.

Our lives are made up of hundreds of thousands of choices. "We have the ability to choose whom we follow," Elder Paul V. Johnson of the Seventy pointed out. "When we follow Satan, we give him power. When we follow God, He gives us power." He went on to speak of being made perfect only through Jesus Christ. "Following every suggestion in every self-help book in the world will not bring it about. There is only one way and one name whereby perfection comes. We are 'made perfect through Jesus the mediator of the new covenant, who wrought out this perfect atonement through the shedding of his own blood' (Doctrine and Covenants 76:69). Our perfection is only possible through God's grace."[5]

"The Atonement of Jesus Christ is at the heart of our message!"

President M. Russell Ballard said to the women of the Church. "It is our core value. It is our doctrinal center. It is the heart and soul of The Church of Jesus Christ of Latter-day Saints. *If you have not yet felt the truth and power of the Savior's Atonement in your life, I invite you to refocus on the central message of the Restoration—a message declaring that we can be 'made perfect through Jesus the mediator of the new covenant, who wrought out this perfect atonement through the shedding of his own blood'* (Doctrine and Covenants 76:69; emphasis added). Sisters [and brothers], please do whatever is necessary to stay focused on the simple and central message of the Restoration. Accept it. Understand it. Embrace it. Love it. Share it. Defend it."[6] This is the strait path, the gospel path, the covenant path, by which we become a holy people.

As readers of the Book of Mormon know, at the very end of the Nephite-Jaredite record, Moroni bears a powerful testimony of the Lord Jesus Christ. He also affirms in a very sober and persuasive manner the truthfulness of the messages contained in the Book of Mormon. He does what a number of the major writers in the book do—he bears witness that "the time speedily cometh that you shall know that I lie not, for ye shall see me at the bar of God; and the Lord God will say unto you: Did I not declare my words unto you, which were written by this man, like as one crying from the dead, yea, even as one speaking out of the dust?" (Moroni 10:27; emphasis added). Only seven verses later, in the very last verse in the Book, Moroni bears witness one final time: "And now I bid unto all, farewell. I soon go to rest in the paradise of God, until my spirit and body shall again reunite, and I am brought forth triumphant through the air, to meet you before the pleasing bar of the great Jehovah, the Eternal Judge of both quick and dead. Amen" (Moroni 10:34; emphasis added).

## CONCLUSION

# The Transformative Power of the Book of Mormon

We are given little indication in the biblical record that the prophet-writers delivered and preserved their messages for any day other than their own. To be sure, such prophets as Isaiah, Jeremiah, Ezekiel, Daniel, Malachi, Peter, Paul, John, and others spoke of the distant future; by the power of the Spirit, they saw and described the doings of peoples of another time and place. While their words were given to the people of their own time, their writings have and will yet find application and fulfillment both now and in the future. And yet we never see a particular prophet from the Bible address himself directly to those who will one day read his pronouncements.

How very different is the Book of Mormon. It was prepared and preserved by seers, those who saw things not visible to the natural eye (see Moses 6:36), who wrote and spoke to us; they saw and knew our day and addressed themselves to specific issues that a people in the last days would confront. The poignant words of Moroni alert us to the contemporary relevance of the Book of Mormon: "Behold, I speak unto you as if ye were present, and yet ye are not. But behold, Jesus Christ hath shown you unto me, and I know your doing" (Mormon 8:35). Later Moroni said: "Behold, I speak unto you as though I spake from the dead; for I know that ye shall have my words" (Mormon 9:30). President Ezra Taft Benson taught that the Book of Mormon "was written for our day. *The Nephites never had the book; neither did the Lamanites of ancient times. It was meant for us.* Mormon wrote near the end of the Nephite civilization. Under the inspiration of God, who sees all things from the beginning, he abridged centuries of records, choosing the stories, speeches, and events that would be most helpful to us."[1]

I love the Bible. I have taught the Old and New Testaments for half a century, and I find great joy in doing so. These testaments contain numerous witnesses of our Lord and Savior. I cherish the Doctrine and Covenants, glory in its plain and pure doctrinal pronouncements and clarifications, and feel a deep sense of gratitude and thanksgiving for this "capstone" of our religion.[2] The Pearl of Great Price is exactly what its name implies—it is worth more than silver and gold. It is an inspired collection of some of the distinctive points of Latter-day Saint doctrine. It bears a powerful witness of Christ's eternal gospel, of the restoration in the last days, and of the divine calling of the Prophet Joseph Smith.

These holy books are true, and they are inspired. They come from God. In an interesting sort of way, however, the Book of Mormon has a spirit all its own. "Something powerful happens when a child of God seeks to know more about Him and His Beloved Son," President Russell M. Nelson declared. "Nowhere are those truths taught more clearly and powerfully than in the Book of Mormon. . . . I've made lists of what the Book of Mormon *is*, what it *affirms*, what it *refutes*, what it *fulfills*, what it *clarifies*, and what it *reveals*. Looking at the Book of Mormon through these lenses has been an insightful and inspiring exercise! I recommend it to each of you. . . . When I think of the Book of Mormon, I think of the word *power*. The truths of the Book of Mormon have the *power* to heal, comfort, restore, succor, strengthen, console, and cheer our souls."[3]

The Book of Mormon is far more than just another theological treatise, more than a collection of great doctrinal sermons. (It would be worth its weight in gold, even if that was all it was!) It is not just a book that helps us *feel good*; it is a heavenly document that has been given to help us *be good.* It is as though the Nephite prophet-leaders are beckoning and pleading to us from the dust: "We sought for the Lord. We found him. We applied the gospel of Jesus Christ and have partaken of its sweet fruits. We know the joy of our redemption and have felt to sing the song of redeeming love. And now, O reader, go and do likewise!" The Book of Mormon is of course an invitation to come unto Christ, but it is also a pattern and roadmap for how to achieve that consummate privilege. This invitation is extended to all humankind, the rank and file as well as the prophets and apostles.

The Book of Mormon does more than teach with plainness and persuasion the effects of the Fall and the absolute necessity for the blessed Atonement of Jesus Christ. It cries out to us that unless we acknowledge our fallen state, put off the natural man, apply the atoning blood of Christ, and be born again, we can never be like or live with our Lord. Nor can we ever hope to establish Zion, a society of the pure in heart. Stated differently, this book is not just another book *about* religion. It *is* religion. Our challenge, therefore, is not just to read and study the Book of Mormon; *we must live it and accept it and apply the very points of its doctrine* (see 1 Nephi 15:14).

As both a bishop and a stake president, I have worked closely with members of the Church who have struggled with their faith or been involved in serious transgression. In some cases, I have asked members to read significant portions of the Book of Mormon and to prepare to discuss the teachings found therein with me. One incident in particular comes to mind. While serving as a stake president, one of my bishops spoke with me at some length about a young man in his ward, a returned missionary. He described the situation as "strange." He mentioned that the man had come into his office, made the comment that he was guilty of some "pretty serious stuff" but that he had no intention of discussing specifics with the bishop. The bishop asked if he would be willing to speak with me as the stake president, and he replied: "Sure. I'll talk with him, but I won't be confessing any sins!"

Several days later, the young man had been in my office for only a matter of moments before I could see that pride and self-assurance dripped from him; he was brash and cocky. We chatted for a bit, and I asked him if he was ready to discuss his transgressions with me. He simply replied, "Nope." I said, "That's too bad, because I had a few things I wanted you to do that I think would have really blessed your life, but it's obvious that you're not prepared for that." He came right back with, "What do you mean I'm not prepared? What did you want me to do?"

I replied: "I wanted you to read the Book of Mormon, but I'm pretty sure you won't get out of it what you need." He responded, "Look, I read the Book of Mormon twice on my mission." I said, "Well, that's fine, but I wanted you to come at the book a little differently." "Like what?" he inquired. I looked him in the eyes and said: "I challenge you to read the entire Book of Mormon in two weeks. I don't want you to mark anything—just read and think carefully about everything you read. Could you handle something like that?" There was a pause of about thirty seconds before he spoke up: "Okay. I'll do it." I said, "Good. I'll see you right here two weeks from tonight."

Boy, did I do some serious praying and fasting during those two weeks! The impression to have him do a very serious reading of the Book of Mormon had come to me in the first fifteen minutes of our interview. But then my mind conceived of all kinds of disastrous scenarios that could take place. Well, the two weeks passed, and he came into my office. I didn't say anything for the first few moments, and he didn't either. I then asked if he had read the entire Book of Mormon. He nodded his head affirmatively but remained silent. I let a few more moments pass without saying anything but then asked: "What are you feeling right now?" He said, "I had a really different experience than what I thought I would have." "What do you mean?" I asked. Tears came to his eyes, and he replied: "I think I want to talk about some of my problems."

He did so, for the next hour or so. He unburdened his heart, confessed his sins, and left my office a new man. He began to work closely with his bishop, repented sincerely, and within a few months had a light in his countenance that hadn't been there for some time. More than once as a priesthood leader I have had this kind of experience, where a serious study of the Book of Mormon proved to be spiritually therapeutic—where hearts were touched, contrition followed, and eventually forgiveness and peace came. Why would the Book of Mormon affect this young man in so profound a way? "The Book of Mormon provides the fullest and most authoritative understanding of the Atonement of Jesus Christ to be found anywhere," President Russell M. Nelson declared. "It teaches what it really means to be born again. . . . These and other truths are more powerfully and persuasively taught in the Book of Mormon than in any other book. *The full power of the gospel of Jesus Christ is contained in the Book of Mormon.*"[4]

Elder Ronald A. Rasband of the Quorum of the Twelve Apostles spoke of his own experience with the Book of Mormon as a young missionary. "There was much more to my reading [of the book] than just marking scriptures. With each reading of the Book of Mormon, front to back, I was filled with a profound love for the Lord. I felt a deeply rooted witness of the truth of His teachings and how they apply to 'this day.' This book fits the title, 'Another Testament of Jesus Christ.' With that study and the spiritual witness that was received, I became a Book of Mormon missionary and a disciple of Jesus Christ."[5]

In the generations following the planting of the Lehite colony in America, leader after leader, prophets and kings, came and led this branch of Israel in truth and righteousness. Though they were inspired by a singular cause, their styles and their approaches to leadership no doubt varied. One thing, however, one symbol and type, remained constant. The military leaders among the Nephites wielded the sword of Laban in defense of their people. That sword was a sign, an ensign, a banner, and an ever-present reminder that only through the Lord's divine assistance can individuals or nations be delivered from their enemies. It stood for something else as well—the price to be paid for scriptural and thus spiritual literacy. The Nephites needed the plates of brass to preserve their language and their religious integrity. There was, however, an impediment—a wicked man who blocked the way. God thus commanded that this man's blood be shed so that Nephi could obtain the sacred record (see 1 Nephi 4). The scriptures are always bought with a price.

And so it is with the Book of Mormon itself. Too much effort has been expended over too many centuries, too much blood has been shed, too many tears have watered the pillows, and too many prayers have ascended to the ears of our Heavenly Father; too great a price has been paid for the Book of Mormon record to be destroyed. Or discarded. Or ignored. No, it must not be ignored, either by the Latter-day Saints (the present custodians of the stick of Joseph) or by a world that desperately needs its message and transforming power. No less than God Himself has borne solemn witness of the Book of Mormon. To Oliver Cowdery, who was raised up to serve as the principal scribe in the book's translation, the Lord affirmed: "I tell thee, that thou mayest know that there is none else save God that knowest thy thoughts and the intents of thy heart. I tell thee these things as a witness unto thee—that *the words or the work which thou hast been writing are true*" (Doctrine and Covenants 6:16–17; emphasis added; compare 18:2). The Almighty set His own seal of truthfulness upon the Nephite record by an oath when He said: "And he [Joseph Smith] has translated the book, even that part which I have commanded him, and *as your Lord and your God liveth it is true*" (Doctrine and Covenants 17:6; emphasis added).

So here we are today. In compliance with prophetic mandates, millions of Latter-day Saints across the world search and pray and teach each day from the Book of Mormon. Many Saints are finding answers to their questions and solutions to their problems. Many have begun to understand, as a result of their study of Restoration scripture, some of the more difficult passages in the Bible. Many have begun to feel that subtle but certain transforming influence that flows from the Book of Mormon—they have begun to sense its sanctifying power. Theirs is a greater yearning for righteousness and the things of the Spirit, a heightened sensitivity to people and feelings, and a corresponding abhorrence for the sins of the world. Many have come to the point where they honestly and truly desire to maintain an eye single to the glory of God (see Doctrine and Covenants 88:67–68).

The day is within reach when the Lord's words—as found in the Book of Mormon—will, in the words of Nephi, "hiss forth unto the ends of the earth for a standard unto [the Lord's] people, which are of the house of Israel (2 Nephi 29:2). The covenant people of the Lord who are scattered among the nations will respond to that voice from the dust that speaks with a familiar spirit. Multitudes of our Father's children will gather to Christ, to the doctrine of Christ, to Christ's Church and kingdom, and thereafter to the congregations of the Saints wherever they reside. All nations will, as the ancients foresaw, gather to the mountain of the Lord's house (see Isaiah 2:2–3; 2 Nephi 12:2–3)—to the stakes of Zion to receive the covenants and ordinances of the holy temple—in preparation for the establishment of the New Jerusalem. And the Book of Mormon will play an integral role in that process (see Moses 7:60–62).

It is my conviction that our minds and hearts can be shaped by the Book of Mormon, by its lessons and logic, testimony and transforming power. It can provide us with the judgment and discernment that is so essential to perceiving the false doctrines of the world as well as those matters that are downright irrelevant. When we abide by the precepts taught in the Book of Mormon, we will gradually begin to acquire faith like the ancients, the faith that strengthens resolve and provides courage and peace in a time of unrest. So much of the anxiety, fear, apprehension, exhaustion, and doubt that now exists in society is so very unnecessary; we can have the right to that lifting and liberating Spirit that produces hope and peace and rest. We need not walk in darkness at noonday or traverse the path of life in twilight when we can instead bask in the bright light of the Son.

The scriptures testify that perilous times lie ahead before the Son of Man will set His foot upon this earth to reign as King of kings and Lord of lords. Before the Savior comes in glory, it is absolutely essential that those who call themselves after Christ's name and seek to acquire the divine nature stand and remain in holy places. Only the sanctified—those Saints who have yielded their hearts unto God and who, like God, have come to abhor sin (see Helaman 3:35; Alma 13:12)—will be able to withstand the taunting and pull of the worldly wise who beckon and belittle from the great and spacious building. I am convinced that the Book of Mormon will be one of the few mainstays to which we can rivet ourselves and one of the few constants and standards to which we can hold in a relativistic world. It is holy and solid ground in a world that continues to slide on the sinking sands of secularity, and it is one of the few ensigns around which a weary people can rally in that future day when demons and mischievous mortals join hands to destroy the faithful. Truly, those who "treasure" up the word of the Lord "shall not be deceived" (Joseph Smith—Matthew 1:37).

God has been gracious to me in planting within my heart a testimony of the grand Restoration, which has a tangible and solid evidence of its truthfulness—namely, the Book of Mormon. I know that this book is the word of God and that the Lord God is its author. It speaks peace and joy to my soul. It is a quiet, steadying influence in my life. My day is not complete until I have read at least a few chapters. Reading it is like coming home. It is a gift of God that we are expected to receive, understand, and experience. I feel a deep sense of kinship with its writers, particularly Mormon and Moroni. I know that they are as concerned now with what is done with their book than they were when they etched their messages onto the gold plates some sixteen centuries ago. I know, by the whisperings of the Holy Ghost to my soul, that the Almighty expects us to read and teach from the Book of Mormon and to devote significant time to considering and applying the doctrine and principles it contains.

President Russell M. Nelson taught that "as you prayerfully study the Book of Mormon *every day*, you will make better decisions—*every day*. I promise that if you ponder what you study, the windows of heaven will open, and you will receive answers to your own questions and direction for your own life. I promise that as you daily immerse yourself in the Book of Mormon, you can be immunized against the evils of the day."[6]

God grant that we might be wise in the day of our probation. May He strengthen us in our sacred care and keeping of the timely and timeless Book of Mormon. Having done all we can to read it, study it, understand it, teach it, testify of it, and live according to its precepts, we can then rest our souls everlastingly with our Father in Heaven and His Son, Jesus Christ, together with those who paid such a dear price to preserve and bring forth this precious book.

APPENDIX 1

# Powerful Precepts from the Book of Mormon

"Anyone who has done much reading," Elder Neal A. Maxwell said, "finds himself grateful for books that contain two or three significant truths or great ideas. Sometimes we gladly settle for articulate restatement or rephrasings. . . . Thus the density of the spiritual truths of the Book of Mormon is especially impressive."[1]

The following is merely a sample of the great doctrinal treasures to be found in the Book of Mormon. These are doctrinal gems. Careful reflection on these truths will edify many and astonish others. Those with an asterisk (*) are distinctive teachings within the Book of Mormon.

1. God will always provide a way for His children to accomplish whatever He commands them (1 Nephi 3:7).
2. Very often we are led by the Spirit, not knowing beforehand the things we should do (1 Nephi 4:6).

*3. Israel is "grafted in" as they come to the knowledge of the true Messiah (1 Nephi 10:14).

*4. The Holy Ghost, or Spirit of the Lord, is in the form of a man (1 Nephi 11:11).

*5. The tree of life is a symbol of Jesus Christ (1 Nephi 11: 4–7, 21–22).

6. Jesus is the God of Abraham, Isaac, and Jacob (1 Nephi 19:10).
7. Salvation is free (2 Nephi 2:4; 26:25, 27–28).
8. We are saved through the merits, mercy, and grace of the Holy Messiah (2 Nephi 2:8; Helaman 14:13).

*9. In a sense, all of God's children will be redeemed. Following the Resurrection, all are brought back into the presence of God to be judged (2 Nephi 9:15; Helaman 14:15–18).

*10. The ordinances of salvation, including baptism, are essential (2 Nephi 31).

*11. The doctrine of Jesus Christ, or gospel of Christ, consists of faith, repentance, baptism, reception of the Holy Ghost, enduring to the end, resurrection, and eternal judgment (2 Nephi 31; 3 Nephi 27).

*12. Israel is scattered when it rejects the true Messiah. Israel is gathered whenever it accepts the true Messiah, His gospel, His Church, and His doctrine (1 Nephi 15:12–19; 2 Nephi 6:8–11; 9:1–2; 10:5–7; 15).

*13. The Fall of Adam and Eve is as much a part of the plan of salvation as is the Atonement of Jesus Christ. "Adam fell that men might be, and men are, that they might have joy" (2 Nephi 2:25).

*14. Joseph Smith is the foreordained "choice seer" in the last days (2 Nephi 3).

15. The Atonement of Christ is infinite because it overcomes physical death and brings to pass the resurrection of all men and women (2 Nephi 9:6–15).

16. If there were no Resurrection, there would be no Atonement; we would all be subject to Satan forever (2 Nephi 9:8–9).

*17. We are to worship God the Father in the name of Jesus Christ (2 Nephi 25:16; Jacob 4:5).

18. Satan is versatile. With some of us, he rages in our hearts and stirs us up to anger against the things of God. Others he pacifies and lulls away into a state of carnal security: they perceive that "all is well in Zion" (2 Nephi 28:20–24).

*19. Those who are truly built on the rock of Christ are eager for new revelation, even new scripture (2 Nephi 28–29).

*20. Remission of sins comes after baptism by immersion and through the conferral of the Holy Ghost; the Holy Ghost is the Sanctifier (2 Nephi 31:17).

21. The members of the Godhead are so united that they are occasionally referred to as "one eternal God" (2 Nephi 31:21; Alma 11:44; 3 Nephi 11:23–25; Mormon 7:7).

*22. People speak with the tongue of angels when they speak the words of Christ—that is, when they speak by the power of the Holy Ghost (2 Nephi 31:13–14; 32:1–5).

*23. True disciples *experience* Christ—they believe in Him, view His death, suffer His cross, and bear the shame of the world (Jacob 1:8).

24. Before we seek for riches, we should seek for the kingdom of God. After we have obtained a hope in Christ, we will obtain riches if we seek them, and we will seek them so that we may clothe the naked, feed the hungry, liberate the captive, and administer relief to the sick and afflicted (Jacob 2:18–19).

*25. Christ and his Atonement have been preached since the beginning of time (Jacob 4:5; 7:11; Jarom 1:11; Alma 39:17–19).
*26. Spiritual darkness comes by looking beyond the mark (Jacob 4:14).
27. God has an everlasting love for His chosen people; He simply will not let Israel go (Jacob 5–6).
*28. We become unshaken in the faith as we have regular spiritual experiences (Jacob 7:5; Enos 1:2–11).
29. We are eternally indebted to God and, even if we should serve God with all the faculties we possess, we would still be unprofitable servants (Mosiah 2:20–25).
30. The natural man is an enemy to God and to himself (Mosiah 3:19; Alma 41:11).
*31. We know that we have been forgiven of our sins when the Spirit dwells with us once again, and when we feel joy and peace of conscience (Mosiah 4:3).
*32. When we are born again, we become the sons and daughters of Jesus Christ (Mosiah 5:7).
*33. Jesus Christ is designated as the Father and the Son—the Father because He was conceived by the power of the Father, and the Son because of the flesh, His physical body (Mosiah 15:1–4; Alma 11:38–39; Helaman 14:12; Mormon 9:12; Ether 3:14).
*34. The First Resurrection will include the prophets and those who heeded their words (Mosiah 15:21–22).
*35. At the time of baptism, we covenant to bear one another's burdens, mourn with those that mourn, comfort those who stand in need of comfort, stand as witnesses of God at all times and in all places; in addition, we take upon us the name of Christ (Mosiah 18:8–10).
36. The Lord can lighten the burdens we bear without removing the burdens from us (Mosiah 24:13–14).
37. When we are born again, we are changed from a carnal and fallen state to a state of righteousness; we become "new creatures" in Christ (Mosiah 27:23–26).
38. The only way to reclaim some who have wandered or left the faith is to bear pure testimony (Alma 4:19).
39. Christ came to earth to experience all that every other mortal experiences—pains, afflictions, temptations, sicknesses, and infirmities—so that He could empathize and thus succor His people (Alma 7:11–13).
*40. All those who receive the Melchizedek Priesthood in this life were foreordained to do so in the premortal existence (Alma 13:1–12).
41. We become persons of sound understanding and are able to teach the

gospel with power and authority as we search the scriptures, pray, and fast (Alma 17:1–3).

*42. Predestination is a false doctrine (Alma 31).

43. Faith is not to have a perfect knowledge but rather to have hope for things that are not seen but are true (Alma 32:21).

*44. The Atonement of Christ is infinite because Jesus Christ is an infinite being (Alma 34:13–14).

45. This life is the time to prepare to meet God, the time for men and women to perform their labors (Alma 34:32).

*46. The same spirit we have at the time of our death will continue with us as we go into the post–mortal spirit world (Alma 34:33–35).

47. By small and simple means great things are brought to pass (1 Nephi 16:29; Alma 37:6).

*48. The only sins more serious to God than sexual immorality are murder and the sin against the Holy Ghost (Alma 39:5).

*49. At the time of death, one experiences a partial judgment and either goes to paradise or to hell/outer darkness (Alma 40:11–14).

50. In the Resurrection, the body and the spirit will be reunited, and the body will be raised in its perfect form (Alma 11:43; 40:23).

51. Wickedness never was happiness; this is what is known as the law of restoration (Alma 41).

52. Mercy cannot rob justice (Alma 42:12–15).

*53. We are sanctified by yielding our hearts to God (Helaman 3:35).

54. We must build our foundation on the rock of our Redeemer if we wish to withstand the onslaught of the devil (Helaman 5:12).

55. Those who seek all their days to be happy while caught up in iniquity will find that their destruction is made sure (Helaman 13:38).

56. The offering we are to make to God is a broken heart and a contrite spirit (3 Nephi 9:20).

*57. When the fullness of the times of the Gentiles comes, the gospel will then be taken on a preferential basis to the house of Israel (3 Nephi 16:10–12).

58. When we take the sacrament of the Lord's Supper, we take the emblems into our soul; that soul will never hunger nor thirst but will always be filled (3 Nephi 18:4–9).

*59. The sign that the work of the Father (the work of gathering Israel) has commenced in the last days is the coming forth of the Book of Mormon (3 Nephi 21:1–7; 29:1; Ether 4:17).

*60. Those who reject the Lord's latter-day servant (Joseph Smith) will be cut off from the Lord's covenant (3 Nephi 21:11).

61. Jesus expounded all the scriptures in one (3 Nephi 23:14).

*62. In order for a church to be the Lord's church it must (1) be called after His name and (2) be built on His gospel. Then the works of the Father will be manifest in it (3 Nephi 27:7–10).

63. The gospel is the good news that Christ came into the world to do the will of the Father and to be lifted up on the cross that He might draw all men unto Him, that they might be raised from the dead and then stand before Him to be judged (3 Nephi 27:13–16).

64. Only those whose garments have been washed clean in the blood of the Lamb can enter the kingdom of God and enter into his rest (3 Nephi 27:19–20).

*65. Translated beings are changed so that they do not experience death or the pains of this life (except sorrow for the sins of the world). They remain in a translated state until the Second Coming of Jesus Christ, at which point they are changed in the twinkling of an eye from mortality to resurrected immortality (3 Nephi 28).

66. True and lasting happiness comes as people are converted to the Lord; they then deal justly with one another and look to the needs of their neighbors. Such persons are made truly free and become partakers of the heavenly gift (4 Nephi 1:2–3).

67. Sorrow that does not lead to repentance is merely the sorrowing of the damned—people simply cannot find happiness in sin (Mormon 2:13).

68. There is an awful fear of death that fills the breasts of the wicked (Mormon 6:7).

69. The eternal purposes of the Lord will roll on, until all His promises are fulfilled (Mormon 8:22).

70. God has not ceased to be a God of miracles (Mormon 9:15, 19–20).

71. We have been charged to do all things in worthiness and to do them in the name of Jesus Christ (Mormon 9:29).

72. Although, because of the Fall, our natures have become evil, we have been commanded to call upon God, and we will receive according to our desires (Ether 3:2).

*73. We should not dispute God's word simply because we cannot see, for we receive no witness until after the trial of our faith (Ether 12:6).

74. If we come unto Christ, He will make known unto us our weakness; if we have faith in Him then He will make weak things become strong unto us (Ether 12:27).

75. Christ laid down His life for the world and went to prepare a place for us; the love that motivated this selfless sacrifice is charity (Ether 12:33–34).

76. If we seek Christ, then the grace of the Father, Son, and Holy Ghost will abide in us forever (Ether 12:41).

*77. We remain spiritually vigilant, watchful unto prayer, through relying alone upon the merits of Christ, who is the author and finisher of our faith (Moroni 6:4).

78. Members of the Church of Jesus Christ are charged to be the peaceable followers of Christ who have sufficient hope to enter into the rest of the Lord here, in preparation for entering into His rest hereafter (Moroni 7:3).

*79. The Spirit of Christ is given to every person that they may know good from evil. Everything that invites to do good and to believe in Christ is sent forth by the gift and power of Christ and is of God (Moroni 7:16).

*80. Angels have not ceased to minister to the children of God. They are subject to Christ and minister to those who have strong faith and a firm mind. The office of their ministry is to call people to repentance, first by declaring the word of Christ to the chosen vessels, who then minister to the rest of humankind (Moroni 7:29–31).

81. Miracles cease and angels do not minister only when faith has ceased also (Moroni 7:36–37; 10:24).

82. Charity is the pure love of Christ and endures forever. We are to pray unto the Father with all the energy of our hearts to be filled with this love, which the Father always bestows upon all who are true followers of his Son. By and through the transforming power of this love, we will be like Him when He appears, and we will see Him as He is (Moroni 7:47–48).

*83. Infant baptism is a false doctrine and a wicked practice, for baptism is only for those who have faith and require repentance, those who are accountable. Since little children are redeemed from the foundation of the world, they are innocent (Moroni 8:10–12).

84. It does not matter how bleak a situation may appear to be or how wicked the world may become; we have a labor to perform while we are in this mortal condition—namely, to conquer the enemy of all righteousness and rest our souls in the kingdom of God (Moroni 9:6).

85. By the power of the Holy Ghost we may know the truth of all things (Moroni 10:5).

*86. We must never deny the gifts of God or gifts of the Spirit; they are given for our profit (Moroni 10:8–18).

87. If we deny ourselves of all ungodliness and love God with our whole soul, then His grace is sufficient for us, so that by that grace we become perfected and sanctified in Christ (Moroni 10:32–33).

APPENDIX 2

# A Topical Study of the Book of Mormon

1. Divine Attributes of God
    - He is from eternity. (Mosiah 3:5; Moroni 7:22)
    - His knowledge and passions (1 Nephi 19:12; 2 Nephi 9:17–20; Jacob 4:8–10; Words of Mormon 1:7; Alma 7:13; 13:3, 7; 18:32; 26:35; Mormon 8:17)
    - He prepares the way for His servants. (1 Nephi 3:7; 9:5–6; 17:50–51)
    - Those who are righteous are favored of God. (1 Nephi 17:35–40)
2. The Godhead: the Father and the Son
    - Separate personages (1 Nephi 10:4; Mosiah 2:34; Alma 12:33–34; 33:11–17; Helaman 5:10–11; Mormon 7:5; Moroni 4:3 [5:2])
    - Worship of and prayer to the Father (2 Nephi 25:16, 28–29; 32:9; Jacob 4:5; 3 Nephi 18:19–20; Ether 4:15; Moroni 8:3; 10:4)
    - Jesus Christ as both the Father and the Son (Mosiah 3:8; 15:1–5; 16:15; Alma 11:26–39; 3 Nephi 1:14; Ether 3:14; 4:12)
3. The Godhead: The Holy Spirit
    - Forever the same (1 Nephi 10:17–19, 22)
    - The Light of Christ or Spirit of Jesus Christ (Moroni 7:12–19, 22–27; 10:17)
    - The Holy Ghost is in the form of a man. (1 Nephi 11:10–11)
    - Baptism by fire (2 Nephi 31:10–15; 32:1–5; Helaman 5:28–50; 3 Nephi 9:20)
    - When the Spirit ceases to strive (1 Nephi 7:14; 2 Nephi 26:11; Mormon 5:16; Ether 2:15; Moroni 8:28; 9:4)
4. Revealed Knowledge vs. Human Knowledge

- God's grand perspective (Jacob 4:8–13; compare 1 Corinthians 1:18–2:16)
- The wisdom of man (1 Nephi 2:12 [cf. Jude 1:10]; 2 Nephi 9:28–29; 28:4–6, 14, 31; Mosiah 12:26–27; Helaman 16:13–22)
- Man's refusal to seek light and truth (2 Nephi 32:4, 7; Mosiah 8:20; 26:1–4)
- Man's sign seeking (Jacob 7:11–20; Alma 30:43, 48)
- The anti-Christ (Jacob 7:1–23; Alma 1:2–15; 30:6–18, 24–28, 37–56, 60)
- The parable of the paths (1 Nephi 8:1–38; 11:7, 20–23, 25, 35–36; 12:16–18; 15:21–24, 26–30, 36)
- Gospel prerequisites (Alma 11:21–22; 12:8–11)
- How revelation comes (Jacob 7:8–12; Enos 1:1–12; Alma 5:43–48; 17:1–4, 9; 18:33–35; 24:8–10; 36:3–4, 25–26 [38:5–6]; Moroni 10:3–7)

5. Pride: The Great Sin
   - The unsteadiness of man (Helaman 12:1–8)
   - The great and spacious building (1 Nephi 8:24–28, 31–34; 11:35–36; 12:18)
   - Unevenness in society (3 Nephi 6:9–16; 24:5; 4 Nephi 1:19–26)
   - Pride in the Church (2 Nephi 28:12–15; Alma 4:4–10; Helaman 3:23–26, 33–36)
   - Contention (Alma 1:19–24; 3 Nephi 11:28–30)
   - A false doctrine of election (Alma 31:12–25)
   - The antidote (2 Nephi 9:28–29, 42; Mosiah 3:19; 4:9–12; Alma 37:33; 38:13–14; Helaman 3:35; 6:5; Moroni 8:10)
6. The Nature of Fallen Humanity
   - Adam and Eve's fall (2 Nephi 2:17–25; Alma 12:19–27)
   - Spiritual death (Alma 5:40–42; 12:16, 32; 40:24–26; 42:9; Helaman 14:17–18)
   - Fall and Atonement linked (2 Nephi 2:25–26; 9:6; Mormon 9:10–12)
   - All humankind as lost, fallen, and hardened (1 Nephi 10:4–6; Mosiah 16:3–8; Alma 10:4–6; Alma 34:9; 42:2–10; Helaman 14:16; Ether 3:1–2; compare Psalm 51:5; Moses 6:55)
   - The natural man (Mosiah 3:17–19; Alma 41:11–13; compare 1 Corinthians 2:11–14)
7. Redemption through the Holy Messiah
   - Retroactive nature of the Atonement (Jarom 1:10–12; Mosiah 3:13; 16:5–6; Alma 24:12–13; 39:17–19)

- The gospel or doctrine of Christ (2 Nephi 31; Jacob 7:6; 3 Nephi 11:31–41; 27:13–21)
- The nature of Christ's suffering (1 Nephi 19:7–12; Mosiah 3:5–9; Alma 7:11–13; 3 Nephi 11:9–11)
- Unconditional benefits; salvation of little children (2 Nephi 9:25–26; Mosiah 3:11, 15–18, 20–21; 15:21–25; Moroni 8)
- An infinite Atonement (2 Nephi 9:6–7; 25:15–16; Alma 34:8–14; compare Doctrine and Covenants 76:40–42; Moses 1:31–35)
- Washed in the blood; forgiveness (1 Nephi 12:10–11; Mosiah 4:1–3; Alma 5:21, 27; Ether 13:10–11)
- Sanctification (Alma 5:54; 13:10–12; Helaman 3:35; 3 Nephi 27:19–21)
- Obtaining and Retaining a remission of sins (Mosiah 4:1–3, 11–12; Alma 4:11–14)
- Justice and mercy (2 Nephi 9:45–46; Mosiah 3:23–27; 15:6–9, 27; Alma 10:20–21; 41:14; 42:12–26; 3 Nephi 26:1–5)
- Salvation and perfection by grace (2 Nephi 2:3–9; 10:24–25; 25:23; 31:19; Mosiah 13:27–28; Alma 22:12–14; 24:10–15; Moroni 6:1–4; 10:30–34)

8. Faith unto Life and Salvation
    - The process of faith (Alma 32; 33:19–23; 34:1–5; Helaman 15:5–8)
    - Faith in Christ, forgiveness, and overcoming (Enos 1:5–8; Alma 36:16–22; 37:33; Helaman 5:12; Moroni 7:20–39)
    - Faith like the ancients (Ether 12; compare Hebrews 11)
9. Repentance, Forgiveness, and the Mighty Change of Heart
    - No unclean thing (1 Nephi 10:20–21; 15:34–35; Alma 7:20–21; 11:34–37; Helaman 5:9–10; 3 Nephi 27:19)
    - Sons and daughters of Christ (Mosiah 5:1–7; 14:10; 15:10–19; 27:23–26; Moroni 7:19)
    - Three dramatic illustrations of spiritual rebirth (Mosiah 27:1–26 [Alma 36]; Alma 19:6; 22:15–18)
    - Alma's spiritual checklist (Alma 5)
    - No more disposition to sin (Mosiah 5:1–3; Alma 13:9–12; 19:33)
    - Do not procrastinate; wickedness never was happiness. (Alma 34:30–41; 41:8–13; Helaman 13:38)
    - Repentance and discipline (Mosiah 26:1–39; Moroni 6:5–8; 3 Nephi 18:26–33)
10. Hope in Christ; Charity
    - Hope in Christ (Jacob 2:19; 4:4, 6, 11; Alma 27:27–28; 34:40–41; 58:10–11; Moroni 7:40–44; 9:25–26)
    - The love of God (2 Nephi 4:16–21; 31:19–20; Moroni 7:44–48)

- Faith, hope, and charity (Alma 7:23–24; 13:27–29; Moroni 7:1, 21–26, 37–48; 10:20–22)

11. Miracles and Spiritual Gifts; the Ministry of Angels; Priesthood
    - Spiritual gifts (3 Nephi 29:5–7; Mormon 9:7–10; Moroni 10:6–26, 30)
    - The ministry of angels (Moroni 7:27–32)
    - Priesthood (2 Nephi 5:26; 6:2; Jacob 1:18–19; Alma 4:20; 5:44; 6:8; 13:1–19; 43:2; 49:29–30; Helaman 8:18)
12. Service, Sacrifice, and Consecration
    - Serving others and serving God (Jacob 2:17–19; Mosiah 2:17; 4:16–27; Alma 1:26–31)
    - Consecration (3 Nephi 26:17–21; 4 Nephi 1:1–3, 15–18)
13. The Book of Mormon on Scripture
    - Spiritual literacy (1 Nephi 3:19–20; 4:11–16; Omni 1:17)
    - The brass plates (1 Nephi 5:10–19; 13:19–23; Mosiah 1:3–5; Alma 37:1–12)
    - The Bible (1 Nephi 13:19–42; 14:18–30; Mormon 7:8–9)
    - The Book of Mormon and modern scripture (2 Nephi 3:10–12; 27:6–23; 29:1–14; 33:10–11; Ether 3:21–28; 4:4–17
    - The record of the lost tribes (2 Nephi 29:12–14)
14. God's Covenant with Israel
    - Scattering and gathering (Title page; 1 Nephi 10:11–14; 15:12–20; 17:36–40; 19:13–19; 2 Nephi 6:4–13; 10:20–22; 21:1–16; 3 Nephi 20:10–13, 24–33)
    - The Lehites (2 Nephi 30:3–8; 33:8; 3 Nephi 15:11–24)
    - Gathering to Christ, His Church, and His doctrine (Title page; 1 Nephi 15:6–20; 2 Nephi 9:1–4; 10:1–12; 25:9–21; 30:3–8; 3 Nephi 5:20–26; Mormon 7:1–10)
    - The Jews (1 Nephi 10:11; 2 Nephi 10:3–8; 25:9–19; 30:1–7; Jacob 4:14–17; 3 Nephi 29:8; Mormon 3:21; 5:12–14)
    - The latter-day and millennial gathering (1 Nephi 22:20–28; 2 Nephi 21:11; 25:17–18; 30:8–18; 3 Nephi 21:1–11, 25–29)
    - The Allegory of Zenos (Jacob 4:13–6:13; compare Romans 11:13–27)
15. Life before Birth; Paradise and Hell; Translation
    - Premortal existence; foreordination (Alma 13:1–5)
    - The postmortal spirit world (2 Nephi 9:8–14; Alma 3:25–26; 34:33–35; 40:6–21; 48:23; Moroni 10:34)
    - Translation (Alma 45:17–19; 3 Nephi 1:1–3; 28 [compare Doctrine and Covenants 7]; 4 Nephi 1:14, 29–33; Mormon 8:9–11; Ether 15:34)

16. Resurrection and Judgment
    - The union of body and spirit; the plan of restoration (2 Nephi 9:3–15; Mosiah 16:6–11; Alma 11:40–45; 40:1–5; 41:1–7)
    - Resurrection and Judgment (2 Nephi 9:15–16; Mosiah 26:22–27; Alma 5:15; 11:40–45; 33:21–22; Helaman 14:14–18; 3 Nephi 27:13–17; Mormon 9:10–14)
    - The First Resurrection (Mosiah 15:21–26; Alma 40:16–26; 3 Nephi 11:13–17; 23:7–13)
17. Because of the Book of Mormon, We Know . . .
    - Great doctrine (Doctrine and Covenants 20:5–12, 17–36; 27:5; 42:12)
    - Salvation itself is at stake. (2 Nephi 25:17–18, 22; 29:11; 33:10–15; Ether 12:38–39; Moroni 10:24–29; Doctrine and Covenants 20:13–15; 84:54–61)
    - The destiny of the Book of Mormon (Moses 7:60–64)

# Notes

## Preface

1. Nelson, "Testimony of the Book of Mormon," *Ensign*, November 1999; emphasis in original.
2. Maxwell, *One More Strain of Praise*, x.
3. Young, in *Journal of Discourses*, 13:56; emphasis added.

## Introduction

1. Benson, "New Witness for Christ," *Ensign*, November 1984.

## Chapter 1: "I Will Go and Do . . . , for I Know"

1. Packer, *"That All May Be Edified,"* 339–40; emphasis in original.
2. Joseph Smith, "Wentworth letter," in *Times and Seasons*, 4:709.

## Chapter 3: The Book of Mormon and the Bible

1. *Teachings of Presidents of the Church: Joseph Smith*, 207.
2. Preface to Doctrine and Covenants 76.
3. Oaks, "Scripture Reading, Revelation, and Joseph Smith's Translation of the Bible," 13.
4. Ballard, "Miracle of the Holy Bible," *Ensign* or *Liahona*, May 2007; emphasis added.

## Chapter 4: "There Are Save Two Churches Only"

1. Roberts, in Conference Report, April 1906, 14–15; emphasis added.
2. Whitney, in Conference Report, April 1928, 59; emphasis added.
3. Packer, "Cloven Tongues of Fire," *Ensign*, May 2000.

## Chapter 5: The Scattering and Gathering of Israel

1. Nelson, in "Hope of Israel," June 3, 2018; emphasis in original.
2. *Teachings of Russell M. Nelson*, 100–101.
3. *Teachings of Presidents of the Church: Joseph Smith*, 416; emphasis added.
4. Nelson, "Children of the Covenant," *Ensign*, May 1995; emphasis added.
5. Nelson, in Bengaluru, India, member meeting, April 19, 2018; *Teachings of Russell M. Nelson*, 130; emphasis in original.
6. Bednar, "Put on Thy Strength, O Zion," *Liahona*, November 2022; emphasis in original.

### Chapter 6: The Merits, Mercy, and Grace of Christ

1. Oaks, *With Full Purpose of Heart*, 75.
2. Uchtdorf, "Gift of Grace," *Ensign* or *Liahona*, May 2015.
3. Maxwell, *Notwithstanding My Weakness*, 9–11; emphasis in original.
4. Craig, "Wholehearted," *Liahona*, November 2022.

### Chapter 7: Life in Eden before the Fall

1. Calvin, *Institutes of the Christian Religion*, Book Second, chaps. 2 and 3.
2 Brunner, *Man in Revolt*, 90.
3. Joseph Fielding Smith, *Doctrines of Salvation*, 1:76–77.
4. *Words of Joseph Smith*, 63.
5. Oaks, "Great Plan of Happiness," *Ensign*, November 1993; emphasis added.

### Chapter 8: The Choice Seer

1. McConkie, *New Witness for the Articles of Faith*, 426.
2. Pratt, in *Journal of Discourses*, 16:38; Taylor, *Mediation and Atonement*, 55; McConkie, *Doctrinal New Testament Commentary*, 1:70–71.
3. Young, in *Journal of Discourses*, 5:332; see also 4:54.

### Chapter 9: Resurrection and Judgment

1. President Brigham Young taught that it was the withdrawal of our Heavenly Father's Spirit that caused Jesus to sweat blood. In *Journal of Discourses*, 3:205–6; see also Holland, "None Were with Him," *Ensign* or *Liahona*, May 2009.
2. Oaks, "Trust in the Lord," *Ensign* or *Liahona*, November 2019; emphasis added.

### Chapter 10: Beware the "Precepts of Men": Evil Attitudes

1. Benson, "The Book of Mormon Is the Word of God," *Ensign*, May 1975.
2. Packer, "On the Shoulders of Giants," February 28, 2004; emphasis added.
3. Hinckley, "Standing Strong and Immovable," January 10, 2004; emphasis added.

### Chapter 11: Beware the "Precepts of Men": Treasuring Every Word of God

1. Maxwell, "Becometh as a Child," *Ensign*, May 1996.
2. Oaks, "Scripture Reading, Revelation, and Joseph Smith's Translation of the Bible," 13; emphasis added.

### Chapter 12: Confronting the Anti-Christs: Sherem and Nehor

1. *Webster's 1828 American Dictionary*, s.v. "flatter."

### Chapter 13: Confronting the Anti-Christs: Korihor

1. *Random House College Dictionary*, s.v. "frenzy."
2. Christofferson, "Truth Endures," January 26, 2018.
3. Nelson, "Love and Laws of God," September 17, 2019.
4. Nelson, "Pure Truth, Pure Doctrine, Pure Revelation," *Liahona*, November 2021.
5. Nelson, "What Is True?" *Liahona*, November 2022.

### Chapter 14: The Sufferings and Death of Christ

1. Oaks, "Sins, Crimes, and Atonement," February 7, 1992; see also *Teachings of Spencer W. Kimball*, 88, 89.
2. Young, in *Journal of Discourses*, 3:206; emphasis added.
3. Holland, "None Were with Him," *Ensign* or *Liahona*, May 2009; emphasis added.
4. *Lectures on Faith*, 5:2; p. 59.
5. Gong, "Happy and Forever," *Liahona*, November 2022; emphasis added.

## Chapter 15: Obtaining and Retaining a Remission of Sins

1. "Joseph Smith's Accounts of the First Vision," The Joseph Smith Papers, JosephSmith Papers.org; "The First Vision," The Church of Jesus Christ of Latter-day Saints, Churchof JesusChrist.org.
2. "Joseph Smith's Accounts of the First Vision"; "The First Vision."
3. Eyring, "Remarks at the Dedication of the First Vision Statue in the Atrium of the Joseph Smith Building, Brigham Young University, 1997"; emphasis added.
4. Bednar, "Always Retain a Remission of Your Sins," *Ensign* or *Liahona*, May 2016; emphasis in original.

## Chapter 16: The Mighty Change of Heart

1. Stott, *Life in Christ*, 109; emphasis added.
2. Benson, "Mighty Change of Heart," *Ensign*, October 1989; emphasis added.
3. Yee, "Beauty for Ashes: The Healing Path of Forgiveness," *Liahona*, November 2022.
4. *Teachings of Presidents of the Church: Joseph Smith*, 471.

## Chapter 17: No Salvation by the Law Alone

1. Joseph Smith, "Account of Meeting and Discourse, 5 January 1841."
2. Joseph Fielding Smith, *Doctrines of Salvation*, 3:85.
3. Skinner, "Law of Moses," 378, 380.
4. McConkie, *Mortal Messiah*, 1:71–72; emphasis added.
5. See Joseph Fielding Smith, *Doctrines of Salvation*, 3:87.
6. See McConkie, *Promised Messiah*, 427.
7. McConkie, "What Think Ye of Salvation by Grace?" 48; emphasis added.

## Chapter 18: Jesus Christ: the Father and the Son

1. "The Father and the Son: A Doctrinal Exposition of the First Presidency and the Twelve," June 30, 1916.
2. See *Lectures on Faith*, 5:2; p. 59.

## Chapter 19: Believe, Then Understand

1. *Teachings of Presidents of the Church: Joseph Smith*, 64; emphasis added.
2. Pratt, *Key to the Science of Theology*, 59–60.
3. Joseph Smith, "Letter to the Church, circa February 1834."
4. Hinckley, *Faith: The Essence of True Religion*, 1, 5–6.

## Chapter 20: "Bearing Down in Pure Testimony"

1. Stevenson, "Nourishing and Bearing Your Testimony," *Liahona*, November 2022.
2. Lee, "Be Loyal to the Royal Within You," 103; emphasis added.
3. Oaks, "Testimony," *Ensign* or *Liahona*, May 2008.
4. *Teachings of Spencer W. Kimball* (1982), 138; emphasis added.
5. Kimball, unpublished address, January 2, 1959.
6. *Teachings of Russell M. Nelson*, 213.
7. Hunter, "Eternal Investments," February 10, 1989, 3.
8. *Teachings of Presidents of the Church: Joseph Smith*, 385.

## Chapter 21: God Grants unto All Nations

1. First Presidency, "God's Love for All Mankind," February 15, 1978.
2. Joseph F. Smith, *Gospel Doctrine*, 31, 395, 398–400; see also *Journal of Discourses*, 15:325.
3. Joseph Smith, in "History, 1838–1856, volume E-1 [1 July 1843–30 April 1844],"

1681; Joseph Smith, "Discourse, 23 July 1843, as Reported by Willard Richards"; see also *Words of Joseph Smith*, 234.
4. Young, in *Journal of Discourses*, 2:139.
5. Young, in *Journal of Discourses*, 7:5.
6. *Autobiography of Peter Cartwright*, 342.
7. Joseph Smith, in "History, 1838–1856, volume E-1 [1 July 1843–30 April 1844]," 1666; Joseph Smith, in "History Draft [1 March–31 December 1843]," 2–3.
8. See Joseph F. Smith, *Gospel Doctrine*, 67–68; McConkie, *New Witness for the Articles of Faith*, 260–61.

### Chapter 22: The Experiment of Faith

1. "We Thank Thee, O God, for a Prophet," *Hymns*, no. 19.
2. Lewis, *Mere Christianity*, 130–31; book 3, chap. 12; emphasis added.
3. Ballard, "Follow Jesus Christ with Footsteps of Faith," *Liahona*, November 2022.

### Chapter 23: "This Life Is the Time"

1. Dahl, "Night of Darkness," 612.
2. Joseph Smith, "Discourse, 20 March 1842, as Published in *Times and Seasons*," 3:751–752.
3. "Improve the Shining Moments," *Hymns*, no. 226.
4. Maxwell, "Why Not Now?" *Ensign*, November 1974.
5. Holland, *To My Friends: Messages of Counsel and Comfort*, 31, 33.

### Chapter 24: Alma's Conversion: A Reason for Hope

1. Andersen, *Divine Gift of Forgiveness*, 3.
2. *Teachings of Presidents of the Church: Joseph Smith*, 76.
3. *Teachings of Spencer W. Kimball*, 252.
4. Holland, "Ministry of Angels," *Ensign* or *Liahona*, November 2008.

### Chapter 25: Doctrinal Counsel to Corianton: Repentance and Forgiveness

1. Joseph Smith, in "Discourse, 7 April 1844, as Reported by Wilford Woodruff," [138]; "History, 1838–1856, volume E-1 [1 July 1843–30 April 1844]," 1976.
2. Joseph Smith, in "History, 1838–1856, volume E-1 [1 July 1843–30 April 1844]," 1921.
3. Holland, "Personal Purity," *Ensign*, November 1998; emphasis added.

### Chapter 26: Doctrinal Counsel to Corianton: Life Hereafter; Justice and Mercy

1. Pratt, in *Journal of Discourses*, 16:365.
2. Cannon, *Gospel Truth*, 58.
3. See Joseph F. Smith, *Gospel Doctrine*, 448–49.
4. Joseph Smith, in "History, 1838–1856, volume D-1 [1 August 1842–1 July 1843]," 1574.
5. Joseph Smith, in "Discourse, 7 April 1844, as Reported by Wilford Woodruff," [138].
6. Wright, *Surprised by Hope*, 151; emphasis added.
7. Joseph F. Smith, "Editor's Table: On the Resurrection," 623–24; see also Joseph F. Smith, *Gospel Doctrine*, 23, 447–48.
8. Joseph Fielding Smith, *Doctrines of Salvation*, 2:293–94.

## Chapter 27: Remember, Remember

1. Holland, devotional address delivered at Brigham Young University, March 2, 1999, in *Trusting Jesus*, 170–77; emphasis added.
2. Andersen, *Divine Gift of Forgiveness*, 47.
3. Pearson, "Are You Still Willing?" *Liahona*, November 2022.

## Chapter 28: The Resurrected Christ Appears and Teaches

1. See Holland, "None Were with Him," *Ensign* or *Liahona*, May 2009.
2. McConkie, "Purifying Power of Gethsemane," *Ensign*, May 1985; emphasis added.
3. See Nelson, "Correct Name of the Church," *Ensign* or *Liahona*, November 2018.
4. Cook, "Eternal Everyday," *Ensign* or *Liahona*, November 2017, citing David Brooks, "Finding a Way to Roll Back Fanaticism," *New York Times*, August 15, 2017, A23.
5. See Joseph F. Smith, *Gospel Doctrine*, 116–17.

## Chapter 29: Called to a Higher Righteousness

1. See, for example, 3 Nephi 12:1; 13:25; 14:1. Joseph Smith referred to the Nephite Twelve as apostles in the Wentworth Letter (see *Teachings of Presidents of the Church: Joseph Smith*, 441). Parley P. Pratt also spoke of the Nephite Twelve as apostles in *Key to the Science of Theology*, 15, 42, 69. See also Moroni 2:2.
2. Lee, *Stand Ye in Holy Places*, 343.
3. Hilton, *Founder of Our Peace*, 48–49; emphasis in original.
4. Bonhoeffer, *Cost of Discipleship*, 176–78; emphasis added.

## Chapter 30: The Praying Savior

1. Hinckley, "Till We Meet Again," *Ensign*, November 2001.
2. *Lectures on Faith* 5:2; pp. 59–60.
3. *Teachings of Presidents of the Church: Joseph Smith*, 42.

## Chapter 31: "This Is My Gospel"

1. Joseph Smith, "Journal, December 1842–June 1844; Book 3, 15 July 1843–29 February 1844," [130] (October 15, 1843); Joseph Smith, in "History, 1838–1856, volume E-1 [1 July 1843–30 April 1844]," 1755.

## Chapter 32: The Mission of the Three Nephites

1. Holland, *Christ and the New Covenant*, 305.
2. Joseph Smith, "Instruction on Priesthood, circa 5 October 1840."
3. Joseph Smith, "Discourse, 3 October 1841, as Published in *Times and Seasons*," 577.
4. Joseph Fielding Smith, *Church History and Modern Revelation*, 192.

## Chapter 33: The Nephite Mini-Millennium

1. Benson, *Witness and a Warning*, 20–21.
2. Young, in *Journal of Discourses*, 11:275.
3. Young, in *Journal of Discourses*, 2:316.
4. Holland, "Greatest Possession," *Liahona*, November 2021; emphasis added.
5. Benson, "Beware of Pride," *Ensign*, May 1989.
6. Cannon, *Gospel Truth*, 71.
7. Cannon, in *Journal of Discourses*, 16:120.

## Chapter 34: Mormon's Distillation of the Book of Mormon

1. Nelson, *Perfection Pending*, 183; emphasis added.
2. *Teachings of Presidents of the Church: Joseph Smith*, 64.

### Chapter 35: "Never Have I Shown Myself"

1. See Ludlow, *Companion to Your Study of the Book of Mormon* (1976), 310.
2. "Jaredites," *Juvenile Instructor*, 27:282.
3. McConkie, "Agency or Inspiration?" *New Era*, January 1975.
4. See Sperry, *Answers to Book of Mormon Questions*, 49.
5. Joseph Fielding Smith, *Doctrines of Salvation*, 1:37; see also McConkie, *Promised Messiah*, 47, 599–600.
6. Lee, "To Be on Speaking Terms with God," October 12, 1973.
7. See Ludlow, *Companion to Your Study of the Book of Mormon*, 318.

### Chapter 36: "My Grace Is Sufficient"

1. Remarks of Harold B. Lee to Boyd K. Packer, in Packer, *Holy Temple*, 184.
2. Packer, *Weakness Is the Way*, 15–16.
3. See Uchtdorf, "Gift of Grace," *Ensign* or *Liahona*, May 2015.

### Chapter 37: "Search Diligently in the Light of Christ"

1. Nelson, "Overcome the World and Find Rest," *Liahona*, November 2022.
2. Joseph F. Smith, *Gospel Doctrine*, 448.
3. McConkie, *New Witness for the Articles of Faith*, 70, 257–58.
4. Covey, "Educated Conscience," 128.
5. Uchtdorf, "Bearers of Heavenly Light," *Ensign* or *Liahona*, November 2017.
6. McConkie, "Doctrinal Restoration," 18.
7. Dennis, "His Yoke Is Easy and His Burden Is Light," *Liahona*, November 2022; emphasis added.
8. *Lectures on Faith* 7:9; pp. 75–76.

### Chapter 39: Reflections on Moroni's Promise

1. Roberts, *Defense of the Faith and the Saints*, 1:512–13.
2. Whitney, in Conference Report, April 1928, 59.
3. Packer, *Let Not Your Heart Be Troubled* (1991), 282; emphasis added.

### Chapter 40: "Come unto Christ and Be Perfected"

1. Soares, "Take Up Our Cross," *Ensign* or *Liahona*, November 2019.
2. Lewis, *Mere Christianity*, 166; book 4, chap. 7.
3. Nelson, "Overcome the World and Find Rest," *Liahona*, November 2022.
4. Holland, "Place No More for the Enemy of My Soul," *Ensign*, May 2010; emphasis added.
5. Johnson, "Be Perfected in Him," *Liahona*, November 2022.
6. Ballard, "Essential Role of Women," *Liahona*, March 2021.

### Conclusion: The Transformative Power of the Book of Mormon

1. Benson, *Witness and a Warning*, 6.
2. Benson, *Witness and a Warning*, 30–31.
3. Nelson, "The Book of Mormon: What Would Your Life Be Like without It?" *Ensign* or *Liahona*, November 2017; emphasis in original.
4. Nelson, "The Book of Mormon: What Would Your Life Be Like without It?"
5. Rasband, "This Day," *Liahona*, November 2022.
6. *Teachings of Russell M. Nelson*, 35; emphasis in original.

### Appendix 1: Powerful Precepts from the Book of Mormon

1. Maxwell, *Plain and Precious Things*, 14.

# Sources


Andersen, Neil L. *The Divine Gift of Forgiveness*. Salt Lake City: Deseret Book, 2019.

Ballard, M. Russell. "The Essential Role of Women." *Liahona*, March 2021.

———. "Follow Jesus Christ with Footsteps of Faith." *Liahona*, November 2022.

———. "The Miracle of the Holy Bible." *Ensign* or *Liahona*, May 2007.

Bednar, David A. "Always Retain a Remission of Your Sins." *Ensign* or *Liahona*, May 2016.

———. "Put on Thy Strength, O Zion." *Liahona*, November 2022.

Benson, Ezra Taft. "Beware of Pride." *Ensign*, May 1989.

———. "The Book of Mormon Is the Word of God." *Ensign*, April 1975.

———. "A Mighty Change of Heart." *Ensign,* October 1989.

———. "A New Witness for Christ." *Ensign*, November 1984.

———. *A Witness and a Warning: A Modern-Day Prophet Testifies of the Book of Mormon.* Salt Lake City: Deseret Book, 1988.

Bonhoeffer, Dietrich. *The Cost of Discipleship*. New York: Macmillan, 1963.

Brunner, Emile. *Man in Revolt: A Christian Anthropology*. Translated by Olive Wyon. Philadelphia: Westminster Press, 1947.

Calvin, John. *Institutes of the Christian Religion*. Book Second. Peabody, MA, 2008.

Cannon, George Q. *Gospel Truth: Discourses and Writings of George Q. Cannon, Two Volumes in One.* Compiled by Jerreld L. Newquist. Salt Lake City: Deseret Book, 1987.

Cartwright, Peter. *Autobiography of Peter Cartwright, the Backwoods Preacher.* Edited by W. P. Strickland. New York: Carlton and Porter, 1856.

Christofferson, D. Todd. "Truth Endures." Address to CES educators, January 26, 2018. ChurchofJesusChrist.org.

Cook, Quentin L. "The Eternal Everyday." *Ensign* or *Liahona*, November 2017.

Covey, Stephen R. "An Educated Conscience." *1975 BYU Speeches of the Year*. Provo, UT: BYU Publications, 1975.

Craig, Michelle D. "Wholehearted." *Liahona*, November 2022.

Dahl, Larry E. "Night of Darkness." In *Book of Mormon Reference Companion*. Edited by Dennis L. Largey. Salt Lake City: Deseret Book, 2003.

Dennis, J. Anette. "His Yoke Is Easy and His Burden Is Light." *Liahona*, November 2022.

Eyring, Henry B. "Remarks at the Dedication of the First Vision Statue in the Atrium of the Joseph Smith Building, Brigham Young University, 1997." Cited in Neil L. Andersen, *The Divine Gift of Forgiveness*. Salt Lake City: Deseret Book, 2019.

"The Father and the Son: A Doctrinal Exposition of the First Presidency and the Twelve,"

June 30, 1916. In *Messages of the First Presidency*. 6 vols. Edited by James R. Clark. Salt Lake City: Bookcraft, 1965–75, 5:26–34.
First Presidency, "God's Love for All Mankind," February 15, 1978.
"The First Vision," The Church of Jesus Christ of Latter-day Saints. ChurchofJesusChrist.org.
Gong, Gerrit W. "Happy and Forever." *Liahona*, November 2022.
Hinckley, Gordon B. *Faith: The Essence of True Religion*. Salt Lake City: Deseret Book, 1989.
———. "Standing Strong and Immovable," Worldwide Leadership Training Broadcast, January 10, 2004.
———. "Till We Meet Again." *Ensign*, November 2001.
Hilton, John, III. *The Founder of Our Peace: Christ-Centered Patterns for Easing Worry, Stress, and Fear.* Salt Lake City: Deseret Book, 2020.
Holland, Jeffrey R. *Christ and the New Covenant: The Messianic Message of the Book of Mormon.* Salt Lake City: Deseret Book, 1997.
———. "The Greatest Possession." *Liahona,* November 2021.
———. "The Ministry of Angels." *Ensign* or *Liahona*, November 2008.
———. "None Were with Him." *Ensign* or *Liahona*, May 2009.
———. "Personal Purity." *Ensign*, November 1998.
———. "Place No More for the Enemy of My Soul." *Ensign* or *Liahona*, May 2010.
———. *To My Friends: Messages of Counsel and Comfort*. Salt Lake City: Deseret Book, 2014.
———. *Trusting Jesus*. Salt Lake City: Deseret Book, 2003.
Hunter, Howard W. "Eternal Investments." Address to CES personnel, February 10, 1989.
*Hymns of The Church of Jesus Christ of Latter-day Saints*. Salt Lake City: The Church of Jesus Christ of Latter-day Saints, 1985.
"Jaredites." *Juvenile Instructor* 27:282.
Johnson, Paul V. "Be Perfected in Him." *Liahona*, November 2022.
"Joseph Smith's Accounts of the First Vision." The Joseph Smith Papers. JosephSmithPapers .org.
*Journal of Discourses*. 26 vols. Liverpool: F. D. Richards, 1851–86.
Kimball, Spencer W. *Teachings of Spencer W. Kimball*. Edited by Edward L. Kimball. Salt Lake City: Bookcraft, 1982.
———. Unpublished address delivered in Los Angeles, January 2, 1959. Cited in H. Stephen Stoker and Joseph C. Muren, *Testimony*. Salt Lake City: Bookcraft, 1980.
*Lectures on Faith*. Salt Lake City: Deseret Book, 1985.
Lee, Harold B. "Be Loyal to the Royal Within You." *1973 BYU Speeches of the Year*. Provo, UT: BYU Publications, 1973.
———. *Stand Ye in Holy Places*. Salt Lake City: Deseret Book, 1974.
———. "To Be on Speaking Terms with God." Address given at the University of Utah Institute of Religion, October 12, 1973.
Lewis, C. S. *Mere Christianity*. New York: Touchstone, 1996.
Ludlow, Daniel H. *A Companion to Your Study of the Book of Mormon.* Salt Lake City: Deseret Book, 1976.
Maxwell, Neal A. "Becometh as a Child." *Ensign*, May 1996.
———. *Notwithstanding My Weakness*. Salt Lake City: Deseret Book, 1981.
———. *One More Strain of Praise*. Salt Lake City: Bookcraft, 1999.
———. *Plain and Precious Things*. Salt Lake City: Deseret Book, 1983.
———. "Why Not Now?" *Ensign*, November 1974.
McConkie, Bruce R. "Agency or Inspiration." *New Era*, January 1975.
———. *Doctrinal New Testament Commentary*. 3 vols. Salt Lake City: Bookcraft, 1965–73.
———. "The Doctrinal Restoration." *The Joseph Smith Translation: The Restoration of Plain and Precious Things*. Provo, UT: BYU Religious Studies Center, 1985.

———. *The Millennial Messiah: The Second Coming of the Son of Man.* Salt Lake City: Deseret Book, 1982.
———. *The Mortal Messiah: From Bethlehem to Calvary.* 4 vols. Salt Lake City: Deseret Book, 1981.
———. *A New Witness for the Articles of Faith.* Salt Lake City: Deseret Book, 1985.
———. *The Promised Messiah: The First Coming of Christ.* Salt Lake City: Deseret Book, 1978.
———. "The Purifying Power of Gethsemane." *Ensign*, May 1985.
———. "What Think Ye of Salvation by Grace?" *Brigham Young University Speeches of the Year*. Provo, UT: BYU Publications, 1984.
McConkie, Joseph Fielding and Robert L. Millet. *Doctrinal Commentary on the Book of Mormon.* 4 vols. Salt Lake City: Bookcraft, 1987–92.
Nelson, Russell M. "The Book of Mormon: What Would Your Life Be Like Without It?" *Ensign* or *Liahona*, November 2017.
———. "Children of the Covenant." *Ensign*, May 1995.
———. "The Correct Name of the Church." *Ensign* or *Liahona*, November 2018.
———. In "Hope of Israel." Worldwide Youth Devotional, Conference Center, Salt Lake City, June 3, 2018.
———. "The Love and Laws of God." Devotional address, Brigham Young University Provo, UT, September 17, 2019.
———. In member meeting, Bengaluru, India, April 19, 2018.
———. "Overcome the World and Find Rest." *Liahona*, November 2022.
———. *Perfection Pending.* Salt Lake City: Deseret Book, 1998.
———. "Pure Truth, Pure Doctrine, Pure Revelation." *Liahona*, November 2021.
———. *Teachings of Russell M. Nelson.* Salt Lake City: Deseret Book, 2018.
———. "A Testimony of the Book of Mormon." *Ensign*, November 1999.
———. "What Is True?" *Liahona*, November 2022.
Oaks, Dallin H. "The Great Plan of Happiness." *Ensign*, November 1993.
———. "Scripture Reading, Revelation, and Joseph Smith's Translation of the Bible." In *Plain and Precious Truths Restored.* Edited by Robert L. Millet and Robert J. Matthews. Salt Lake City: Bookcraft, 1995.
———. "Sins, Crimes, and Atonement." Address delivered to CES religious educators, February 7, 1992. In Dallin H. Oaks, *With Full Purpose of Heart.* Salt Lake City: Deseret Book, 2002.
———. "Testimony." *Ensign* or *Liahona*, May 2008.
———. "Trust in the Lord." *Ensign*, November 2019.
———. *With Full Purpose of Heart.* Salt Lake City: Deseret Book, 2002.
Packer, Boyd K. "The Cloven Tongues of Fire." *Ensign*, May 2000.
———. *The Holy Temple.* Salt Lake City: Bookcraft, 1980.
———. *Let Not Your Heart Be Troubled.* Salt Lake City: Bookcraft, 1991.
———. "On the Shoulders of Giants." Devotional address, J. Reuben Clark Law Society, Brigham Young University, Provo, UT, February 28, 2004.
———. *"That All May Be Edified."* Salt Lake City: Bookcraft, 1982.
Packer, J. I. *Weakness Is the Way: Life with Christ Our Strength.* Wheaton, IL: Crossway Books, 2013.
Pearson, Kevin W. "Are You Still Willing?" *Liahona*, November 2022.
Pratt, Parley P. *Key to the Science of Theology.* Salt Lake City: Deseret Book, 1978.
*Random House College Dictionary.* Unabridged Edition. New York: Random House, 1988.
Rasband, Ronald A. "This Day." *Liahona*, November 2022.
Roberts, B. H. *Defense of the Faith and the Saints.* 2 vols. Salt Lake City: Deseret News, 1907.

———. In Conference Report, April 1906.

Skinner, Andrew C. "Law of Moses." In Robert L. Millet, Camille Fronk Olson, Andrew C. Skinner, and Brent L. Top. *LDS Beliefs: A Doctrinal Reference.* Salt Lake City: Deseret Book, 2011.

Smith, Joseph. "Account of Meeting and Discourse, 5 January 1841, as Reported by William P. McIntire." The Joseph Smith Papers. JosephSmithPapers.org.

———. "Discourse, 3 October 1841, as Published in *Times and Seasons.*" The Joseph Smith Papers. JosephSmithPapers.org.

———. "Discourse, 20 March 1842, as Published in *Times and Seasons.*" The Joseph Smith Papers. JosephSmithPapers.org.

———. "Discourse, 7 April 1844, as Reported by Wilford Woodruff." The Joseph Smith Papers. JosephSmithPapers.org.

———. "History, 1838–1856, volume D-1 [1 August 1842–1 July 1843]." The Joseph Smith Papers. JosephSmithPapers.org

———. "History, 1838–1856, volume E-1 [1 July 1843–30 April 1844]." The Joseph Smith Papers. JosephSmithPapers.org.

———. "History Draft [1 March–31 December 1843]," The Joseph Smith Papers. JosephSmithPapers.org.

———. "Instruction on Priesthood, circa 5 October 1840." The Joseph Smith Papers. JosephSmithPapers.org.

———. "Journal, December 1842–June 1844; Book 3, 15 July 1843–29 February 1844." The Joseph Smith Papers. JosephSmithPapers.org.

———. "Letter to the Church, circa February 1834." The Joseph Smith Papers. JosephSmithPapers.org.

———. *Teachings of Presidents of the Church: Joseph Smith.* Salt Lake City: The Church of Jesus Christ of Latter-day Saints, 2007.

———. *The Words of Joseph Smith: The Contemporary Accounts of the Nauvoo Discourses of the Prophet Joseph.* Compiled and edited by Andrew F. Ehat and Lyndon W. Cook. Provo, UT: BYU Religious Studies Center, 1980.

Soares, Ulisses. "Take Up Our Cross." *Ensign* or *Liahona*, November 2019.

Sperry, Sidney B. *Answers to Book of Mormon Questions.* Salt Lake City: Bookcraft, 1967.

Smith, Joseph F. "Editor's Table: On the Resurrection." *Improvement Era*, June 1904, 623–24.

———. *Gospel Doctrine.* Salt Lake City: Deseret Book, 1971.

Smith, Joseph Fielding. *Church History and Modern Revelation, Being a Course of Study for the Melchizedek Priesthood Quorums for the Year 1947.* Salt Lake City: Deseret News Press, 1946.

———. *Doctrines of Salvation.* 3 vols. Compiled by Bruce R. McConkie. Salt Lake City: Bookcraft, 1954–56.

Stevenson, Gary E. "Nourishing and Bearing Your Testimony." *Liahona*, November 2022.

Stott, John. *Life in Christ.* Wheaton, IL: Tyndale House Publishers, 1991.

*Times and Seasons.* Nauvoo, IL: The Church of Jesus Christ of Latter-day Saints, 1839–46.

Uchtdorf, Dieter F. "Bearers of Heavenly Light." *Ensign* or *Liahona*, November 2017.

———. "The Gift of Grace." *Ensign* or *Liahona*, May 2015.

*Webster's 1828 American Dictionary.* Facsimile. San Francisco: Foundation for American Christian Education, 1967.

Whitney, Orson F. In Conference Report, April 1928.

Wright, N. T. *Surprised by Hope: Rethinking Heaven, the Resurrection, and the Mission of the Church.* New York: HarperOne, 2008.

Yee, Kristen M. "Beauty for Ashes: The Healing Path of Forgiveness." *Liahona*, November 2022.

# Index